CURRIER'S GUIDE TO PRICING

AMERICAN ARTISTS

1645—1945

Current Price Ranges On
Over 5000 American Artists

Written and Compiled
by
William T. Currier

**FIRST
EDITION**

ISBN 0-935277-00-5 Softcover
Library of Congress
Catalog Card Number 85-71716

Printed in the United States of America

FIRST EDITION

2 3 4 5 6 7 8 9 10

****
Cover Photo:
Joseph C. Leyendecker (1874-1951)
"The Fourth of July Flagpole"
(31" x 24")
from the **Saturday Evening Post**, July 3, 1937
Courtesy of:
JUDY GOFFMAN
JUDY GOFFMAN AMERICAN PAINTINGS
Galleries in New York and Pennsylvania
****

Additional copies of this book
may be obtained from bookstores and selected
antique dealers. To order directly from the
publisher, remit $14.95 plus $1.00 shipping
(Massachusetts residents add 5% sales tax (.75)
TO:

**CURRIER'S FINE ART
APPRAISALS AND PUBLISHING**
P.O. Box 2098-B
Brockton, MA   02403

[Make check payable to CFAAP]

Acknowledgments

Many thanks to

Bill Beyer, whose contacts, knowledge of advertising and marketing, and continuous encouragement, provided me, intially and continuously, with the confidence that the book would be a success.

Norman Feather, for his expertise and valuable assistance in editing and preparation of the final copy. It would have been so difficult without him.

"Betty," at the Joslin Hall Book Co., for taking her valuable time to explain terms, and provide important contacts which helped me to market my book.

Vose Galleries of Boston, Inc., in general, for providing most of the photographs in this book, and to **Terri Vose** in particular, a special thanks, for his warm reception into the Gallery, and his enthusiastic willingness to help me select appropriate photographs for the book. It is refreshing to have gallery personnel who make you feel at home.

Elizabeth Haff, Curator, and **Joseph Kagle** , Director, of the Brockton Art Center, Fuller Memorial (Brockton, Massachusetts), for their cooperation in providing photographs for this book.

Special thanks to **Judy Goffman, Judy Goffman American Paintings**, an authority on American illustrators, with Galleries in New York and Pennsylvania, for taking, from her hectic schedule, the time to edit the list of over 300 illustrators that I submitted to her. Also, for providing photographs for both the cover and content of the book.

The Harcus Gallery, Boston, for contributing a fine photograph for the book.

The Fischbach Gallery, New York City, for editing prices for artists they represent.

M. Knoedler & Co.,Inc., New York City, for editing prices of artists they represent and for contributing photographs for the book.

Richard and Marianne Cannon, and Robert Elowitch, President of
Barridoff Galleries, Maine, for permission to use the photograph
of the Levi Wells Prentice still life painting for my book.

My parents, **Lillian and William,** for their encouragement and
support - as always.

Finally, a very special thanks to my wife, **Donna,** her mother,
Lorraine, and my daughter, **Danielle,** who from the beginning, all
supported me, encouraged me, and showed, most of all,
understanding. They sacrificed so much every day, every evening,
every weekend, month after month, to make this book possible. I
thank you especially, with love.

With Love To My Wife Donna And
Daughter Danielle

About the author. William T. Currier has been an educator with the Boston Public Schools for over fifteen years. Although his knowledge of art history was not acquired through a "formal" education in art history, he spent thousands of hours during the past twenty years in intense independent study of both art history and the art market. Mr. Currier has been a guest speaker at adult education classes, lecturing on identifying original prints and paintings, and has attended many lectures and professional seminars on art history and art investment. He is presently president of **Currier's Fine Art Appraisals and Publishing** ,a member of The New England Appraisers Association, and works privately as an agent, market liaison, consultant, dealer, appraiser,and publisher.

CONTENTS

Introduction

Until the publication of this book, no antique dealer, auctioneer, art collector, estate lawyer, bank trust officer, art consultant, appraiser, had available to him or her in an inexpensive, compact, concise, and portable format, a practical reference, compiled from the best sources, that could help quickly assess the probable worth of fine examples of American art from the 18th, 19th, and early 20th centuries. **Currier's Guide To Pricing American Artists** may well be the most profitable investment that anyone, who has occasion to buy and sell American art, could ever make.

You will find that you have purchased the most **practical** price guide to 300 years of American art [artists born 1645-1945] available today. The compilation of data here will be useful to even the most seasoned veteran of the American art marketplace: accurate spellings of artists' names; accurate birth and death dates not easily found elsewhere; a "mnemonic" (meaning to assist the memory) list of subject matter typical for each artist "value prioritized" - the most sought after subjects for each artist are listed first - and current, accurate price ranges (compiled from thousands of auction results over the past fifteen years) for America's most sought after artists.

One final note: You are welcome and encouraged to comment, make note of errors, and feel free to suggest changes or additions which will improve **your** guide. Please, write or call:

William T. Currier
Currier's Fine Art
Appraisals and Publishing
P.O. Box 2098
Brockton, MA 02403

(617) 588-4509

* Please see Disclaimer opposite Page 11.

Disclaimer

Every attempt, within reason, has been made to keep the price ranges herein as accurate as possible. There may be mistakes, both typographical and in content. Therefore, this guide should be used only as a **general** guide, not as the final, or ultimate, source of the only prices which may be realized at auction by any particular artist.

Special care must be exercised when examining the prices of **contemporary** artists. Because of the "dynamic" nature of the market as a whole, prices can rise and fall quickly. With living artists, it is best to check with those galleries that represent them for the "final" word on current values. Prices charged in the galleries for the works of living artists can be many times those realized at auction.

Also, the compilation of recommended conservators, auction houses and private galleries in the appendix is only a representative sampling of the hundreds of other conservators, auction houses and private galleries which I am sure may be of equal distinction.

The author and Currier's Fine Art Appraisals and Publishing shall have neither liability nor responsibility to any person with respect to any loss or damage caused or alleged to be caused directly or indirectly by the information contained in this book.

PART ONE

Direct Factors and Outside Influences Affecting Value

****
Please Note: Two assumptions are made throughout this guide: that you are a **novice** in the art marketplace, and that we will always be talking about prices at **fair market value** (auction results).
****

Until your work of art is sold, it has no real value (unlike stocks); only a subjective value based on many factors. No one can guarantee that your piece will bring a specified dollar amount at some future date. All influences on a work of art vary and, for that reason, you can expect a different price at each new auction. Let's look briefly at some of the direct factors and outside influences which, the author feels, most dramatically affect price.

THE SEVEN MOST IMPORTANT FACTORS

ARTIST. The most important factor. When we can **prove** who the artist is, whether or not the piece is signed, it will most directly influence the price realized. Almost without exception, the first question you will get from any major auction house, or dealer, when you call them to look for price information, will be: "Who is the artist?" Once the name is known, everything else follows: "What's the subject matter?", "What's the condition?", etc.

If you buy a piece which is unsigned, but you have been told by the seller that it was painted by a well known artist, obtaining a letter from an authority, which states without question that it is the particular artist the seller said it was, will help immensely in increasing its desirability and value.

Most would consider the signature to be exceedingly

important. The truth is, that it is of the very least value, until it can be proved without question that it is indeed the signature of the artist who painted the particular work.

Signatures can be added to an oil painting by anyone feeling it will increase its value. If you have a magnifying glass of at least 10-30x, examine the signature to be sure that "old" cracks running through the signature do indeed run through – that they are not filled with paint from a "recent" signature. If you suspect a forged signature, another way to check is to rub the signature gently with a little turpentine on a soft cloth – it will usually wash out a recent signature.

An authentic signature with a date is more desirable than one without.

MEDIUM. For any artist who was generally prolific in almost all mediums, a sliding scale of progressive value might be represented as follows:

Of Least Value	■	Pencil● Ink ●Watercolors	Gouaches ● ● ● Pastels	Acrylics Tempera	Oils ▶	Of Greatest Value

There are many good books available which explain the peculiarities of each of the mediums above. The novice to the art market should endeavor to familiarize him/herself with several.

The most popular medium overall today is still oils. It should be mentioned that, in the case of many contemporary artists, mixed media is extremely popular – much to the chagrin of today's conservators. Also, with contemporary artists, it is their mixed media work which often brings the highest prices.

Try to remember, the price ranges in this guide which begin with an asterisk (*) denote mixed media, watercolors, gouaches, pastels, and/or pencil and ink drawings. With such a variety of mediums, you can expect a price range often to start in the hundreds (for drawings) and end in the hundreds of thousands (for contemporary mixed media). Don't be mislead, though, in thinking all drawings will be of least value – there are exceptions. A drawing which is a preparatory study for a painting, which today is historically important, can have great value. One example which comes to mind is the ink and watercolor drawing by Benjamin West, a study for the painting, **The Death of General Wolfe**, which sold at Sotheby's (5/84) for $165,000.

QUALITY. Without question, the most exceptional pieces, as regards quality, in any medium, by any artist, will bring exceptionally high prices. Every dealer will tell you that he has no problem **quickly** moving the pieces of the highest quality.

The work of a much sought after artist will only bring a meager price, if it is of meager quality. Artist were human, of course, and had their good and bad days. During an artist's lifetime, his/her work could have evolved through several style changes, and within each style change can be found works of varying quality. The months or years which represent that style change are called "periods". It may happen that a small work of great quality, from a much sought after earlier,or later period, will be of more value than a much larger work from some other "period" which is not highly sought after.

At the end of the alphabetical listings in this guide, is a separate section entitled: **RECORD PRICES**. Those prices represent values realized for works which were considered of **great** quality. They had to be isolated, because the prices were **well** above the high end of all other works by that artist, and to include them would have distorted a "true" picture of the normal price range of that artist's work.

There are many factors which the novice can consider in determining a "probable" value of a fine painting, but judging quality, style, and period is best left up to the "expert": university scholar, museum curator, art dealer, certain art consultants, qualified appraiser, or some independent author or connoisseur.

SUBJECT. In a broad sense, this is the main theme of a work of art. In a narrower vein, it is the "subject matter" within the subject that can affect value. As an example, the subject of a painting might be a still life, but its "subject matter" might be dead game birds. The subject of another painting might be marine, and the "subject matter", a coastal harbor scene.

Most artists have one or two subjects which they are best known for. These particular subjects (see the section on TYPICAL SUBJECTS in Part 2 for a list with an explanation) are the ones most sought after and bring the highest prices. Robert Spear Dunning is best known for his still lifes; John George Brown is best known as a painter of genre, etc. Knowing the subject(s) most sought after for any particular artist is very important for you in determining the "probable" value of a piece. I have done most of that work for **you** in this guide - more on that in Part 2.

After attending a number of art auctions, you will begin to note which subjects and subject matter are most and least desirable. In general, collectors today want bright colorful, non-offensive pieces for their walls. Let's look more closely at our subjects:

Figures: "Studio" portraits, with the exception of early "Folk portraits" (see Primitives below), and historical figures, hold very little interest for collectors, unless done by a well known artist. The most desirable "Figure" paintings are those in a non-studio setting - groups of people in an interior or outdoors. Collectors often prefer women and children over men in both portraits and figure studies. Religous figures are not very popular, unless they are "Old Master" paintings. For certain collectors, the nude figure is desirable. Western figures are presently very popular, as are many Arabian, and orientalist figure paintings.

Genre: Themes which can be considered genre probably number in the thousands. Some of the more popular themes might be: a public fête, a friendly conversation, the comedies of the household, or the little dramas of private life.

Illustration: Because of the scope of this subject and the endless variety of both subject matter and mediums, it is very difficult to point out a "most" and "least" popular subject matter. It is best to talk to someone who specializes in American Illustration. If you have any questionsabout American illustrators, call or write Judy Goffman (see Appendix). Judy is a leading authority on American Illustration, and she would be happy to help you.

Landscapes: Collectors today prefer bright,colorful landscapes with identifiable landmarks - especially if the landmarks have "local" interest. Of the four seasons, winter scenes seem to draw the most attention. Landscapes with a "luminist" quality are popular. American scenes are usually more desirable than European scenes by the same artist.

Marines: Collectors of marine subjects can be very particular about their ship portraits - the rigging, the position of the sails, the flags that are being flown, and many other details can effect the desirability of a marine painting. American vessels, flying American flags, are always more desirable than foreign. From my own observations, the old side-wheelers and clipper ships under full sail enjoy considerable popularity. As with landscapes, collectors prefer coastal scenes in which there is an identifiable landmark - such as a familiar lighthouse. Again, local interest increases value.

Primitives: Very little of the early "Folk Art" is undesirable - all examples are eagerly collected. Pieces in very poor condition, or poorly restored, have little interest. With primitives, it is best to sell them "as is," rather them having them restored. Collectors usually have their own conservators to whom they entrust their new acquisitions, and prefer no previous restoration.

Still lifes: All types of still lifes are collected, from our earliest primitives to today's paintings of "photographic realism." Floral pieces today are enjoying popularity, as are elaborate fruit and vegetable compositions. The "grander" the composition, the greater the value. When things are introduced into a composition which are not essential to it, they are known as accessories and can often add interest and value to a still life.

Wildlife: Scenes with an abundance of blood will be least desirable. Farm yard fowl don't enjoy much popularity. Of all the animals around the farm, horses are the most popular with collectors. Deer are always popular if not shown being shot, and most hunting and fishing scenes will find buyers if there is no blood and gore.

STYLE. Sir Joshua Reynolds (1723-1792) said,"In painting, style is the same as in writing: some are grand, others plain; some florid and others simple." Styles can be peculiar to a "school," or a master, in design, composition, coloring, expression, and execution, but not necessarily peculiar to the artist. In many instance, artists have changed their personal styles several times during their lifetime. As stated earlier, each new style change was considered a new period. Some periods, or styles, are more sought after than others because of a greater appeal.

Some styles of painting are currently enjoying more popularity than others. Leading the list would be the work of the American Impressionists.

When you're assessing the "probable" value of a painting, it may be necessary to let an "expert" (see QUALITY above) determine the style of the work.

CONDITION. Although "condition" seems a long way down on our list of "factors determing value," it is really the one variable which we must pay the most attention to. No matter who the artist is, a painting in very poor condition, or one that has been heavily restored, will have very little value – at best, a fraction of the worth of a similiar painting in pristine condition.

Before you buy a painting on canvas in need of conservation, consider the following:

1. After you spend anywhere from $100-$1500 for the cost of restoration, will you be able to realize a profit?
2. Are you willing to tie that painting up for what may take as long as six months?
3. If there is paint loss, is any of it in critical areas

which will affect value? For instance, you do not want the paint to be falling away from the faces and bodies of people in a figure painting.
4. Is the overall paint loss greater than 25% ? If so, unless the painting is **extremely** valuable, pass on it!
5. Besides restoration,will the painting need an appropriate frame to make it saleable - another expense?
6. Is the painting covered with a very dark layer of dirt and varnish? Only a professional conservator will be able to ascertain if that painting will "clean up." If she/he says definitely not, you may never see a profit.
7. The cost of restoration can be **very** high, if the conservator has to do a relining and extensive "inpainting" besides a cleaning. Relinings are often neccessary when the canvas is extremely wrinkled, torn, abraded, or too loose and floppy. Inpainting is an expensive and involved process of repainting damaged areas to their original condition.
8. Has the painting **already** had any "bad" restoration?

REMEMBER: Though cleaning may be useful to restore the original brilliancy of an old painting - though relining is sometimes needed to save it from imminent destruction - to let it be attempted by a non-professional is a sacrilege. ALWAYS MAKE SURE THAT THE CONSERVATOR HAS AN IMPECCABLE REPUTATION FOR QUALITY WORK. Also, **never** use water to clean a painting - leave it alone, until an expert can look at it.

If you need to find a conservator, I have compiled a representative list from around the country and abroad in the Appendix of this guide. Your best source for a reputable conservator is the recommendation of an art museum or prestigious art gallery. Some of the latter are also listed in the Appendix - see if there is one near you.

SIZE. All it will take is one afternoon at an art auction to see that there is a definite correlation between size and price. This relation holds true **only** with the paintings by the same artist, and with paintings that are similar in subject matter, quality, and style.
You may never hear of a painting that is too small to be desirable, but you will likely hear of a painting being too big to be desirable. When a painting is larger than sofa size, you will find that your buying audience has shrunk considerably. Of course, there would be exceptions to this, in cases where the artist is an eminent American master.

OUTSIDE INFLUENCES ON VALUE

As discussed above, when you purchase a painting for resale, there are inherent factors - artist, size, medium, condition, quality, subject, style - which can be quickly ascertained for determining an "approximate" value. There are other "outside" influences - historical importance, provenance, time and location of sale, competitive bidding, publicity and fads - which can have a positive or negative affect on value. Let's take a brief look at each.

HISTORICAL IMPORTANCE. All preparatory studies (drawings, watercolors, oil sketches, etc.) for any major historical American painting can be valuable. If you find, while researching your artist, that he/she painted many historically important paintings, check your piece or have an "expert" check your piece, to determine if it could be an important preparatory study. The likelihood of finding an actual canvas which is a **major** historical painting is slim. Most are either in museums, historical societies, or private corporate collections. Don't expect to find one in someone's attic next month.

PROVENANCE. Provenance is simply a pedigree. It can be important to some collectors; not so important with others. Provenance works in reverse when you see a list. The present owner is listed first, the previous owner is listed second, and so on, until we are back, ideally, to the artist himself. This line of ownership can make the piece very desirable, if the list has some important names on it. But there can be a problem. We sometimes have no way of checking the authenticity of this document. Most of the people on the list will probably be dead now - and not available to vouch for their prior ownership of the piece in question.

A provenance is not at all necessary to transact a sale, but if you have supportable evidence that the provenance is unquestionably genuine, then it can be even more important than the signature on the piece.

Sometimes, you will find that names have been "filled" in to complete a gap in its pedigree. Be careful. Always try to judge the piece first on its own merit as a fine work of art. If it turns out later that all the documentation included with it is "right," then the value of the piece will jump up.

The topic of Provenance is closely related to a discussion of authentication. If you feel you have just bought an "important" painting and would like to have it properly authenticated, see the Appendix under **Appraisal Organizations** for a list of authentication services.

SELLING: TIME AND LOCATION OF SALE. Some auction houses do better than others, selling certain artists. It is valuable information to know at which auction an artist continually commands the highest prices. Information of this type is not easily obtainable, unless you have been closely following the market all over the country. If you have a "potentially" valuable painting, I might suggest that you contact some art consultants in your area, to see if they provide that service. If they do not, the author (address is in the front of the book) can help you. Please call or write.

The worst months of the year to sell at auction are in July and August. The best months to sell are April, May, June, October, November, December.

If you plan to send your art to auction at one of the **major** auction houses (see the list in the Appendix), then you'd better keep two things in mind, if you're in a hurry to see your money:

1. From the day you send your piece to auction until the day of the actual sale, two to five months may have passed. Auction officials need that time to research all the paintings, determine estimates, and photograph most of the paintings in the sale for placement in a catalog, which goes out (at a price) to the patrons of the sale, and do the pre-sale advertising.

2. Many of the **major** auction houses do not send you your money (less commission) until 35-40 days after the sale. They wait for buyer's checks to clear.

Be aware that a small number of artists ONLY sell at a high price at a particular auction, due often to a high concentration of collectors in the area for the work of that artist. One name which readily comes to mind is Ralph Cahoon (d.1982), who always does well at the Richard Bourne Auction Gallery, Hyannis, Massachusetts.

Many of the artists who sell in the $500-10,000 range will fare better at auctions in regions where they spent most of their lives painting. The "home-town artist" will do best near his home-town. The big name artist will sell everywhere.

Before you ship your piece to auction, check the offers of dealers who "specialize" in work by your artist - you may get an offer you can't refuse.

COMPETITIVE BIDDING. Almost every major auction has a good number of fine paintings which sell well above the estimates - much to the delight of the consignor. Competitive bidding can drive the price up well above estimate. All that is needed is two or more people who want that piece badly enough that it seems money is no object. In June of 1981, a Charles Sprague Pearce painting sold (with a pre-sale estimate of $10-15,000) for $247,500. Can you imagine how happy that consignor was!

PUBLICITY AND FADS. The resale value of your piece will leap, if it has been an illustration in one or more pieces of literature. If the piece also has a well-documented exhibition record, that will increase its desirability.

Someone once said, "As New York goes, so goes the country." It often seems what starts out popular and fashionable in New York, catches on elsewhere.

If you get a chance to follow the market more closely each year, you'll be able to stay on top of what is currently "fashionable."

PART TWO

How To Use This Guide

AN OVERVIEW

In the process of compiling the over 5000 names, it was found that in many instances, the spelling of names was incorrect, or incomplete, with only initials and a surname, as they appeared in many of the auction house catalogs nationally. This was due in part, understandably, to the haste with which many of these artists were researched and then recorded into the catalog in time for the pre-sale promotion. The full and correct spelling of names was accomplished as accurately as possible by checking more than one dictionary of artists for each name. If no dates were available, the century during which that artist is known to have worked was placed next to the name.

The birth and death dates, when available, were researched for accuracy and recorded next to the name. In many instances a birth and death date are recorded which could not be easily found elsewhere.

Price ranges* and typical subject(s), "value prioritized" and listed, using mnemonic letters, were established by doing what amounted to an appraisal of each individual artist. Vast amounts of biographical data, from my own reference library and sources outside, had to be carefully gone over, in attempts to establish those subjects most typical for each artist in question. From that point, it then had to be ascertained as well as possible which subject(s) consistently brought the highest prices - the most sought after subjects by the collectors. After carefully recording all the auction prices for each artist over a fifteen-year period, it was possible then to record a price range which reflected the "practical" low and high for that particular artist. Any dollar amount which was well above the average high end, and which did not obviously fit into the typical price range for that artist, was recorded alphabetically on a separate list entitled, "RECORD PRICES" - found on page 142.

*Please read the Disclaimer opposite Page 11.

LET'S KEEP IT SIMPLE

The names and dates need no more explanation than you have above. It will be the "price ranges" and the "typical subjects" that need clarification.

PRICE RANGES: You have to remember four things:

> 1. 85% of the price ranges are simply low and high dollar amounts, indicating the range within which you would expect the artist's oils, acrylics, and/or tempera paintings to sell.

Example:

AHL, HENRY HAMMOND (1896-   )   300-2500   L, I

> 2. 14% of the price ranges will be preceded by an asterisk (*), indicating a price range for that artist's drawings, watercolors, gouaches, pastels, and/or mixed media. If an artist's name was listed twice, he/she was prolific enough in all mediums to have "two separate" price ranges.

Example: (Note: when a name is listed twice, the "typical subject" follows the second price range and the birth and death dates also follow the second name.)

ARTIST	PRICE RANGE	TYPICAL SUBJECT
STEVENS, WILLIAM LESTER	*150-1200	
STEVENS, WILLIAM LESTER (1888 - 1969)	400-4500+	L, M, S

> 3. You're probably already asking, "What's that plus (+) sign doing on the previous example?" The plus (+) simply indicates that that artist has a record price which you will find on page 142, entitled RECORD PRICES. The record for W. L. Stevens is $10,450. Obviously, to have said that Steven's price range is 400-10,000 would have distorted the true range within which 99% of his work falls. In all instances where one price was **WELL** above all others appearing at **auction**, it went onto the "RECORD PRICE" page. You will see a plus 51 times from A to Z.

> 4. Less than 1% of the price ranges will not have any prices at all - only six question marks (??????). They indicate an artist who was considered one of Americas's "textbook" artists, but who has had very few paintings, if any, appear at auction in the past 15 years. If their work did appear, it could sell at prices running into the hundreds of thousands of dollars or higher.

TYPICAL SUBJECTS: THE "MNEMONIC" LETTERS

"MNEMONIC" means "assisting or designed to assist the memory." In that respect, you will find after each artist,if the information was available, single letters corresponding to the subjects most typical for the artist, arranged "value prioritized" (see below). Each letter matches the following subjects:

A Avant-Garde
F Figures
G Genre
I Illustration
L Landscapes
M Marines
P Primitives
S Still Lifes
W Wildlife
X Unknown

Shortly, for the benefit of the novice, we will briefly explain with photo examples, each of the subject areas.

"VALUE PRIORITIZED" simply means that you will find the subjects arranged in descending order as regards value. Those subjects by that particular artist, which "generally" bring the highest prices, are listed first, and so on. Please keep in mind that no such list can be compiled with the certainty of "death and taxes" - the author has made a sincere effort to keep the list as accurate as possible. If you are aware of an error and can substantiate it, please bring it to my attention. I will make the correction in **your** guide for the second edition, to the benefit of everyone.

Let's take a closer look at each subject area, with examples:

TYPICAL SUBJECTS

For our purposes,"Avant-Garde" will refer to all the art work which does not easily fit into any of the other categories herein because of their unconventional styles. Such works might typically include the "experimental" works or "fads" of the 20th century - such as Cubism, Dadaism, Surrealism, Abstract Expressionism, Minimal Art, Photorealism, and Pop Art.

****
PLEASE NOTE: It is important to repeat here a statement made earlier in the "Disclaimer." When examining the prices of Contemporary

artists (over 300 in this guide),care must be exercised. Because of the "dynamic" nature of the contemporary market as a whole, prices rise and fall quickly. With living artists,it is **ALWAYS** best to check with those galleries that represent them for the "final" word on current values.
****

The best reference for finding those Galleries which represent many of the artists listed here is Paul Cumming's book, **Dictionary of Contemporary American Artists**, St. Martin's Press, New York (ISBN 0-312-20097-8, $50.00). There are no prices, but it has plenty of biographical material on over 900 contemporary artists.

The following are modern examples of avant-garde work:

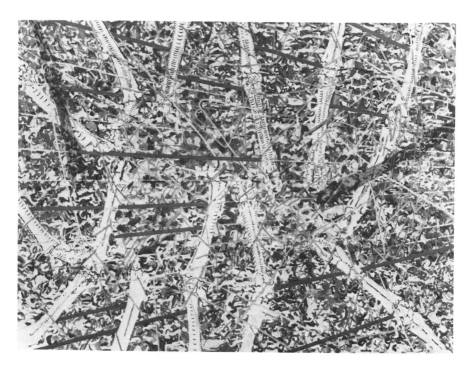

NANCY GRAVES, **Calipers, Legs, Lines**, acrylic and oil on canvas, 64" x 88", Courtesy of M. Knoedler & Co., Inc., New York

HERBERT FERBER, **Harleguin Series III #6**, 1982,
acrylic on canvas, 55 x 84, M. Knoedler & Co., Inc.
New York

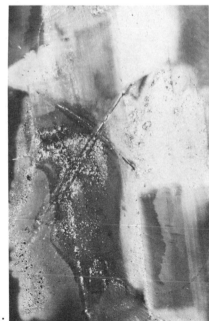

SANDI SLONE,
Blake's Bolt, 1984,
acrylic on canvas,
61 x 41, Courtesy of
The Harcus Gallery, Boston.

Figures

Most typically under this category are works which depict adults and/or children in various studio and non-studio settings. These figure studies may be: portraits (single and/or group),miniatures, historical figures, and people from all walks of life in settings typical for the period and location. Many "experts" will argue, with good reason , that many non-studio figure paintings are "genre."

In figure painting, the artist usually is more interested in depicting the character of the individual, not so much the human situation, as in "genre."

Religious, historical, and allegorical subjects will also be included in this category for our purposes.

Here are three examples of figure painting:

CHAUNCEY FOSTER RYDER, **Over There**, oil on canvas, Courtesy of The Brockton Art Center, Fuller Memorial.

GILBERT STUART,
George Washington,
oil on canvas,
29 x 24, Courtesy of
Vose Galleries
of Boston, Inc.

JOHN GEORGE BROWN,
The Cider Mill,
oil on canvas,
30 x 24, Courtesy of
Vose Galleries
of Boston, Inc.

Genre

"Genre" refers to people of all ages engaged in everyday activities typical for the period and location. "Genre" differs from "figure studies" in that usually the activity in the composition is the main theme. Typical compositions might include: Western, Sporting, City, Country, Seafaring, or Domestic subjects.

Of particular note are the "genre," or "American Scene" paintings of the late 1920's, 30's, and 40's. The scenes were generally a preoccupation with the political and social realities of the day: contemporary morals and manners, the "beauty" found in the drabness and decay of our cities, studies of the poor and underprivileged, studies of the blue-collar worker of the farm and mine - a literal protest against the "pretty" pictures of the 19th century.

Here are two examples of childhood genre:

EDWARD POTTHAST, **Ring Around The Rosey**, oil on canvas, 24 x 30, Courtesy of Vose Galleries of Boston, Inc.

EASTMAN JOHNSON, **Lunch Time**, oil on canvas,
21 x 19, Courtesy of Vose Galleries of Boston, Inc.

Illustration

This is a broad category which typically involves works which were executed for the purpose of reinforcing an idea or theme of a publication and/or advertisement. In this category, you will find the greatest variety of mediums and subject matter.

There are three examples of illustration – the cover, and the two examples which follow:

MAXFIELD PARRISH, **Waterfall**, 1930-1, oil on panel, 32 x 22, Courtesy of Judy Goffman American Paintings.

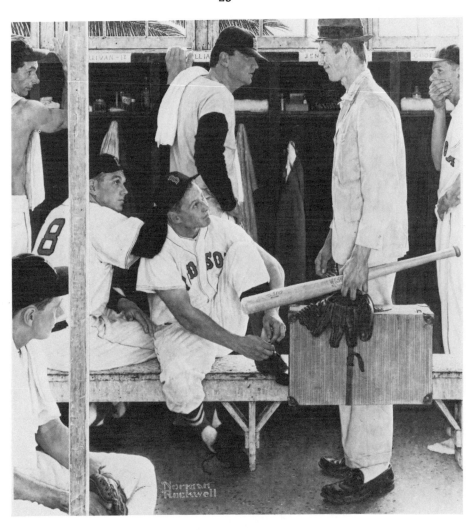

NORMAN ROCKWELL, **The Rookie**, 1957,
oil on canvas, 41 x 39, Courtesy of
Judy Goffman American Paintings.

Landscapes

In this category, you may find compositions which depict natural scenery, and which may or may not include figures and/or man-made objects. All seasons and all times of the day may be depicted, and views might be of any of the following : Scenes West or East of the Mississippi, Seascapes (shoreline views), and Scenes outside the United States. "Genre" may often be combined into a landscape composition.

The following examples show a good cross section of possible subject matter in a landscape: The first is a wonderful example of a highly sought after 19th century composition; the second, a turn-of-the-century coastal landscape which borders on being called a "marine" painting; and an early 20th century landscape by a member of the "ash-can" school who revolted against the "pretty" pictures typical of the 19th century:

ASHER B. DURAND **Haying**, oil on canvas, 36 x 54, Courtesy of Vose Galleries of Boston, Inc.

JOHN JOSEPH ENNEKING, **York Harbor, Maine**, 1887, O/C
18 x 24, Courtesy of Vose Galleries of Boston, Inc.

WILLIAM GLACKENS, **Cannes**, oil on canvas,
13 x 16, Courtesy of Vose Galleries of Boston, Inc.

Marines

This category will be used in instances where the artist's major output was nautical compositions - drawings and/or paintings of vessels of all descriptions and sizes, sea scenes, and coastal or harbor scenes.

Here are two fine examples of a marine subject:

THOMAS BIRCH, **View of Philadelphia from Below the Navy Yard**, O/C, 22 x 33, Courtesy of Vose Galleries of Boston, Inc.

WILLIAM TROST RICHARDS, **Seascape**, oil on canvas, Courtesy of Vose Galleries of Boston, Inc.

Primitive

A term used interchangeably with two other terms: "Folk Art" and "Naive Art." For our purposes here,"primitive" will refer to all those compositions done by "non-professional" artists - typically referred to as "limners."

"Primitive" compositions may depict subjects from any of the other categories listed herein (portraits, landscapes, genre, etc.). Typically, a primitive painting may appear two-dimensional, lack a source of light, and be characterized by an undeveloped spatial sense.

Here are two fine examples of a primitive subject:

THOMAS CHAMBERS, **Undercliff, Coldspring, New York**, oil on canvas, 22 x 30, Courtesy of Vose Galleries of Boston, Inc.

RUFUS HATHAWAY, **Mrs. Joshua Winsor**, oil on canvas, 38 x 25, Courtesy of Vose Galleries of Boston, Inc.

Still lifes

These are most often paintings of inanimate objects done for their beauty of color, line, or arrangement. These compositions are almost always set indoors, and during the 19th and 20th centuries most typically depicted the following: fruit and/or vegetables, flowers, or objects found around the home or farm.

When things are introduced into a composition to add interest and color, they are usually called **accessories**.

Here are three examples of a still life. The first is a fine example of a 20th century still life with accessories; the second, a fine example of a "**trompe l'oeil**" (meaning "to trick the eye") still life; and the third, a fine example of a popular subject matter: fruit (in this case, apples and melons):

FRANK WESTON BENSON, **The Silver Screen**, oil on canvas, 36 x 44, Courtesy of Vose Galleries of Boston, Inc.

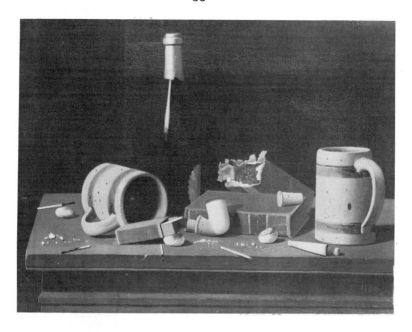

JOHN F. PETO, **Mugs, Bottle , etc.**, oil on canvas,
12 x 16, Courtesy of Vose Galleries of Boston, Inc.

LEVI WELLS PRENTICE, **Apples and Melons**, oil on canvas,
12 x 18, Courtesy of Richard and Marianne Cannon.

Wildlife

Many artists made a career of drawing and painting wildlife subjects (animals, fish, and/or birds) set in their natural habitat. Also included in this category will be animal subjects in a domestic or farm setting - such as horse portraits, the family pets, and farmyard animals and fowl.

Here is one example of a typical wildlife composition:

THOMAS HINKLEY, **The Family,** oil on canvas, 60 x 50, Courtesy of Vose Galleries of Boston, Inc.

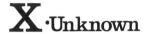

Sufficient data were not available at this time, to determine the type of subject matter "most" typical for this artist. If the "X" is followed by a letter(s) A thru W in parentheses, then that artist is known to have executed "some" works in that particular category. If you have verifiable information as regards prices or subject matter for any artists listed here with an "X", please send it along. The address is at the front of this guide.

****

EXPERT OR SLEUTH?

Now that you are familiar with the use of this guide, what next? When you want to quickly estimate the "probable" value of a certain work of art, you'll want to use this guide first. After determining that you may have a **very** valuable painting, and before you sell (privately, to a dealer, on consignment, through advertisement, or in your shop, etc.), you will want to determine **more accurately** what the painting may be worth (fair market value). You have two choices. Either you consult with an "expert" (art appraiser, qualified auctioneer, art dealer, art consultant), or you try to research it yourself. Whichever route you decide on, you will find help in the Appendix of this guide under **Resources For Pricing**, and **Appraisal Organizations**.

One last comment. If you are a complete novice to the art market, I would recommend seeking the help of an expert. Only they will have the trained eye and the references on hand, to make the most accurate estimate of the value of your piece.

AMERICAN ARTISTS

```
ABBEY, EDWIN AUSTIN                              *500-3000
ABBEY, EDWIN AUSTIN (1852 - 1911)               2000-25000    I,G,F
ABBOTT, SAMUEL NELSON                            *100-1000
ABBOTT, SAMUEL NELSON (1874 - 1953)             500-3500      I
ABBOTT, YARNALL (1870 - 1938)                   100-500       X (G,F)
ABDY, ROWENA MEEKS (1887 - 1945)                *200-700      L,G,I
ABEL, MYER (1904 -      )                        100-600       F,G
ABERCROMBIE, ?    (20TH C)                       200-500       X (S)
ABRAMOFSKY, ISRAEL (20TH C)                      200-1200      L,F
ABRAMOVITZ, ALBERT (1879 - 1963)                400-1000      L,F
ACHEFF, WILLIAM (20TH C)                         5000-60000    X (G,F)
ACHESON, GEORGINA ELLIOT (19TH - 20TH C)        *300-600      X (F)
ADAM, JOHN (19TH - 20TH C)                       100-300       G,L
ADAM, RICHARD B. (20TH C)                        200-600       X (G)
ADAMS, CATHERINE LONGHORNE                       600-3000      L
ADAMS, CHARLES PARTRIDGE                         *100-1000
ADAMS, CHARLES PARTRIDGE (1858 - 1942)          500-3500      L
ADAMS, JOHN OTTIS (1851 - 1927)                 600-3500      L
ADAMS, JOSEPH ALEXANDER (1803 - 1880)           300-1000      X (L)
ADAMS, WAYMAN (1883 - 1959)                      400-2500      F
ADAMS, WILLIS SEAVER (1842 - 1921)              300-1200      L
ADDY, ALFRED (19TH - 20TH C)                     200-800       L
ADOLPHE, ALBERT JEAN (1865 - 1940)              150-3500      L,F,G,S
ADOLPHE, VIRGINIA (1880 -      )                 100-500       X (S)
ADOMEIT, GEORGE G. (1879 - 1967)                200-600       X (L)
AGOSTINI, TONY (20TH C)                          100-300       A
AHL, HENRY CURTIS (20TH C ?)                     100-400       M,L,S
AHL, HENRY HAMMOND (1896 -      )                300-2500      L,I
AHLBORNE, EMIL (early 20TH C)                    100-300       X (L)
AIKEN, CHARLES AVERY                             *100-400      I
AIKEN, CHARLES AVERY (1872 - 1965)              200-1000      I,S
AIKEN, CHARLES G. (20TH C)                       100-200       X
AINSLEY, DENNIS (20TH C)                         100-400       X (L)
AITKEN, HARRY G. (19TH - 20TH C)                100-300       L
AKIN, LOUIS B. (1868 - 1913)                    500-3000      L,G,I
ALAJALOV, CONSTANTIN (1900 -      )             *200-1000      I
ALBEE, PERCY F. (1883 - 1959)                   *100-500      G,F
ALBERS, JOSEF (1888 - 1976)                      3500-75000    A
ALBERT, ERNEST (1857 - 1946)                     800-10000     L
ALBRICH, W. (early 20th c)                       100-200       X (L)
```

* -Denotes Mixed Media,Watercolors,Gouaches,Pastels,and/or Drawings

40

Name	Price	Media
ALBRIGHT, ADAM EMORY (1862 - 1957)	800-6000	G
ALBRIGHT, IVAN LE LORRAINE	*800-4000	
ALBRIGHT, IVAN LE LORRAINE (1897 -)	1500-20000	A,F,S
ALDEN, REBECCA B. (early 19TH C)	*100-400	X (S)
ALDERMAN, GEORGE P.B. (1862 - 1942)	*200-600	I
ALDRICH, GEORGE AMES (1872 - 1941)	500-5000	L,F
ALEX, KOSTA (1925 -)	400-2000	F
ALEXANDER, CLIFFORD GREAR (1870 -)	300-800	L,I
ALEXANDER, ESTHER FRANCES (19TH C)	*200-800	X (F)
ALEXANDER, FRANCIS	*200-700	F
ALEXANDER, FRANCIS (1800 - 1880)	400-8000	F
ALEXANDER, HENRY (1860 - 1895)	2000-6500	X (F,G)
ALEXANDER, JOHN WHITE (1856 - 1915)	1000-25000	F,I
ALF, MARTHA (1930 -)	1000-3000	X
ALLEN, CHARLES CURTIS (1886 - 1950)	500-3500	L
ALLEN, COURTNEY (1896 -)	200-600	I
ALLEN, DOUGLAS (20TH C)	1000-3000	X (W)
ALLEN, F.B. (early 20TH C)	*100-200	X (L)
ALLEN, HOWARD (19TH - 20TH C)	100-600	X (G)
ALLEN, J.D. (1851 - 1947)	400-3000	X (G)
ALLEN, JUNIUS (1898 - 1962)	200-2500	L,G
ALLEN, MARION BOYD (1862 -)	100-600	F,L
ALLEN, THOMAS (1849 - 1924)	300-3000	L,G
ALLIS, C. HARRY (- 1938)	300-3000	L
ALLSTON, WASHINGTON (1779 - 1843)	5000-??????	F,G,L,M
ALTEN, MATHAIS JOSEPH	*100-400	
ALTEN, MATHIAS JOSEPH (1871 - 1938)	400-2000	F,L
ALTOON, JOHN (1925 - 1969)	*500-2500	A
AMANS, JACQUES (1801 - 1888)	500-3000	F
AMES, DANIEL E. (active 1840-55)	800-3500	F
AMES, EZRA (1768 - 1836)	500-4500	F
AMICK, ROBERT WESLEY	*400-1200	
AMICK, ROBERT WESLEY (1879 - 1969)	2500-15000	G,I
ANDERSON, ALEXANDER (1775 - 1870)	600-3000	F,G
ANDERSON, FRED (early 20TH C)	100-300	X (G)
ANDERSON, FREDERIC A. (19TH - 20TH C)	500-1200	X (G)
ANDERSON, HAROLD EDGERLY (1899 -)	100-400	X (G)
ANDERSON, HAROLD N.(1894 -)	500-2000	X (I)
ANDERSON, KARL (1874 - 1956)	500-5000	F,G,I
ANDERSON, LENNART (1928 -)	500-1500	X (L)
ANDERSON, M.J.(19TH - 20TH C)	100-300	X (F,S)
ANDERSON, RONALD (1886 - 1926)	*200-400	X (F,S)
ANDERSON, RUTH A.(1884 - 1939)	300-2000	F,L
ANDERSON, VICTOR COLEMAN (1882 -)	*100-600	X (G,I)
ANDRADE, MARY FRATZ (early 20TH C)	300-800	X (L,G)
ANDREW, INEZ LANGDEN (late 19TH C)	100-400	L
ANDREW, RICHARD (1867 -)	500-1500	X (F,L)
ANDREWS, AMBROSE (active 1825-60)	500-5000	L,F
ANDREWS, BENNY (1930 -)	100-500	X
ANGEL, RIFKA (1899 -)	100-600	X (G)
ANISFELD, BORIS (1879 - 1973)	400-2000	X (F,I)
ANNES, HECTOR L. (20TH C)	100-250	L
ANSHUTZ, THOMAS POLLACK	*500-10000	
ANSHUTZ, THOMAS POLLOCK (1851 -1912)	5000-100000	F,L,G,M
ANUSZKIEWICZ, RICHARD (1930 -)	3000-20000	A

* -Denotes Mixed Media,Watercolors,Gouaches,Pastels,and/or Drawings

```
APPEL, CHARLES P. (1857 -      )              500-2500     L
APT, CHARLES (1933 -       )                 1500-3000     X
ARCANGELO, ALLAN D'(1930 -       )            500-5000     A
ARCENZA, NICOLA D' (19TH C)                  *100-300      X (L)
ARDLEY, A.A.(19TH C)                          100-300      X (S)
ARENTZ, JOSEF M. (1903 - 1969)                300-1500     X (G,L)
ARMS, JESSIE (1883 -       )                  100-450      X (F,G)
ARMSTRONG, DAVID MAITLAND (1836 - 1918)       400-4500     G,F,M
ARMSTRONG, WILLIAM G. (1823 - 1890)           800-4000     L
ARMSTRONG, WILLIAM W. (1822 - 1914)           400-2500     L
ARNO, PETER (1904 - 1968)                    *100-1000     I
ARNOLD, JAMES (20TH C)                        300-600      X
ARNOLD, JAY (19TH - 20TH C)                   200-600      M
ARONSON, BORIS (1900 -       )               *500-2000     X (I)
ARONSON, DAVID (1923 -       )               *300-2500     F
ARRIOLA, FORTUNATO (1827 - 1872)             1000-7000     X (L)
ARTER, J. CHARLES (      - 1923)              150-600      F
ARTHURS, STANLEY MASSEY (1877 - 1950)         300-7500     I
ARTIGES, EMILE (20TH C)                       200-900      L
ARTSCHWAGER, RICHARD (1924 -       )         3000-18000    A
ARY, HENRY (1802 - 1859)                     1000-6500     L
ASCENZO, NICOLA D'(1869 -       )            *200-800      I,L
ASHBROOK, PAUL (1867 -       )                200-600      X (F)
ASHE, EDMUND M.(20TH)                        *250-700      X (F,I)
ASHLEY, CLIFFORD WARREN (1881 - 1947)        1500-6000     M,L,I
ASHLEY, FRANK N.                             *150-700
ASHLEY, FRANK N. (20TH C)                     300-700      X (G,F)
ASPLYND. TARE (20TH C)                        100-300      X (G)
ATCHISON, JOSEPH ANTHONY (1895 -       )     *100-200      X (M)
ATHERTON, JOHN C. (1900 - 1952)              200-1200      L,I
ATKEN, JAMES (19TH C )                        500-3000     G,L
AUDUBON, JOHN JAMES (1785 - 1851)            *2500-125000  W
AUDUBON, VICTOR GIFFORD (1809 - 1862)        1000-5000     L
AUERBACH-LEVY, WILLIAM (1889 -       )        200-500      F
AULISIO, JOSEPH (1910 - 1974)                2000-25000    P,L
AULMANN, THEODORA (1882 -       )             100-300      L
AULT, GEORGE C.                              *300-6500
AULT, GEORGE C. (1891 - 1941)                 500-25000    L
AUSTIN, CHARLES PERCY (1883 - 1929)           500-1200     X (G,L)
AUSTIN, DARREL                               *100-500
AUSTIN, DARREL (1907 -       )                500-4000     F
AUSTIN, EDWARD C.(20TH C)                    *100-300      X (M)
AUSTRIAN, BEN (1870 - 1921)                   400-4500     L,W
AVEDISIAN, EDWARD (1936 -       )             500-6500     A
AVERY, ADDISON E. (19TH C)                   *100-300      S
AVERY, MILTON                               *1000-50000
AVERY, MILTON (1893 - 1965)                  1000-100000   A
AVINOFF, ANDRE (1884 - 1949)                 *200-600      X (L)
AYERS, H. MERVIN (1902 - 1975)               *100-300      X (F)
AYLWARD, WILLIAM JAMES (1875 - 1956)          400-1500     G,M,I
```

* -Denotes Mixed Media,Watercolors,Gouaches,Pastels,and/or Drawings

B

BABBIDGE, JAMES GARDNER (1844 - 1919)	2000-6000	M
BABCOCK, WILLIAM P.(1826 - 1899)	300-1500	S,G,L
BABER, ALICE (1928 -)	800-6500	A
BACH, ESTHER E.(20TH)	*150-350	X (W)
BACHER, OTTO HENRY (1856 - 1909)	1500-45000	L,S,I,M
BACON, C.E. (19TH C)	100-600	L
BACON, CHARLES ROSWELL (1868 - 1913)	400-4500	L
BACON, FRANK A. (1803 - 1887)	500-2500	L
BACON, HENRY	*300-1500	
BACON, HENRY (1839 - 1912)	1500-18000	F,G,L
BACON, I.L.(late 19TH C)	100-250	X (S)
BACON, IRVING R. (1875 - 1962)	*300-800	X (G)
BACON, PEGGY B.	*100-2000	I
BACON, PEGGY B.(1895 -)	1000-3500	F,G,
BADGER, FRANCIS (19TH - 20TH C)	500-1500	X (G)
BADGER, JOSEPH (1708 - 1765)	1500-6000	P
BADGER, S.F.M.(19TH C)	1000-6000	M
BADGER, THOMAS (1792 - 1868)	250-600	F
BAER, JO (1929 -)	3000-10000	A
BAER, MARTIN (1894 - 1961)	200-1200	A
BAER, WILLIAM JACOB (1860 - 1941)	400-3500	F,G,S
BAILEY, JAMES G. (1870 -)	200-600	I,L
BAILEY, S.S. (19TH C)	*100-350	L
BAILEY, T.(19TH - 20TH C)	100-500	M,L
BAILEY, WILLIAM H.	*1000-4500	
BAILEY, WILLIAM H. (1930 -)	5000-35000	A
BAIRD, WILLIAM BABTISTE (1847 -)	500-6000	L,W,M
BAKER, CHARLES (1844 - 1906)	*100-400	L,M
BAKER, ELISHA TAYLOR (1827 - 1890)	200-700	M
BAKER, ELIZABETH GOWDY (1860 - 1927)	*100-500	F
BAKER, ERNEST (19TH C)	300-1200	M
BAKER, G.A. (19TH - 20TH C)	800-9000	M
BAKER, GEORGE A. (1821 - 1880)	200-700	F
BAKER, J. ELDER (19TH C)	*300-3000	G,S
BAKER, O.F. (19TH C)	300-1000	M
BAKER, SAMUEL BURTIS (1882 - 1967)	100-500	L,F
BAKER, T.E. (19TH - 20TH C)	1000-6500	M
BAKER, W.B. (19TH C)	*500-1000	M
BAKER, WILLIAM BLISS (1859 - 1886)	600-7000	L,M
BALDWIN, ALBERTUS H.(1865 -)	*100-350	X (M)
BALDWIN, G.B. (19TH C)	300-1500	F
BALINK, HENDRICUS C.(1882 - 1963)	3000-20000	L,F
BALL, ALICE WORTHINGTON (- 1929)	200-1200	M,S
BALL, L. CLARENCE	*200-500	
BALL, L. CLARENCE (1858 - 1915)	300-2000	L,S
BALLIN, HUGO (1879 - 1956)	300-2000	F
BAMA, JAMES ELLIOTT	*4000-20000	
BAMA, JAMES ELLIOTT (1926 -)	8000-25000	G,F,S
BANKS, RICHARD (20TH C)	500-2500	X (F)
BANNARD, (WALTER) DARBY (1934 -)	1000-20000	A

* -Denotes Mixed Media,Watercolors,Gouaches,Pastels,and/or Drawings

```
BANNISTER, EDWARD MITCHELL (1828 - 1901)      1000-15000    L,F
BANNISTER, J. (1821 - 1901)                    500-2000     M,S
BANTA, WEART (19TH C)                          100-1800     L,F
BARBER, JOHN (1898 - 1965)                     500-6000     G,L
BARBER, JOHN WARNER (1798 - 1885)             *150-400      I
BARBER, JOSEPH (1915 -     )                   *100-300      M
BARCHUS, ELIZA R. (1857 - 1959)                200-2500     L
BARCLAY, MCCLELLAND                           *100-400
BARCLAY, MCCLELLAND (1891 - 1943)              400-2500     I,G,S
BARD, JAMES (and JOHN) (1815 - 1897)           10000-50000  M
BARDAZZI, PETER (1943 -     )                  500-3000     A
BARILE, XAVIER J. (1891 -     )                200-1500     X (A)
BARKER, GEORGE (1882 - 1965)                   100-500      L
BARLOW, JOHN NOBLE (1861 - 1917)               500-6000     L
BARLOW, MYRON (1873 - 1938)                    800-3000     G,F
BARNARD, EDWARD HERBERT (1855 - 1909)          500-2000     S,L
BARNES, ERNEST HARRISON (1873 -     )          500-3000     L
BARNES, GERTRUDE (1865 -     )                 500-2500     L
BARNES, JOHN PIERCE (1893 -     )              800-4000     L
BARNES, PENELOPE BIRCH (early 19TH C)         *300-800      S
BARNET, WILL (1911 -     )                     1000-6000    X (A)
BARNETT, BJORN (JR) (1887 -     )              300-1200     L
BARNETT, HERBERT (1910 - 1978)                 500-3000     A,L
BARNETT, RITA WOLPE (20TH C)                   150-400      X (L,S)
BARNETT, THOMAS P.(1870 - 1929)                200-1500     L,M
BARNETT, WILLIAM (20TH C)                      100-800      A
BARNITZ, A.M. (19TH C)                         150-400      X (L)
BARR, WILLIAM (1867 - 1933)                    400-1000     L,G
BARRAUD, ALFRED T. (1849 - 1925)               100-400      L
BARRETT, ELIZABETH HUNT (1863 -     )          100-500      L
BARRETT, MARY E. (19TH C)                     *500-3000     L
BARRETT, OLIVER GLEN (20TH C)                  100-500      L
BARRETT, WILLIAM S. (1854 - 1927)              600-3000     L,M
BARRON, ROS (1933 -     )                      300-700      X (A)
BARROW, JOHN DOBSON (1827 - 1907)              400-2000     L
BARRY, EDITH CLEAVES (early 20TH C)            150-500      L
BARSE, GEORGE RANDOLPH (JR) (1861 - 1938)      1000-5000    L
BARTHOLOMEW, WILLIAM N.(1856 - 1919)          *100-500      L
BARTLETT, DANA (1878 - 1957)                   400-2000     L
BARTLETT, FREDERICK EUGENE (1852 - 1911)      *100-200      X (M,L)
BARTLETT, JONATHAN ADAMS (1817 - 1902)         3000-10000   P
BARTLETT, PAUL WAYLAND (1881 - 1925)           400-2000     L
BARTOLL, WILLIAM THOMPSON (1817 - 1859)        250-2500     P
BARTON, LOREN R.                              *300-800
BARTON, LOREN R. (1893 - 1975)                 500-2000     L,G,M
BARTON, MINETTE (1889 - 1976)                  600-5000     X (G)
BARTON, RALPH (1891 - 1931)                   *200-800      S,I
BARTOO, CATHERINE R. (1876 - 1949)             100-300      X
BASCOM, RUTH HENSHAW (1772 - 1848)            *2000-10000   P
BASHFIELD, EDWIN HOWLAND (1848 - 1936)         800-4000     F
BASING, CHARLES (1865 -     )                  500-3000     X (L)
BASKERVILLE, CHARLES (1896 -     )             800-3000     X (F,G)
BASKIN, LEONARD (1922 -     )                 *400-4000     A
BATCHELLER, FREDERICK S.(1837 - 1889)          600-3500     S,L
BATTY, ROLAND W. (20TH C)                      300-900      X
```

* -Denotes Mixed Media,Watercolors,Gouaches,Pastels,and/or Drawings

BAUCHMANN, C.(late 19TH C)	100-500	L
BAUER, WILLIAM (1888 -)	200-800	L
BAUM, CARL (CHARLES ?)(19TH C)	500-6500	S,L
BAUM, CHARLES (1812 - 1877)	500-6500	S,L
BAUM, WALTER EMERSON (1884 - 1956)	350-3000	L,I
BAUMANN, GUSTAVE (1881 - 1971)	200-800	L
BAUMGARTEN, WILLIAM (19TH - 20TH C)	*500-2000	I
BAUMGRAS, PETER (1827 - 1904)	500-1500	L,S,F
BAXTER, ELIJAH (JR) (1849 - 1939)	300-1000	L,S
BAYARD, CLIFFORD ADAMS (1892 - 1934)	400-1500	L
BAYER, HERBERT	*200-800	
BAYER, HERBERT (1900 -)	1000-6000	X (A)
BAYLES, ? (19TH C)	100-400	X (L)
BAYLINSON, A.S. (1882 - 1950)	200-700	X (S)
BAZIOTES, WILLIAM A.	*4000-75000	
BAZIOTES, WILLIAM A. (1912 - 1963)	5000-275000	A
BEAL, GIFFORD	*400-1200	
BEAL, GIFFORD (1879 - 1956)	1000-20000	L,G
BEAL, JACK (1931 -)	1500-20000	X (A)
BEAL, REYNOLDS	*150-2000	
BEAL, REYNOLDS (1867 - 1951)	1000-15000	L,G,M
BEALL, CECIL CALVERT (1892 -)	*100-750	I
BEAMAN, GAMALIEL WILLIAM (19TH C)	400-1800	L
BEAMAN, WILLIAM (19TH C)	100-400	L
BEAME, W. (19TH C)	150-800	L
BEAN, CAROLINE VAN HOOK (1880 - 1970)	400-1000	X (G)
BEAN, HANNAH (early 19TH C)	*250-800	P
BEAR, JESSIE DREW (20TH C)	100-400	X
BEARD, ADELIA BELLE (- 1920)	400-2000	L,F,I
BEARD, ALICE (19TH - 20TH C)	300-2500	X (G)
BEARD, HARRY (19TH C)	250-1200	X (W,S)
BEARD, JAMES HENRY (1812 - 1893)	1500-25000	F,G,L,W
BEARD, WILLIAM HOLBROOK (1824 - 1900)	1500-25000	F,G,L
BEARDEN, ROMARE (1914 -)	*1000-30000	A
BEATON, CECIL (20TH C)	*300-1500	X (I,S)
BEATTIE, ALEXANDER (20TH C)	100-400	X
BEATTY, FRANK T. (1899 -)	*800-2500	X (M)
BEATTY, JOHN WILLIAM (1851 - 1924)	400-5500	L
BEAUCHAMP, ROBERT (1923 -)	300-4000	A
BEAUFORT, JOHN (19TH C)	800-7500	L
BEAUMONT, ARTHUR EDWAINE (1879 - 1956)	350-1500	M,F
BEAUREGARD, C.G.(19TH C)	250-900	X (G)
BEAUX, CECILIA	*400-4500	
BEAUX, CECILIA (1863 - 1942)	1000-25000	F,L
BEBIE, HENRY (1824 - 1888)	800-3500	L,F
BECHER, ARTHUR E. (1877 - 1941)	300-1800	I,L,G
BECHTLE, ROBERT (1932 -)	5000-35000	A
BECKER, FREDERICK W. (1888 - 1953)	300-1200	L
BECKER, J. (19TH C)	500-30000	S
BECKETT, CHARLES E. (active 1840-50	100-600	L,M
BECKHOFF, HARRY (1901 - 1979)	*400-2500	I
BECKINGHAM, ARTHUR (19TH C)	300-1200	G,F
BECKMANN, MAX	*500-75000	
BECKMANN, MAX (1884 - 1950)	3500-275000	A
BECKWITH, ARTHUR (1860 - 1930)	250-1000	L

* -Denotes Mixed Media,Watercolors,Gouaches,Pastels,and/or Drawings

BECKWITH, JAMES CARROLL (1852 - 1917)	400-18000	F,G
BEELER, JOE	*1500-10000	
BEELER, JOE (1931 -)	5000-30000	L,G
BEERS, JULIE HART (1835 - 1913)	800-3000	L
BEHRE, FREDERIC JOHN (19TH - 20TH C)	400-2000	X (S)
BELKNAP, ZEDEKIAH (1781 - 1858)	1000-30000	P
BELL, CECIL C. (1906 - 1970)	200-1000	X (L,F)
BELL, CHARLES (1874 - 1935)	1000-35000	A
BELL, EDWARD AUGUSTE (1862 - 1953)	800-4500	F
BELL, LARRY (1939 -)	500-3500	A
BELLOWS, ALBERT F.	*400-7500	
BELLOWS, ALBERT F.(1829 - 1883)	800-5000	L,G
BELLOWS, GEORGE W.	*500-24000	
BELLOWS, GEORGE W.(1882 - 1925)	6000-125000	G,F,L
BEMELMANS, LUDWIG (1898 - 1962)	*150-3000	I
BEMISH, R. HILLS (19TH - 20TH C)	*100-300	L
BEN-ZION, (1897 -)	250-1500	A
BENBRIDGE, HENRY (1743 - 1812)	2000-10000	F
BENDA, WLADYSLAW T. (1873 - 1948)	*150-500	I
BENDER, BILL (1920 -)	300-2000	X (A)
BENEDICT, A.C.(19TH - 20TH C)	800-3500	L
BENEDUCE, ANTIMO (1900 -)	*100-250	L,S
BENEKER, GERRIT ALBERTUS (1882 - 1934)	500-3500	G,I,F
BENGSTON, BILLY AL (1934 -)	800-10000	A
BENJAMIN, KARL (1925 -)	500-2500	A
BENJAMIN, NORA (1899 -)	*100-300	X
BENJAMIN, SAMUEL G.W. (1837 - 1914)	500-2000	M
BENN, BEN (1884 - 1983)	500-4500	F,S
BENNETT, LYLE HATCHER (19TH - 20TH C)	400-900	X
BENNETT, RAINEY (1904 -)	*100-300	L
BENSELL, GEORGE FREDERICK (1837 - 1879)	500-8000	F,G
BENSON, EUGENE (1839 - 1908)	400-5000	F,L
BENSON, FRANK WESTON	*500-15000	
BENSON, FRANK WESTON (1862 - 1951)	2000-100000	F,W,L,S
BENSON, JOHN P.(1865 - 1947)	200-800	M
BENSON, LESLIE (1885 -)	200-1500	G,I
BENTLEY, JOHN W.(1880 -)	300-1500	L
BENTON, DWIGHT (1834 -)	250-1000	L
BENTON, THOMAS HART	*500-70000	
BENTON, THOMAS HART (1889 - 1975)	3000-375000	G,F,L,I
BERKE, ERNEST (1921 -)	800-10000	F,L
BERMAN, EUGENE	*200-3500	
BERMAN, EUGENE (1899 - 1972)	1000-8000	I,F
BERMAN, SAUL (1899 -)	800-3500	X (G)
BERMAN, WALLACE (1926 - 1976)	400-2500	A
BERNEKER, LOUIS FREDERICK (1876 - 1937)	300-2000	F,L
BERNINGHAUS, J. CHARLES (1905 -)	250-900	X (L)
BERNINGHAUS, OSCAR E.(1874 - 1952)	2500-200000	G,L,I
BERNSTEIN, RICHARD (1930 -)	400-3200	X
BERNSTEIN, THERESA (1895 -)	200-6000	X (L)
BERRY, CARROLL THAYER (1886 - 1978)	100-1500	M,L
BERRY, PATRICK VINCENT (1843 - 1913)	300-1200	L,W
BERS, JULIE HART (1835 - 1913)	500-3000	L
BERTHELSEN, JOHANN	*300-800	
BERTHELSEN, JOHANN (1883 - 1969)	500-6000	L,M

* -Denotes Mixed Media,Watercolors,Gouaches,Pastels,and/or Drawings

```
BERTHOT, JAKE                                    *300-2500
BERTHOT, JAKE (1939 -       )                    1000-10000    A
BERTRAM, H.C. (19TH C)                           *100-400      G
BESS, FORREST CLEMENGER (1911 - 1977)            2500-20000    A
BEST, ARTHUR WILLIAM (1859 - 1935)               200-2000      L
BEST, HARRY CASSIE (1863 - 1936)                 500-1500      L
BETTS, HAROLD HARRINGTON (1881 -       )         300-4500      F,L
BETTS, LOUIS (1873 - 1961)                       800-30000     F,G,S
BETTS, VIRGINIA BATTLE (20TH C)                  150-500       X
BEWICK, WILLIAM (1795 - 1866)                    600-1200      X (G)
BEWLEY, MURRAY PERCIVAL (1884 - 1964)            400-3500      F
BEYER, WILLIAM E. (1929 -       )                *200-800      L,M
BIANCHI, A. (20TH C)                             100-350       X (S)
BICKERSTAFF, ? (20TH C)                          100-650       L
BICKNELL, ALBION HARRIS (1837 - 1915)            400-5000      F,G,S
BICKNELL, E. (19TH - 20TH C)                     *150-400      X (L)
BICKNELL, FRANK ALFRED (1866 - 1943)             400-3000      L
BICKNELL, WILLIAM H.W. (1860 -       )           400-1200      X (G)
BIDDLE, GEORGE (1885 - 1973)                     500-6000      G,I,L
BIDWELL, A.(19TH C)                              100-400       X (G)
BIERSTADT, ALBERT (1830 - 1902)                  1500-350000+  L,M
BIGELOW, CHARLES C. (1891 -       )              100-250       F
BIGELOW, DANIEL FOLGER (1823 - 1910)             300-1500      L
BIGELOW, THOMAS (1849 - 1924)                    600-2000      L
BIGGS, ROBERT OLDHAM (1920 -       )             500-1800      L,G
BIGGS, WALTER (1886 - 1968)                      *100-2500     I
BILLING, FREDERICK W. (1835 - 1914)              500-2500      X (G)
BILLINGS, HENRY (1901 -       )                  *800-4500     I
BINGHAM, GEORGE CALEB (1811 - 1879)              5000-1000000  G,F,L
BINKS, WARD (20TH C)                             400-3000      W
BINNEY, H.N. (19TH C)                            *250-800      X (M)
BINTONI, ROLLIN (19TH C)                         100-350       L
BIRCH, THOMAS (1779 - 1851)                      3500-180000   L,M,F
BIRCH, WILLIAM (1755 - 1834)                     *500-3500     L,G
BIRCHALL, WILLIAM MINSHAL (1884 -       )        *100-1200     M
BIRDSALL JR, AMOS (1865 - 1938)                  400-6000      M
BIRMELIN, ROBERT (1933 -       )                 200-800       A,M
BIRNEY, WILLIAM VIERPLANCK (1858 - 1909)         800-10000     F,G
BIRREN, JOSEPH P. (1864 - 1933)                  250-1200      L
BISBING, HENRY SINGLEWOOD (1849 - 1919)          600-3000      L,W
BISCHOFF, FRANZ ALBERT (1864 - 1929)             500-10000     L,M
BISHOP, ALBERT F. (1855 -       )                800-5000      L,M
BISHOP, ISABEL                                   *200-1500
BISHOP, ISABEL (1902 -       )                   1000-4000     G,F
BISPHAM, HENRY COLLINS (1841 - 1882)             250-1200      L
BISSELL, EDGAR JULIAN (1856 -       )            300-1000      L
BISTRAM, EMIL (1895 -       )                    500-1500      X (F)
BIXBEE, WILLIAM JOHNSON (1850 - 1921)            250-2000      L
BLACK, LAVERNE NELSON (1887 - 1938)              2000-50000    F,G
BLACK, OLIVE PARKER (1868 - 1948)                500-3000      L
BLACKBURN, JOSEPH (1700 -       )                800-45000     P
BLACKMAN, WALTER (1847 - 1928)                   400-8000      G,L,F
BLACKWELL, TOM (1938 -       )                   3000-25000    A
BLAIR, STREETER (1888 - 1966)                    400-12000     L
BLAKE, LEO B. (20TH C)                           250-600       L
```

* -Denotes Mixed Media,Watercolors,Gouaches,Pastels,and/or Drawings

BLAKELOCK, RALPH A.(1847 - 1919)	500-35000	L
BLANCH, ARNOLD (1896 - 1968)	300-1200	F,S
BLANEY, DWIGHT (1865 - 1944)	100-800	L,M
BLANKENSHIP, ROY (20TH C)	300-1200	L
BLASHFIELD, EDWIN HOWLAND (1848 - 1936)	800-18000	G,F
BLASS, CHARLOTTE L.(1908 -)	100-400	F,L
BLAUVELT, CHARLES F. (1824 - 1900)	800-6500	G,F
BLECKNER, ROSS (20TH C)	500-3500	A
BLEIMAN, MAX (19TH - 20TH C)	200-1000	L
BLENNER, CARLE JOHN (1864 - 1952)	500-8000	F,S,G,L
BLOCH, ALBERT (1882 - 1961)	700-6000	A
BLOMFIELD, C. (19TH C)	250-1000	L
BLOODGOOD, MORRIS S. (1845 - 1920)	250-2500	L
BLOOM, HYMAN (1913 -)	1000-10000	A
BLOOMER, HIRAM REYNOLDS (1845 - 1910)	300-2500	L
BLUEMNER, OSCAR F.	*350-15000	
BLUEMNER, OSCAR F. (1867 - 1938)	2500-50000	A,L
BLUHM, NORMAN (1920 -)	1200-15000	A
BLUM, JEROME (1884 - 1956)	250-1500	A,L
BLUM, ROBERT FREDERICK	*1000-50000+	
BLUM, ROBERT FREDERICK (1857 - 1903)	1000-50000+	L,F,I
BLUME, PETER (1906 -)	*500-5000	A
BLUMENSCHEIN, ERNEST LEONARD	*1500-8000	
BLUMENSCHEIN, ERNEST LEONARD (1874 - 1960)	1500-80000	F,I,L
BLUMENSCHEIN, HELEN GREENE (1909 -)	600-2500	X (L)
BLUNT, JOHN S. (1798 - 1835)	800-8000	P,M
BLYTHE, DAVID GILMOUR (1815 - 1865)	3000-60000	G,F
BOARDMAN, WILLIAM G. (1815 - 1865)	350-5000	L
BOCHERO, PETER (1895 - 1962)	700-6000	P
BODWELL, A.V. (early 20TH C)	100-500	X (L)
BOEHM, HENRY (- 1914)	300-1500	L
BOESE, HENRY (active 1845-65)	400-3000	L
BOGERT, GEORGE HIRST (1864 - 1944)	400-2500	L
BOGGS, FRANK MEYERS	*500-2000	
BOGGS, FRANK MEYERS (1855 - 1926)	1500-12000	L,M
BOHAN, RUTH HARRIS (1891 - 1981)	250-1000	X
BOHLER, HANS (20TH C)	100-450	L
BOHM, MAX (1868 - 1923)	500-5000	G,F
BOHROD, AARON	*200-2500	
BOHROD, AARON (1907 -)	600-10000	G,L,S
BOICE, BRUCE (1941 -)	500-5000	A
BOILEAU, PHILIP (1864 - 1917)	*300-2500	F,I
BOISSEAU, ALFRED (1823 - 1903)	350-3500	X (G,F)
BOIT, EDWARD DARLEY (1840 - 1916)	*350-8000	L
BOLEGARD, JOSEPH (20TH C)	*500-3500	I
BOLMER, M. DEFOREST (1854 - 1910)	200-1200	L
BOLOTOWSKY, ILYA (1907 - 1981)	2500-15000	A
BOLSTER, JANETTE WHEELER (1821 - 1883)	200-500	X (L)
BONFIELD, GEORGE R. (1802 - 1898)	500-6000	L,M
BONFIELD, WILLIAM VAN DE VELDE (19TH C)	400-3000	L
BONGART, SERGEI R. (20TH C)	300-2500	L
BONHAM, HORACE (1835 - 1892)	600-5000	G
BONIN, R. (20TH C)	600-2500	X
BONNET, LEON (20TH C)	400-2000	L
BONTECOU, LEE (1931 -)	*500-5000	A

* -Denotes Mixed Media,Watercolors,Gouaches,Pastels,and/or Drawings

```
BOOG, CARLE MICHEL (1877 -     )              150-600      X (G)
BOOTH, FRANKLIN (1874 - 1943)                *600-3500     I
BORBINO, J. (1905 - 1964)                     800-4000     L,M
BOREIN, EDWARD (1872 - 1945)                 *400-30000    G,L
BOREN, JAMES                                 *2500-25000
BOREN, JAMES (1921 -     )                     5000-40000   G,L
BORG, CARL OSCAR (1879 - 1947)                700-14000    L,I
BORGLUM, J. GUTZON (1867 - 1941)              400-2000     X (L)
BORGO, LOUIS (1867 -     )                    *100-500      I
BORGORD, MARTIN (1869 - 1935)                 600-3000     F,G
BORONDA, LESTER D.(1886 - 1951)               500-2000     L,G
BOSA, LOUIS (1905 -     )                      200-2500     L,G
BOSKERCK, ROBERT WARD VAN (1855 - 1932)       300-4000     L
BOSLEY, FREDERICK A.(1881 - 1942)             2500-20000   F
BOSS, HOMER (1882 - 1956)                     250-1500     L
BOSTELLE, THOMAS (1921 -     )                *100-400      L
BOSTON, F.D. (20TH C)                         200-700      L
BOSTON, FREDERICK JAMES (1855 - 1932)         350-3500     F,L,S
BOSTON, JOSEPH H.(     - 1954)                300-2500     L,F
BOTKE, CORNELIUS (1887 - 1954)                300-2000     L,S
BOTKE, JESSIE ARMS (1883 - 1971)              600-3000     W,I
BOTT, E.F.E.V. (19TH C)                       400-1500     L,G
BOUCHE, LOUIS (1896 - 1969)                   600-15000    L,G,I
BOUGHTON, GEORGE HENRY (1833 - 1905)          800-6000     L,G,F
BOUGUEREAU, E.J.G.(1837 - 1922)               1200-8000    F
BOUNDEY, BURTON SHEPARD (1879 - 1962)         300-2000     L
BOUTELLE, DEWITT CLINTON (1820 - 1884)        800-7500     L,G,F
BOVEE, I.A. (19TH - 20TH C)                   100-400      L
BOWDOIN, HARRIETTE (19TH - 20TH C)            200-1200     G,I
BOWEN, BENJAMIN JAMES (1859 -     )           100-500      M
BOWER, ALEXANDER                             *100-600
BOWER, ALEXANDER (1875 - 1952)                300-3000     M,L
BOWIE, FRANK LOUISVILLE (1857 - 1936)         100-350      L .
BOWMAN, ADRIANUS M.(19TH C)                   200-700      S
BOWYER, ALAN (19TH - 20TH C)                  100-600      X (G)
BOXER, STANLEY ROBERT (1926 -     )           2000-10000   A
BOYENHART, C. (19TH C)                        100-400      X (F)
BOYER, RALPH LUDWIG (1879 - 1952)             200-1000     F,I
BOYES, G.E. (19TH C)                          500-5000     F
BOYLE, CHARLES WELLINGTON (1864 - 1925)       600-3000     L
BOYLE, FERDINAND THOMAS LEE (1820 - 1906)     400-1000     F
BOYLE, JOHN J. (1852 - 1917)                  600-2000     S
BOYLE, W.W. (19TH C)                          250-2500     X (L)
BRAAM, G. (19TH C)                           *100-500      P
BRACE, REEVES (19TH - 20TH C)                 500-2000     L
BRACH, PAUL (1924 -     )                      800-5000     A
BRACKETT, A. LORING (19TH - 20TH C)           500-2500     X (W)
BRACKETT, WALTER M. (1823 - 1919)             500-3500     W
BRACKMAN, ROBERT (1898 - 1980)                500-7000     S,F
BRADFORD, WILLIAM                            *800-4500
BRADFORD, WILLIAM (1823 - 1892)               1500-75000   M,L
BRADISH, ALVA (1806 - 1901)                   500-1000     P
BRADLEY, ANNE CARY (1884 -     )              300-1500     X
BRADLEY, JOHN (     - 1874)                   18000-50000  P
BRADLEY, PETER (1940 -     )                   500-1500     A
```

* -Denotes Mixed Media,Watercolors,Gouaches,Pastels,and/or Drawings

```
BRADSTREET, JOSIE E. ( ? )                        100-500       L,S
BRADY, MATTHEW (1823 - 1892)                     *500-2500      F
BRAGG, CHARLES (20TH C)                            500-2000      X (G)
BRAINARD, ANN ELIZABETH (19TH C)                   100-800       L
BRANCHARD, EMILE PIERRE (1881 - 1938)              200-3000      L
BRANDIEN, CARL W. (20TH C)                         100-700       X
BRANDRIFF, GEORGE KENNEDY (1890 - 1936)            200-11000     L
BRANDT, CARL LUDWIG (1831 - 1905)                  700-8000      L,F
BRANSOM, PAUL (1885 - 1981)                        300-4000      I
BRAUN, MAURICE (1877 -1941)                        600-5000      L
BRAZINGTON, WILLIAM CAREY (1865 - 1914)           *400-1200      F
BRECK, JOHN LESLIE (       - 1899)
BRECKENRIDGE, HUGH HENRY (1870 - 1937)             800-7500      S,L,F
BREDIN, RAY SLOAN (1881 - 1933)                    800-12000     L,F
BREEM, PAUL (19TH)                                 300-3500      M
BREENE, ALEXANDER (20TH C)                         100-350       M
BREHM, GEORGE (1878 - 1966)                       *200-1000      I
BRENNER, CARL CHRISTIAN (1838 - 1888)              800-5500      L
BRENNER, F.H. (19TH C)                             200-1000      L
BRENNERMAN, GEORGE W. (1856 - 1906)                500-5000      L,W,I
BRETT, DOROTHY (1882 - 1977)                       700-8000      A
BRETT, HAROLD MATHEWS (1880 - 1955)                350-3000      I,G,F
BREUER, HENRY JOSEPH (1860 - 1932)                 400-3500      L
BREUER, THEODORE A. (19TH - 20TH C)                500-12000     F
BREUL, HUGO (1854 - 1910)                          700-3500      F,G
BREVITT, GEORGE (1854 -       )                    700-5500      L
BREVOORT, JAMES RENWICK (1832 - 1918)              500-4500      L
BREWER, NICHOLAS RICHARD (1857 - 1932)             1000-4500     F,L
BREWERTON, GEORGE DOUGLAS                         *250-1500
BREWERTON, GEORGE DOUGLAS (1820 - 1901)            600-5000      L,M
BREWSTER, ANNA RICHARDS (1870 - 1952)              300-1500      L,I
BREWSTER JR.,JOHN (1766 - 1854)                    2500-120000   P
BRICE, WILLIAM (1921 -       )                     5000-20000    A
BRICHER, ALFRED THOMPSON                          *350-25000
BRICHER, ALFRED THOMPSON (1837 - 1908)             1500-110000   M,L
BRIDGEMAN, R. (19TH C)                             100-500       P
BRIDGES, CHARLES (active 1730-45)                  2500-8000     P
BRIDGES, FEDILIA                                  *300-2000
BRIDGES, FIDELIA (1835 - 1923)                     800-5500      L,W,M
BRIDGMAN, FREDERICK ARTHUR (1847 - 1928)           800-40000     F,L,G
BRIGANTI, NICHOLAS P. (1895 -       )              350-3500      L,F
BRIGGS, LUCIUS A. (1852 - 1931)                   *250-800       M
BRIGGS, WARREN C. (1867 - 1903)                    250-1800      L
BRIGHAM, WILLIAM COLE (1870 -       )              500-2500      L
BRILL, GEORGE REITER (1867 - 1918)                 100-400       F
BRINDLE, E. MELBOURNE (1904 -       )             *600-5000      I
BRINLEY, DANIEL PUTNAM (1879 - 1963)               2000-8000     L,F
BRISCOE, DANIEL (1826 - 1883)                      250-800       X (M)
BRISCOE, FRANKLIN D.(1844 - 1903)                  400-7000      M
BRISTOL, JOHN BUNYON (1826 - 1909)                 500-5000      L
BROAD, A.H. (20TH C)                               100-300       L
BROCKMAN, ANN (1899 -       )                      250-3000      X (F)
BRODERSON, MORRIS GAYLORD (1928 -       )          500-5000      A
BRODIE, GANDY (1924 - 1975)                        600-3500      X (A)
BROMLEY, F.C.(19TH C)                              200-2500      L
```

* -Denotes Mixed Media,Watercolors,Gouaches,Pastels,and/or Drawings

```
BROMLEY, J.W. (19TH C)                              400-1500      F
BROOK, ALEXANDER                                    *150-600
BROOK, ALEXANDER (1898 -      )                     500-6000      F,L
BROOKE, RICHARD NORRIS (1847 - 1920)                400-4500      L,G
BROOKES, SAMUEL MARSDEN (1816 - 1892)               3500-50000    S
BROOKS, ALDEN FINNEY (1840 - 1931)                  1000-4000     S,F,G
BROOKS, CORA SMALLEY (     - 1930)                  100-500       L
BROOKS, HENRY H. (1898 -      )                     100-800       X (S)
BROOKS, JAMES (1906 -     )                          2500-30000    A
BROOKS, NICHOLAS ALDEN (active 1880-1905)           1000-7500     S
BROUGIER, ADOLF (1870 - 1926)                       300-1500      X (L)
BROWERE, ALBURTIS DELL ORIENT (1814 - 1887)         1200-12000    G,L,S
BROWN, ANNA (19TH - 20TH C)                         300-1500      X
BROWN, BENJAMIN CHAMBERS (1865 - 1942)              350-3500      L
BROWN, BOLTON (1865 - 1936)                         400-2000      X (L)
BROWN, BRADFORD (20TH C)                            *150-600      X
BROWN, CHARLES V. (1848 -      )                    500-2500      X (F)
BROWN, DOUGLAS EDWIN (1904 -      )                 *150-500      X
BROWN, ETHELBERT (1870 -      )                     100-400       X (G)
BROWN, F. GRISWOLD (20TH C)                         100-400       L
BROWN, FRANCIS F.(1891 -      )                     400-1200      L
BROWN, FRANK A.(1876 -      )                       150-700       F,G
BROWN, GEORGE ELMER (1871 - 1946)                   350-6000      L
BROWN, GEORGE LORING (1814 - 1889)                  500-10000     L,M
BROWN, GRAFTON TYLER (1841 - 1918)                  250-1500      L
BROWN, HARLEY (20TH C)                              *500-8000     X (F)
BROWN, HARRISON BIRD (1831 - 1915)                  500-6000      L,M
BROWN, J. APPLETON (1844 - 1902)                    600-15000     L,M
BROWN, J. HENRY (1818 - 1891)                       450-2000      F,L
BROWN, J. RANDOLPH (1861 -      )                   350-2000      X (M)
BROWN, J. (active 1800-35)                          5000-35000    P
BROWN, JAMES (mid 19TH C)                           700-4000      X (G)
BROWN, JOAN (1938 -      )                          3000-15000    A
BROWN, JOHN BUNYAN (1826 - 1909)                    400-3500      L
BROWN, JOHN GEORGE (1831 - 1913)                    4000-115000   G
BROWN, MANNEVILLE E.D. (1810 - 1896)                800-4000      L,F
BROWN, MATHER (1761 - 1831)                         400-7500      F
BROWN, MAURICE (1877 - 1941)                        150-700       X (L)
BROWN, MCALPIN (20TH C)                             100-500       F,L
BROWN, P. (19TH - 20TH C)                           100-400       X (M)
BROWN, ROGER (1941 -      )                         5000-25000    A
BROWN, ROY (1879 - 1956)                            350-2000      L
BROWN, SAMUEL JOSEPH (1907 -      )                 400-3000      A,F
BROWN, W. WARREN (19TH C ?)                         250-1500      M
BROWN, W.H. (active 1875-1890)                      200-750       X (L)
BROWN, WALTER (1853 - 1929)                         100-500       X
BROWN, WALTER FRANCIS (1853 - 1929)                 350-1500      L,I
BROWN, WILLIAM ALDEN (1877 -      )                 100-500       L
BROWN, WILLIAM MARSHALL (1863 - 1929)               750-2500      G
BROWN, WILLIAM MASON (1828 - 1898)                  800-20000     S,L
BROWNE, BYRON (1907 - 1961)                         450-10000     A
BROWNE, CHARLES FRANCIS (1859 - 1921)               500-3500      L
BROWNE, GEORGE ELMER (1871 - 1946)                  500-6000      M,L,G
BROWNE, HAROLD PUTNAM (1894 - 1931)                 *150-400      X (L)
BROWNE, MARGARET FITZHUGH (1884 - 1972)             350-3000      X (L)
```

* -Denotes Mixed Media,Watercolors,Gouaches,Pastels,and/or Drawings

```
BROWNE, MATILDA (1896 -      )                    350-1800    S,L
BROWNELL, CHARLES DE WOLF (1822 - 1909)          650-15000   L,S
BROWNELL, MATILDA AUCHINLOSS (1869 -  )  1000-6000   L
BROWNING, COLLEEN (1927 -    )                    300-1800    X
BROWNSCOMBE, JENNIE                               *300-2500
BROWNSCOMBE, JENNIE (1850 - 1936)                800-20000   F
BRUCE, EDWARD (1879 - 1943)                      350-3500    L
BRUCE, GRANVILLE (20TH C)                        *200-800    X
BRUCE, JAMES CHRISTIE (19TH - 20TH C)            150-600     M
BRUCE, JOSEPHINE (19TH C)                        100-300     X (S)
BRUCKMAN, LODEWYK (1903 -    )                    500-3000    X (S)
BRUESTLE, BERTRAM G. (1902 -    )                 200-1200    L
BRUESTLE, GEORGE M.(1872 - 1939)                 350-4000    L
BRUMIDI, CONSTANTINO (1805 - 1880)               2000-30000  X (F)
BRUNDAGE, WILLIAM TYSON (1849 - 1923)            200-2500    M
BRUNET, ADELE LAURE (1879 -    )                 100-250     F
BRUNNER, FREDERICK SANDS (1886 -    )            350-3000    I
BRUNTON, RICHARD (    - 1832)                    800-4000    P
BRUSH, GEORGE DE FOREST (1855 - 1941)            1000-70000  F
BRUTON, MARGARET (    - 1983)                    200-600     X
BRUZZI, ?    (19TH C)                            100-500     X (W)
BRYANT, EVERETT LLYOD (1864 - 1945)              100-1000    S,L
BRYANT, HAROLD E.(1894 - 1950)                   800-4500    X (F)
BRYANT, HENRY C.(1812 - 1881)                    1000-7000   L,F
BRYANT, WALLACE (19TH - 20TH C)                  150-600     M,F
BUCHTERKIRCH, ARMIN (1859 -    )                 *100-500    F,L,M
BUCK, WILLIAM H. (1840 - 1888)                   2000-18000  L,G
BUDGEON, T. (19TH C)                             500-2500    L
BUDNER, T. (20TH C)                              100-400     X (G)
BUDSEY, ALFRED (20TH C)                          *100-400    X (F)
BUEHR, G.F. (early 20TH C)                       100-400     X (L)
BUFF, CONRAD (1886 - 1975)                       100-400     L
BULL, CHARLES LIVINGSTON (1874 - 1932)           *150-1000   I,W,M
BULLARD, OTIS A. (1816 - 1853)                   800-4500    F,G,L
BUNCE, WILLIAM GEDNEY (1840 - 1916)              200-1500    L,M
BUNDY, HORACE (1814 - 1883)                      350-5000    F
BUNDY, JOHN ELWOOD (1853 - 1933)                 300-3000    L
BUNKER, DENNIS MILLER (1861 - 1890)              1200-35000  F
BUNNER, ANDREW FISHER (1841 - 1897)              800-5000    L,M
BURBANK, ELBRIDGE AYER (1858 - 1949)             700-10000   F,S
BURCHFIELD, CHARLES E.(1893 - 1967)              *800-150000 L,A
BURDICK, HORACE ROBBINS (1844 - 1942)            100-800     F,S
BUREN, AEBURN L. VAN (1891 -    )                *100-750    I
BURGDORFF, FERDINAND (1881 -    )                200-2000    L
BURGESS, GEORGE H. (1831 -    )                  1500-8000   X (L)
BURGESS, RUTH PAYNE (19TH C)                     250-800     F
BURKHARDT, HANS GUSTAV (1904 -    )              *200-2000   A
BURLEIGH, SIDNEY RICHMOND                        *900-7500
BURLEIGH, SIDNEY RICHMOND (1853 - 1931)          1500-8500   L,F
BURLIN, PAUL (1886 - 1969)                       250-5000    A
BURLIUK, DAVID                                   *150-800
BURLIUK, DAVID (1882 - 1966)                     350-20000   G,S,L,F
BURNS, CHARLES H. (1932 -    )                   200-1000    X
BURNS, MILTON (1853 - 1933)                      *100-300    X (G,M)
BURNS, PAUL (20TH C)                             *100-500    L
```

* -Denotes Mixed Media,Watercolors,Gouaches,Pastels,and/or Drawings

```
BURNSIDE, CAMERON (1887 -    )          *250-700       X (L)
BURPEE, WILLIAM PARTRIDGE               *250-1000
BURPEE, WILLIAM PARTRIDGE (1846 -    )   800-5000      M,L
BURR, GEORGE BRAINARD (1876 - 1939)      700-5000      L
BURR, GEORGE ELBERT                     *200-750
BURR, GEORGE ELBERT (1859 - 1939)        600-2500      L,S
BURRIDGE, WALTER WILCOX (1857 -    )    *200-600       L
BURRILL JR., E. (late 19TH C)            100-500       X (G)
BURROUGHS, BRYSON (1868 - 1934)          600-2000      F
BURT, JAMES (19TH C)                     800-4000      L,M
BUSBY, C.A. (active 1810-30)            *1000-4000     P ?
BUSCH, CLARENCE FRANCIS (1887 -    )     500-2000      X (F)
BUSH, JACK (1909 - 1977)                5000-65000     A
BUSH, NORTON (1834 - 1894)               500-10000     L,M
BUTEAU, W.A. (19TH C)                    100-400       L
BUTLER, B.L. (19TH - 20TH C)             100-400       X
BUTLER, CHARLES E. (19TH C)              800-3500      G
BUTLER, EDITH EMERSON (late 19TH C)     *100-400       L
BUTLER, GEORGE BERNARD (1838 - 1907)     700-5000      F,S
BUTLER, H.D. (early 20TH C)              250-800       L
BUTLER, HOWARD RUSSELL (1856 - 1934)     300-4000      L,M
BUTLER, MARY (20TH C)                    100-400       L
BUTLER, THEODORE E.(1876 - 1937)         900-35000     L,F
BUTMAN, FREDERICK (active 1855-70)       350-2000      L
BUTTERSWORTH, JAMES E.(1817 - 1894)     1500-45000     M
BUTTON, JOHN (1929 -    )                600-10000     A
BUXTON, HANNAH P. (19TH C ?)             600-2500      X (F̄)
```

C

```
CABOT, AMY (    - 1934)                   200-700      X
CABOT, EDWARD CLARKE (1818 - 1901)       *350-1500     L
CADENASSO, GIUSEPPE (1858 - 1918)         200-700      L
CADMUS, PAUL                             *350-3500
CADMUS, PAUL (1904 -    )                2500-25000     G,F
CADY, EMMA JANE (19TH C)                 *1500-6500     X (S)
CADY, HENRY N.                           *150-450
CADY, HENRY N. (1849 -    )               400-3500      M,L
CADY, WALTER HARRISON (1877 - 1970)       350-1800      I
CAFFERTY, JAMES H. (1819 - 1869)          250-4500      G,F,S
CAHILL, WILLIAM VINCENT (    - 1924)      750-5000      L
CAHOON, CHARLES (1861 - 1951)             400-4500      L
CAHOON, MARTHA (20TH C)                   300-2000      L,S
```

* -Denotes Mixed Media,Watercolors,Gouaches,Pastels,and/or Drawings

```
CAHOON, RALPH (      - 1982)                    500-12000    P
CALCAGNO, LAWRENCE (1916 -      )              200-700      A
CALDER, ALEXANDER (1898 - 1976)              *450-8500
CALDER, ALEXANDER (1898 - 1976)               1500-45000   A
CALDER, ALEXANDER STERLING (1870 - 1945)    *1000-5000    A
CALIFANO, JOE (1864 -      )                   350-1800     X
CALIGA, ISAAC HENRY (1857 -      )             500-5500     F
CALLAHAN, JAMES (20TH C)                      *100-400      L
CALLE, PAUL                                   *5000-15000
CALLE, PAUL (20TH C)                          10000-90000   L,I
CALLOWHILL, JAMES (19TH - 20TH C)             150-800      L
CALYO, NICCOLINO VICOMTE (1799 - 1884)        800-5000     L,M
CAMERON, EDGAR SPIER (1862 - 1944)            300-800      L
CAMERON, JOHN (1828 -      )                   2500-15000   L,M
CAMP, JOSEPH RODEFER DE (1858 - 1923)         2500-65000   L
CAMPBELL, BLENDON REED (1872 -      )          300-1200     I
CAMPBELL, C.M. (active c.1900)               *600-1800     G
CAMPBELL, COLIN (20TH C)                       100-300      L
CAMPBELL, GEORGE F. (20TH C ?)                400-1500     X (M)
CAMPBELL, HARRY (20TH C)                       100-250      X
CANFIELD, ABIJAH (1769-1830)                 *2000-15000   P
CANIFF, MILTON (1907 -      )                 *250-600      X (F)
CANTEY, MAURINE (1901 -      )                 200-1000     X
CANTRALL, HARRIET M. (20TH C)                  100-600      M
CAPLES, ROBERT (20TH C)                       *200-700      L
CAPP, AL (20TH C)                             2500-18000    A
CARBEE, J.C. (19TH - 20TH C)                  400-1200     X (F)
CARBEE, SCOTT (1860 -      )                   300-800      X (F)
CARDELL, MRS. FRANK HALE (1905 -      )        200-700      X (S)
CARDENASSO, GIUSEPPE (1858 - 1918)            200-700      L
CARISS, HENRY T. (1840 - 1903)                3500-10000   G
CARL, KATHERINE AUGUSTA (      - 1938)        200-650      F
CARLES, ARTHUR B. (1882 - 1952)               1200-65000   A,S,F
CARLETON, CLIFFORD (1867 - 1946)             *100-500      I
CARLEY, S.G. (late 19TH C)                    100-350      X (S)
CARLIN , ANDREW B. (19TH C)                   800-5000     F
CARLIN, JOHN (1813 - 1891)                    500-6000     G,L,F
CARLO, GIRARDO DE (20TH C)                    100-300      L
CARLSEN, DINES (1901 - 1966)                  500-7000     S,L
CARLSEN, SOREN EMIL (1853 - 1932)             650-85000    S,L
CARLSON, JOHN FABIAN (1875 - 1945)            250-14000    L
CARLTON, ANNE (19TH - 20TH C)                 250-2500     L,G
CARLTON, WILLIAM TOLMAN (1816 - 1888)         750-3500     G
CARMIENCKE, JOHANN HERMANN (1810 - 1867)      300-8500     L
CARPENTER, DUDLEY (1870 -      )               100-400      X
CARPENTER, ELLEN MARIA (1836 - 1909)          300-1500     L,F,S
CARPENTER, FRED GREEN (1882 - 1965)           200-6000     L,F
CARR, JOHN (      - 1837)                      800-4000     X (S,L)
CARR, LYELL (1857 - 1912)                     650-7000     G,F
CARR, SAMUEL S. (1837 - 1908)                 800-35000    G
CARROL. ROBERT (20TH C)                        350-2500     X
CARROLL, JOHN WESLEY                          *100-600
CARROLL, JOHN WESLEY (1892 - 1959)            250-2500     F,S
CARSMAN, JON (20TH C)                          400-4500     X
CARSON, W.A. (early 20TH C)                    100-350      L
```

* -Denotes Mixed Media,Watercolors,Gouaches,Pastels,and/or Drawings

```
CARSTAIRS, JAMES STEWART (19TH - 20TH C)       200-700        X (L)
CARTER, CLARENCE HOLBROOK (1904 -       )       500-5000       F
CARTER, DENNIS MALONE (1827 - 1881)             800-6000       G,F
CARTER, HENRY (1821 - 1880)                    *100-500        X (G)
CARTER, JAMES (1817 - 1873)                     350-800        F
CARTER, PRUETT A. (1891 - 1955)                 200-4000       I,F
CARY, WILLIAM DE LA MONTAGNE (1840 - 1922)      700-50000      G,S
CASE, EDMUND E. (1840 - 1919)                   350-2500       L
CASER, ETTORE (1880 - 1944)                     100-650        F,S
CASH, HERBERT (19TH - 20TH C)                   100-500        X (S)
CASHELL, V. (19TH - 20TH C)                    *400-1000       L
CASILEAR,JOHN WILLIAM (1811 - 1893)            1200-20000      L
CASNELLI, VICTOR (19TH C)                      *600-3000       F,G
CASS, GEORGE NELSON (1831 - 1882)               750-3500       W,L,S
CASS, KAE DORN (1901 - 1971)                   *100-450        L
CASSATT, MARY                                  *400-475000
CASSATT,MARY (1844 - 1926)                     1800-1250000    F
CASSIDY, IRA D. GERALD (1879 - 1934)           5000-20000      F,L,I
CASSIN, F.B. (20TH C)                           300-1000       X
CASTANO, JOHN (20TH C)                          500-2000       X (G)
CASTELLON, FEDERICO (1914 - 1971)              1000-6000       A
CASTLE-KEITH, WILLIAM (19TH - 20TH C)           200-850        L
CATHCART, JOHN (19TH C)                         100-500        X (F)
CATLIN, GEORGE                                 *2500-30000
CATLIN, GEORGE (1796 - 1872)                   2000-300000     F,L,M
CAULDWELL, LESLIE GRIFFEN (1861 - 1941)         500-4500       F
CAVALLON, GIORGIO                              *400-1800
CAVALLON, GIORGIO (1904 -       )              4000-35000      A
CEDERQUIST, ARTHUR E. (1884 - 1955)             250-800        L
CHACE, HELEN B. ( 20TH C ?)                     100-350        X (M)
CHADWICK, ELLEN N. ( ? )                        100-600        X (L)
CHADWICK, WILLIAM (1879 - 1962)                 650-15000      L,F
CHAESE, EMILIE (18TH C)                          800-8000       X (G)
CHAESE, NORA (19TH C)                           250-1200       G,F
CHAFFEE, OLIVER (1881 - 1944)                   350-3000       X (S)
CHAFFEE, SAMUEL R. (19TH - 20TH C)             *100-850        L
CHALFANT, JEFFERSON DAVID (1846 - 1931)        6500-65000      G,F
CHALIAPIN, BORIS (20TH C)                       100-600        X (F)
CHALLEE, S.R. (late 19TH C)                    *100-400        X (L)
CHALLONER, WILLIAM L. (20TH C ?)                600-3000       X (L,M)
CHAMBERLAIN, NORMAN STILES (1887 - 1961)        800-4500       X (L)
CHAMBERLAIN, WYNN (1929 -       )               400-3000       X (S,F)
CHAMBERLIN, FRANK TOLLES (1873 - 1961)         *250-800        X
CHAMBERLIN, PRICE A. (19TH C)                  *100-400        L
CHAMBERS, C. BOSSERON (1882 -       )           250-2500       F,I
CHAMBERS, CHARLES EDWARD (1892 - 1942)          300-2500       I
CHAMBERS, THOMAS (1805 - 1866)                  600-30000      P
CHAMPNEY, BENJAMIN (1817 - 1909)                450-5000       L,G,S
CHAMPNEY, JAMES WELLS                          *400-3500
CHAMPNEY, JAMES WELLS (1843 - 1903)             500-45000      G,F,L
CHAN, GEORGE (20TH C)                           200-750        L
CHANDLER, HENRY DALAND (19TH C)                *250-2500       I
CHANDLER, JOSEPH GOODHUE (1813 - 1880)          450-4500       F
CHANDLER, MRS. JOSEPH GOODHUE (1820-1868)       100-1000       X (F,S)
CHANDLER, WINTHROP (1747 - 1790)              10000-75000      P
```

* -Denotes Mixed Media,Watercolors,Gouaches,Pastels,and/or Drawings

Name	Price	Media
CHANDLER, (? late 19TH - 20TH C)	100-350	L,M
CHANEY, LESTER JOSEPH (1907 -)	200-650	M
CHANLER, ROBERT WINTHROP (1872 - 1930)	*600-1800	X (W)
CHAPEL, GUY MARTIN (1871 -)	200-600	L
CHAPIN, ALPHEUS (1787 - 1870)	400-1200	F
CHAPIN, BRYANT (1859 - 1927)	150-3500	S,L
CHAPIN, C.H. (active 1850-85)	500-3000	L
CHAPIN, FRANCIS (1899 - 1965)	*100-500	G,F
CHAPIN, JAMES ORMSBEE (1887 -1975)	300-6500	X (G)
CHAPLIN, SARAH (19TH C)	*250-650	X (S)
CHAPMAN, CARLTON THEODORE (1860 - 1926)	300-5000	M,L
CHAPMAN, CHARLES SHEPARD (1879 - 1962)	200-2500	F,L,I
CHAPMAN, CONRAD WISE (1842 - 1910)	900-13000	G,L,M
CHAPMAN, CYRUS DURAND (1856 - 1918)	650-2500	X (S)
CHAPMAN, JOHN GADSBY (1808 - 1889)	800-8500	G,L,I,M
CHAPMAN, JOHN LINTON (1839 - 1905)	1000-10000	G,L,M
CHAPMAN, MINERVA JOSEPHINE (1858 -)	300-1200	G,S,L
CHAPPEL, ALONZO	*200-750	
CHAPPEL, ALONZO (1828 - 1887)	350-1500	F,M
CHARTRAND, ESTEBAN (19TH C)	300-3000	L
CHASE, ADELAIDE COLE (1868 - 1944)	100-650	F,S
CHASE, C.H. (19TH C)	600-2500	M
CHASE, FRANK SWIFT (1886 - 1958)	350-1200	L,M
CHASE, HENRY (HARRY) (1853 - 1889)	650-5000	M
CHASE, LILA ELIZABETH (19TH - 20TH C)	350-1500	X (F)
CHASE, WILLIAM MERRITT	*1200-300000+	
CHASE, WILLIAM MERRITT (1849 - 1916)	2000-475000	L,F,S
CHATTERTON, CLARENCE K. (1880 - 1973)	750-7000	L,F
CHECK, R.S. (19TH C)	200-600	F
CHEN, CHI (1912 -)	*350-3200	L
CHEN, HILO (20TH C)	1000-6500	X (F)
CHENEY, RUSSELL (1881 - 1945)	350-2500	X (L)
CHERNEY, MARVIN (1925 - 1967)	200-1200	A
CHERNOW, ANN (20TH C)	*300-1500	A
CHESTER, C. (19TH C)	150-500	P
CHICHESTER, CECIL (1891 -)	250-3000	L,I
CHICKERING, CHARLES R. (1934 -)	250-650	X (G)
CHILD, EDWIN BURRAGE (1868 - 1937)	250-3000	F,L,I
CHIRIACKA, ERNEST (1920 -)	1000-8500	X (L,F)
CHITTENDEN, ALICE BROWN (1860 - 1934)	150-1000	F,S
CHRISTENSEN, DAN (1942 -)	3000-20000	A
CHRISTOPHER, WILLIAM (1924 - 1973)	*300-1200	X
CHRISTY, F. EARL (1883 -)	*300-1200	X
CHRISTY, HOWARD CHANDLER	*250-3500	
CHRISTY, HOWARD CHANDLER (1873 - 1952)	500-20000	I,F
CHUMLEY, JOHN WESLEY (1928 -)	*400-5500	X (L,G)
CHURCH, FREDERIC EDWIN (1826 - 1900)	2500-350000+	L,M
CHURCH, FREDERICK STUART (1842 - 1923)	250-4000	L,I
CHURCHILL, WILLIAM WORCESTER (1858 - 1926)	2500-6500	F
CICERI, ERNEST (1817 - 1866)	*150-500	X (M)
CIKOVSKY, NICOLAI (1894 - 1934)	250-750	L,F,S,M
CIMIOTTI, GUSTAVE (1875 -)	250-2000	L
CIPRICO, MARGUERITE (20TH C)	100-400	L
CLAGHORN, JOSEPH C.	*150-850	
CLAGHORN, JOSEPH C. (1869 -)	900-7500	L

* -Denotes Mixed Media,Watercolors,Gouaches,Pastels,and/or Drawings

CLAIR, R.A. (19TH C)	750-2000	L
CLAITON, J (19TH - 20TH C)	150-650	X (M)
CLAPP, WILLIAM HENRY (1879 - 1954)	750-6500	L,F
CLARK, ALSON SKINNER (1876 - 1949)	1200-18000	L,I
CLARK, BENTON (1895 - 1964)	300-3500	I
CLARK, C. MYRON (1876 - 1925)	100-850	L,M
CLARK, ELIOT CANDEE (1883 - 1980)	400-5000	L
CLARK, EMERSON (19TH C)	200-850	X (G)
CLARK, FREEMAN (19TH C)	200-750	L
CLARK, GEORGE MERRITT (- 1904)	350-1500	G
CLARK, MATT (1903 - 1972)	200-1200	I
CLARK, ROY C. (1889 -)	100-600	L
CLARK, VIRGINIA KEEP (1878 -)	100-400	F
CLARK, WALTER (1848 - 1917)	200-1500	L
CLARK, WALTER APPLETON (1876 - 1906)	200-1200	X
CLARK, WALTER LEIGHTON (19TH C ?)	150-750	X
CLARKE, J.V. (late 19TH C)	100-600	X (L)
CLARKE, JOHN CLEM (1937 -)	500-15000	A
CLARKE, ROBERT A. (early 19TH C)	3500-25000	G
CLARKSON, EDWARD (active 1845-60)	750-3000	X (G)
CLAY, MARY F.R. (- 1939)	250-1000	F,L
CLEAVES, W.R. (late 19TH C)	200-800	L
CLIME, WINFIELD SCOTT (1881 - 1958)	450-2500	L
CLINEDINST, BENJAMIN WEST	*100-600	
CLINEDINST, BENJAMIN WEST (1859 - 1931)	350-4500	I,G,F
CLINTON, C.F. (19TH C)	500-2000	X (F)
CLONESSY, W. (19TH C)	100-600	X (G)
CLONNEY, JAMES GOODWYN (1812 - 1867)	25000-275000	G,F
CLOSSON, WILLIAM BAXTER PALMER (1848-1926)	250-1500	X (G)
CLOUGH, STANLEY THOMAS (1905 -)	100-500	L
CLOUGH, GEORGE L. (1824 - 1901)	700-6500	L,M,F
CLOVER, LEWIS P. (1819 - 1896)	250-1500	F,G
CLYMER, JOHN FORD (1907 -)	1000-130000	I,G
CLYNE, A.J. (20TH C)	100-500	L
COALE, GRIFFITH BAILAY (1890 - 1950)	300-1500	I,F
COAST, OSCAR REGAN (1851 - 1931)	200-750	L
COATES, EDMOND C. (1816 - 1871)	500-5000+	L,G,M
COATES, JOHN (19TH C)	400-1500	L,G
COATS, RANDOLPH (1891 -)	150-750	L
COB, LYMUSES E. (19TH C)	650-2000	X (F)
COBB, CYRUS (1834 - 1903)	150-650	L,F,M
COBB, DARIUS (1834 - 1919)	200-1800	L,S,F,M
COBURN, FREDERICK SIMPSON	*350-1500	
COBURN, FREDERICK SIMPSON (1871 - 1960)	2500-30000	L
COCHRAN, ALLEN DEAN (1888 - 1935)	150-500	X (F)
COCHRANE, CONSTANCE (20TH C)	150-650	L,M
CODMAN, CHARLES (1800 - 1842)	1000-12000	L,M
CODMAN, EDWIN E. (19TH C)	100-600	M
CODMAN, JOHN AMORY (1824 - 1886)	650-3500	L,M,F
COFFEE, WILL J. (20TH C)	100-350	L,F
COFFIN, ELIZABETH R. (1851 - 1930)	1200-2000	X
COFFIN, GEORGE ALBERT (1856 - 1922)	100-600	M
COFFIN, WILLIAM ANDERSON (1855 - 1925)	400-15000	L,M,F
COFFIN, WILLIAM HASKELL	*200-850	
COFFIN, WILLIAM HASKELL (- 1941)	250-5000	M,L,F

* -Denotes Mixed Media,Watercolors,Gouaches,Pastels,and/or Drawings

COGGELSHALL, JOHN I. (1856 - 1927)	250-900	X (G)
COGGESHALL, K.M. (20TH C)	100-350	L
COGSWELL, WILLIAM (1819 - 1903)	250-750	F
COHEN, GEORGE (1919 -)	350-1500	X (G)
COHEN, LEWIS (1857 - 1915)	350-2000	L,F
COIT, CAROLINE (- 1934)	*150-500	M,L
COLBY, GEORGE E. (1859 -)	450-1800	L
COLE, ALPHAESUS PHILEMON (1876 - 1900)	100-850	F,L
COLE, JOSEPH FOXCROFT (1837 - 1892)	450-2800	L,F
COLE, JOSEPH GREENLEAF (1803 - 1858)	350-1000	F
COLE, THOMAS (1801 - 1848)	3500-900000	L
COLEGROVE, M.B. (19TH C)	100-650	L
COLEMAN, CHARLES CARYL (1840 - 1928)	700-150000	L,G,F
COLEMAN, GLENN O. (1887 - 1932)	3500-20000	L
COLEMAN, MARION (20TH C)	150-650	X (F)
COLEMAN, R. CLARKSON (1884 -)	200-1200	M
COLEMAN, RALPH PALLEN (1892 -)	200-1200	I,F
COLEMAN, SAMUEL (1832 - 1920)	1500-35000	L,M
COLLIER, B.L. (19TH - 20TH C)	100-400	L
COLLIER, WILLIAM R. (19TH C)	*300-1500	X (L)
COLLINS, EARL (1925 -)	400-1500	X (L)
COLLINS, FRANK H. (- 1935)	100-750	X (F)
COLLVER, ETHEL BLANCHARD (1875 - 1955)	750-4500	F
COLMAN, ROY CLARKSON (1884 -)	200-750	L
COLMAN, SAMUEL	600-3500	
COLMAN, SAMUEL (1832 - 1920)	1500-35000	L,M
COLT, MORGAN (1876 - 1926)	450-2000	L
COLTMAN, ORA (1860 -)	*100-400	L
COMAN, CHARLOTTE BUELL (1833 - 1924)	150-850	L
COMEGYS, GEORGE H. (early 19TH C)	350-3500	G
COMINS, ALICE R. (- 1934)	300-650	L
COMPERA, ALEXIS (1856 - 1906)	400-1200	L
COMSTOCK, ENOS BENJAMIN (1879 - 1945)	600-2500	X (I)
CONANT, ALBAN JASPER (1821 - 1915)	650-2500	F,M
CONANT, LUCY SCARSBOROUGH (1867 - 1921)	200-750	L
CONARROE, GEORGE W. (1803 - 1882)	600-2500	F
CONELY, WILLIAM B. (1830 - 1911)	200-750	X (S,F)
CONGDON, ADAIRENE VOSE (19TH C)	600-1800	X (G)
CONGDON, THOMAS RAPHAEL (1862 - 1917)	*200-750	X (G)
CONGER, WILLIAM (early 20TH C)	*200-600	X (G)
CONKLIN, S. (19TH - 20TH C)	350-1200	X (M)
CONNAWAY, JAY HALL (1893 - 1970)	250-850	L,M
CONNELL, EDWIN D. (1859 -)	800-2500	F,W
CONNER, ALBERT CLINTON (1848 - 1929)	150-850	L
CONNER, JOHN ANTHONY (20TH C)	150-600	L
CONNORS, BRUCE G. (1909 -)	*250-800	X (L)
CONSTANT, GEORGE (1892 - 1978)	*150-500	I
CONTI, GINO EMILIO (1900 -)	100-350	G
CONWAY, FRED (1900 - 1972)	*150-850	X (L)
COOK, C.M. (19TH C)	150-650	X (M)
COOK, CAPTAIN (19TH - 20TH C)	1000-6000	P
COOK, CHARLES BAILEY (early 20TH C)	200-900	X (L)
COOK, MARION (19TH C ?)	300-1200	X (L)
COOK, NELSON (1817 - 1892)	500-5000	F
COOKE, GEORGE (1793 - 1849)	700-4500	L,M

* -Denotes Mixed Media,Watercolors,Gouaches,Pastels,and/or Drawings

COOKMAN, CHARLES EDWIN (1856 -1913)	250-2000	F
COOLEY, B. (19TH C)	800-3500	X
COOLIDGE, CASSIUS M. (19TH - 20TH C)	500-1800	X
COOMBS, DELBERT DANA (1850 - 1938)	150-2500	L,M
COOPER, ASHLEY DAVID MONTAGUE (1856 - 1924)	400-8500	L,G
COOPER, COLIN CAMPBELL (1856 - 1937)	400-12000+	G,F,L
COOPER, EMMA LAMPERT (- 1920)	*400-1000	X (G)
COOPER, GEORGE VICTOR (1810 - 1878)	150-650	L
COOPER, J. (18TH - 19TH C)	200-850	F
COPE, GEORGE (1855 - 1929)	500-30000	S,L
COPE, GORDON (20TH C)	150-600	L
COPELAND, ALFRED BRYANT (1840 - 1909)	850-4500	X (G,L)
COPELAND, CHARLES (1858 - 1945)	*100-800	L,I,M
COPELAND, JOSEPH FRANK (1872 -)	*100-400	L
COPLEY, JOHN SINGLETON (1737 - 1815)	2500-650000	F,M
COPLEY, WILLIAM (BILL) NELSON (1919-)	1500-15000	A
COPPEDGE, FERN ISABELL (1888 -)	150-1500	L
CORBINO, JOHN (1905 - 1964)	150-3500	F,G,L
CORDREY, EARL SOMERS (1902 -)	*150-500	X (I)
COREY, BERNARD (20TH C)	250-800	L
CORNE, MICHELE FELICE (1752 - 1845)	*3000-12000	F,M
CORNELL, JOSEPH (1903 - 1972)	1000-20000	A
CORNOYER, PAUL (1864 - 1923)	500-20000	L
CORNWELL, DEAN (1892 - 1960)	400-30000	I
CORSON, ALICE VINCENT (- 1915)	750-2500	X (F)
CORSON, CHARLES SCHELL (- 1921)	400-6000	L
CORWIN, CHARLES ABEL (1857 - 1938)	500-3000	G,L
COSTELLO, DAVID (20TH C)	300-800	X
COSTIGAN, JOHN EDWARD (1888 - 1972)	450-13000	L,F
COSTSANEN, J. (1888 -)	1200-6000	G
COTE, ALAN (1937 -)	500-3000	A
COTTINGHAM, ROBERT	*1000-6000	
COTTINGHAM, ROBERT (1935 -)	5000-45000	A
COTTON, WILLIAM H.	*200-600	
COTTON, WILLIAM H. (1880 - 1958)	250-6500	F,I
COUGHLIN, A.T. (late 19TH C)	400-2000	L
COULON, EMMA (19TH - 20TH C)	800-3500	L,G
COULON, GEORGE DAVID (1823 - 1904)	850-4500	L,F
COULON, PAULINE (19TH C)	*400-1200	X (W)
COULTER, MARY J. (20TH C)	100-700	L
COULTER, WILLIAM ALEXANDER (1849 - 1936)	1200-18000	M
COUSE, EANGER IRVING (1866 - 1936)	1000-75000	F,G
COUTER, FRANKLYN C. (19TH C)	700-2000	X (F)
COUTTS, ALICE (1865 - 1937)	400-1800	L,G
COUTTS, GORDAN (1880 - 1937)	450-4000	L,F
COWLES, FLEUR (20TH C)	250-900	X
COX, ALBERT SCOTT (1863 - 1920)	500-3200	G,L,F,I
COX, ALLYN (1896 - 1982)	100-250	L,F,S
COX, ARTHUR (late 19TH C)	*150-650	X (L)
COX, CHARLES BRINTON (1864 - 1905)	400-4000	X (G)
COX, KENYON (1856 - 1919)	500-5500	F,I
COX, L.M. (19TH - 20TH C)	100-400	X (L)
COZZENS, FREDERICK SCHILLER (1846 - 1928)	*400-5000	M,I
CRAFFT, R.B. (active 1835-65)	600-2000	F
CRAIG, CHARLES (1846 - 1931)	850-6000	F,L

* -Denotes Mixed Media,Watercolors,Gouaches,Pastels,and/or Drawings

```
CRAIG, ISAAC EUGENE (1830 -     )           500-2000      F,L
CRAIG, J.W. (20TH C ?)                      *100-400       L
CRAIG, ROBERT (19TH C)                       200-1000      L
CRAIG, THOMAS BIGELOW (1849 - 1924)          350-4000      L
CRAIG, WILLIAM (1829 - 1875)                *150-650       L
CRANCH, CHRISTOPHER PEARSE (1813 - 1892)     500-6500      L,F,S
CRANDELL, BRADSHAW (1896 - 1966)            *400-3000      I
CRANE, ANN (20TH C)                          250-850       L
CRANE, (ROBERT) BRUCE (1857 - 1937)          800-9500      L
CRANE, JAMES (20TH C)                        800-4500      P
CRANE, STANLEY WILLIAM (1905 -     )         450-1800      L,S
CRAWFORD, ALICE BERLE (20TH C)              *100-400       X (L)
CRAWFORD, EARL STETSON (1877 -     )         600-2500      F
CRAWFORD, JAMES W. (1832 -     )             100-750       S
CRAWFORD,RALSTON (1906 - 1978)               10000-170000 A
CRIEFELDS, RICHARD (1853 - 1939)             400-2000      S,F
CRISP, ARTHUR WATKINS (1881 -     )          600-3000      G,I
CRISS, FRANCIS H.(1901 - 1973)               1000-15000    A,L
CRITCHER, CATHERINE CARTER (1868 -     )     5000-32000    F
CROCKER, JOHN DENISON (1823 - 1879)          650-6000      L,F
CROCKWELL, DOUGLAS S. (1904 -1968)           600-6000      I
CROCKWELL, SPENCER DOUGLAS (1904 - 1968)     600-6000      I
CROMWELL, CHARLES (1838 -     )              700-3000      I
CROOKS, R. (20TH C)                          400-1500      X (G)
CROPSEY,JASPER FRANCIS (1823 - 1900)         1500-675000   L,M
CROSBY, GEORGE L. (1833 -     )              300-2500      G,M
CROSBY, RAYMOND MOREAU 1875 -     )         *150-500       F
CROSKEY, W.H. (19TH C)                       500-1500      X (G)
CROSS, HENRY H. (1837 - 1918)                1200-6500     L,G,F
CROSSMAN, WILLIAM HENRY (1896 -     )        350-1200      L,G
CROW, LOUISE (20TH C)                        100-400       X (S)
CROWLEY, J.M. (active c.1830-40)            *1200-2500     P
CROWNINGSHIELD, FREDERIC (1845 - 1918)       400-4500      L
CRUSET, SEBASTIEN (20TH C)                   700-2000      X (L)
CRUTCHFIELD, WILLIAM (1932 -     )          *500-1800      X
CUCARO, PASCAL (1915 -     )                 100-500       X
CUCCHI, ANTHONY (20TH C)                     200-750       X
CUCUEL, EDWARD (1875 - 1951)                 1500-35000    F
CULLINGANE, A.C. (19TH C)                    100-300       P
CULMER, HENRY L.A. (1854 - 1914)             800-3500      X
CULVER, CHARLES (1908 - 1967)               *100-400       L,W,F
CULVERHOUSE, JOHANN MONGELS (1820 - 1891)    3000-14000    G,L
CUMMING, ARTHUR (19TH C)                     150-500       X (S)
CUNEO, CYRUS C. (1878 - 1916)                150-1200      X (L,G)
CUNEO, RINALDO (RICHARD) (1877 - 1939)       200-1500      L
CUNNINGHAM, EARL (1893 - 1978)               300-3000      P
CUNNINGHAM, FERN FRANCES (1889 -     )       100-650       X (L,S)
CUNNINGHAM, PATRICIA STANLEY (1919 -     )   200-900       X
CUPREIN, FRANK W. (1871 - 1948)              250-1200      L,M
CURRAN, CHARLES COURTNEY (1861 - 1942)       500-70000     F,L,S
CURRAN, J. (19TH -20TH C)                    500-4000      F,L
CURRIER, JOSEPH FRANK (1843 - 1909)          600-2500      G,L
CURRIER, WALTER BARRON (1879 - 1934)         250-1200      L
CURRY, JOHN STEUART                         *500-6500
CURRY, JOHN STEUART (1897 - 1946)            700-25000     G,L
```

* -Denotes Mixed Media,Watercolors,Gouaches,Pastels,and/or Drawings

```
CURRY, ROBERT F. (1872 - 1945)               500-2500    L
CURTIS, ASA (    - 1858)                      100-450     M
CURTIS, CALVIN (1822 - 1893)                 250-1200    L
CURTIS, ELIZABETH (1873 -      )             250-3000    L,M
CURTIS, EMILE (20TH C)                        150-600    X (F)
CURTIS, LELAND (1897 -      )                200-1000    L,M
CURTIS, MARIAN (1912 -      )               *100-400     L
CURTIS, RALPH WORMELEY (late 19TH C)        2500-40000  F,L
CUSHING, HOWARD GARDINER (1869 - 1916)       450-1200    L,F
CUSHING, J.C. (19TH C)                       200-1000    X (S)
CUSHING, MARY A. (19TH C)                   *200-600     F
CUSTER, EDWARD L. (1837 - 1880)              250-900     P,W,L
```

D

```
D'ARCANGELO, ALLAN (1930 -      )                       3000-20000   A
DABB, RAYMOND (19TH C)                                   650-2000    M
DABO, LEON (1868 - 1960)                                 600-8500    M,L,S
DABO, THEODORE SCOTT (1877 -      )                      150-500     M,L
DAGGY, RICHARD S. (1892 -      )                        *200-750     L
DAHLAGER, JULES (20TH C)                                 700-2500    X
DAHLGREEN, CHARLES W. (1864 - 1955)                      400-2000    L
DAHLGREN, CARL CHRISTIAN (1841 - 1920)                   300-1800    L
DAHLGREN, MARIUS (1844 - 1920)                           250-850     L
DAINGERFIELD, ELLIOTT (1859 - 1932)                      500-5500    L,F,I
DAKEN, SIDNEY TILDEN (1876 - 1935)                       100-750     L
DALBIAC, F. (20TH C)                                     200-750     F
DALE, GEORGE EDWARD (1840 - 1873)                        300-900     X (G)
DALE, WILLIAM (19TH - 20TH C)                            500-2500    L
DALLAS, WILLIAM WILKINS (19TH C)                         100-600     L
DALLIN, CYRUS EDWIN (1861 - 1944)                        200-1200    L
DAMROW, CHARLES (1916 -      )                           350-3500    G,L
DANA, WILLIAM PARSONS WINCHESTER (1833-1927)            600-2000    L,G,M
DANIEL, WILLIAM SWIFT (1865 -      )                     150-500     L
DANIELS, ELMER HARLAND (1905 -      )                    100-300     L,F
DANLON, F. (JR.) (19TH - 20TH C)                         600-5000    X (I,S)
DANNAT, WILLIAM TURNER (1853 - 1929)                     500-3500    F,G
DANNER, SARA KALB (1894 -      )                         150-650     L
DAPHNIS, NASSOS (1914 -      )                           100-1200    A
DARBY, ELIZABETH CLORINDA (    - 1906)                   500-2500    X (S)
DARGE, FRED (1900 -      )                               100-400     G,L
```

* -Denotes Mixed Media,Watercolors,Gouaches,Pastels,and/or Drawings

```
DARLEY, FELIX OCTAVIUS CARR (1822 - 1888)   *200-6500         I,G
DARLING, ROBERT (19TH C)                     2500-10000        F
DARRAH, ANN SOPHIA TOWNE (1819 - 1881)       250-2500          L,M,S
DART, RICHARD POUSETTE (20TH C)              1500-7000         X (F)
DASBURG, ANDREW                             *500-3000
DASBURG, ANDREW (1887 - 1979)                1200-50000        A,L
DASH, ROBERT (1932 -      )                  350-1200          L
DATZ, ABRAHAM MARK (1891 - 1969)             100-450           L
DAUGHERTY, JAMES HENRY                      *350-1200
DAUGHERTY, JAMES HENRY (1889 - 1974)         600-25000         A,I
DAUGHERTY  PAUL (1877 - 1947)                700-2800          L
DAVENPORT, W.S. (19TH - 20TH C)              150-900           X
DAVEY, RANDALL (1887 - 1964)                 650-7500          W,F
DAVID, S.S. (DE SCOTT EVANS)(1847 - 1898)    2000-30000        S,G,F
DAVIDSON, ALLAN D. (19TH - 20TH C)           100-400           X (G)
DAVIDSON, GEORGE (1889 - 1965)               250-750           L,G
DAVIDSON, JO (1883 - 1952)                  *100-500           F
DAVIDSON, MORRIS (1898 -      )             *100-450           A
DAVIES, ALBERT WEBSTER (1889 - 1967)         400-3500          P
DAVIES, ARTHUR BOWEN                        *100-3000
DAVIES, ARTHUR BOWEN (1862 - 1928)           450-15000         A,F,L,
DAVIES, HAROLD CHRISTOPHER ( ? )             500-3000          X (L)
DAVIES, KEN (1925 -      )                   1000-4500         X (S)
DAVIS, A.C. (19TH - 20TH C)                  100-500           X (S)
DAVIS, A.F. (20TH C ?)                       150-750           L
DAVIS, ALEXANDER JACKSON (1803 - 1892)      *5000-15000        L
DAVIS, CHARLES HAROLD (1856 - 1933)          800-15000         L,G
DAVIS, FLOYD MACMILLAN (1896 - 1966)        *250-3000          I
DAVIS, GENE (1920 -      )                   1500-12000        A
DAVIS, GLADYS ROCKMORE (1901 - 1967)         500-4500          F
DAVIS, H.A. (19TH C)                         500-1800          L
DAVIS, HARRY JR. (20TH C)                    350-1500          X (G)
DAVIS, JANE A. (active 1825-55)             *1000-7500         P
DAVIS, JAMES EDWARD (1901 -      )           900-5000          X (G)
DAVIS, JOHN STEEPLE (19TH - 20TH C)          150-500           X (G)
DAVIS, JOSEPH H. (active 1830-35)           *500-14000         F
DAVIS, LEONARD MOORE (1864 - 1938)           200-2500          L
DAVIS, RONALD (RON) WENDELL (1937 -      )   2500-20000        A
DAVIS, STUART                               *450-55000
DAVIS, STUART (1894 - 1964)                  12000-225000      A
DAVIS, VESTIE E. (1904 - 1978)               400-8500          P
DAVIS, WARREN B.                            *100-800
DAVIS, WARREN B. (1865 - 1928)               400-3500          F
DAVIS, WILLIAM M. (1829 - 1920)              3000-65000        L,G
DAWES, EDWIN M. (1872 -      )               350-1500          L
DAWSON, GEORGE WALTER (1870 -      )         300-1200          L,G,S
DAWSON, MARK (19TH C)                        100-600           X (L)
DAWSON-WATSON, DAWSON (1864 - 1939)          350-9000          L
DAY, FRANCIS (1863 -      )                  500-7500          L,G,F
DAY, NELLIE M. (19TH C)                      150-850           L,G
DAY, W. PERCY (20TH C)                       500-2500          L
DE CAMP, JOSEPH RODEFER (1858 - 1923)        2500-65000        L
DE DIEGO, JULIO (1900 - 1979)               *100-750           X
DE HAVEN, FRANKLIN (1856 - 1934)  (See "DEHAVEN")
DE RIBCOWSKY, DEY (1880 - 1935)              200-1500          M,L
```

* -Denotes Mixed Media,Watercolors,Gouaches,Pastels,and/or Drawings

```
DE THULSTRUP, THURE                              *250-2000
DE THULSTRUP, THURE (1849 - 1930)                 700-6500      F,M,I
DEAKIN, EDWIN (1838 - 1923)                       500-6500      L,S
DEAN, EDWARD CLARENCE (1879 -      )             *250-850       X (L)
DEAN, SOPHIA (19TH C)                             800-2500      P
DEAN, WALTER LOFTHOUSE (1854 - 1912)              300-1500      M,G,L
DEARBORN, SAMUEL H. (actice 1800-25)            *200-500       F
DEARTH, HENRY GOLDEN (1864 - 1918)               1200-9500      L,F
DEAS, CHARLES                                    *600-12000
DEAS, CHARLES (1818 - 1867)                      1000-65000     G,F
DECHAR, PETER (1942 -      )                       800-4500      A
DECKER, JOSEPH (1853 - 1924)                      7500-200000   S
DECKER, ROBERT M. (1847 -      )                  300-900       L
DEFREES, T. (late 19TH C)                         200-850       L
DEHAAS, M.F.H. (1832 - 1895)                      600-12000     M
DEHAVEN, FRANKLIN (1856 - 1934)                   350-5000      L
DEHN,ADOLPH ARTHUR                               *350-4500      G,L
DEHN, ADOLPH ARTHUR (1895 - 1968)                 500-6500
DEKLYN, CHARLES F. (20TH C ?)                     150-600       L
DELANEY, BEAUFORD (1902 - 1979)                   250-850       X (M)
DELANEY, JOSEPH (1904 -      )                     300-900       X (G)
DELANO, GERARD CURTIS (1890 - 1972)               8000-30000    L,G
DELANOY, ABRAHAM (1740 - 1786)                   *750-1500      P,F
DELBOS, JULIUS                                   *100-750
DELBOS, JULIUS (1879 -      )                      450-2000      M,L
DELEROISE, C. (19TH C)                            100-650       X (L)
DELLENBAUGH, FREDERICK S. (1853 - 1935)           400-15000     G,L
DEMEAUX, M. (20TH C)                              100-300       F,L
DEMING, EDWIN WILLARD                            *350-2500
DEMING, EDWIN WILLARD (1860 - 1942)               500-12000     F,G,I,W
DEMUTH, CHARLES (1883 - 1935)                    *500-125000    A,F,L,I
DENNY, GIDEON JACQUES (1830 - 1886)               600-2500      L,G,M
DENSLOW, WILLIAM WALLACE (1856 -      )          *100-350       L
DERBY, HORACE B. (19TH C)                        *150-850       M
DERIJCKE, J.L. (20TH C)                           100-600       X (G)
DERRICK, WILLIAM ROWELL (      - 1941)            350-1200      X (L)
DES PORT, A. (19TH C)                             750-4500      X (G)
DESATNICK, MIKE (20TH C)                          5000-15000    X
DESSAR, LOUIS PAUL (1867 - 1952)                  400-3000      G,L
DESVARREUX-LARPENTEUR, JAMES (1847 -      )       400-1500      L,W
DETWILLER, FREDERICK K. (1882 - 1953)             200-1000      I
DEVLAN, F.D. (1835 - 1870)                        400-2000      L
DEVOLL, F. USHER (1873 -      )                    250-750       L
DEWEY, CHARLES MELVILLE (1849 - 1937)             400-2800      L
DEWEY, EDWARD H. (1850 - 1939)                    500-3000      L,W
DEWING, THOMAS WILMER                            *650-20000
DEWING, THOMAS WILMER (1851 - 1938)               3000-20000    F
DEWING, MARIA OAKEY (1857 -      )                850-18000     G
DIAO, DAVID (1943 -      )                         350-2500      A
DICK, M.G. (19TH - 20TH C)                        200-750       X (S)
DICKERMAN, ALBERT (19TH - 20TH C)                 250-3000      L
DICKINSON, ANSON (1780 - 1852)                   *300-800       F
DICKINSON, DAROL (1942 -      )                    1500-4500     X (G)
DICKINSON, EDWIN W. (1891 - 1978)                 3000-15000    A,F
DICKINSON, J.S. (19TH C)                          150-600       X (G)
```

* -Denotes Mixed Media,Watercolors,Gouaches,Pastels,and/or Drawings

DICKINSON, HOWARD CLINTON (20TH C)	100-500	L
DICKINSON, PRESTON	*850-6500	
DICKINSON, PRESTON (1891 - 1930)	1000-20000	A
DIEBENKORN, RICHARD	*30000-80000	
DIEBENKORN, RICHARD (1922 -)	150000-500000A	
DIEHL, ARTHUR VIDAL (19TH - 20TH C)	150-850	L
DIELMAN, FREDERICK (1847 - 1935)	*100-1200	I
DIETRICH, ADELHEID (1827 -)	5000-65000	S
DIKE , PHILIP LATIMER (1906 -)	100-600	L
DILLAWAY, THEODORE M. (1874 -)	100-600	L
DILLER, BURGOYNE (1906 - 1964)	5000-25000	A
DILLON, JULIA MCENTEE (1834 - 1919)	400-1500	X (L)
DILLWORTH, C. (19TH C)	100-750	L
DINE, JIM	*2000-40000	
DINE, JIM (1935 -)	10000-75000	A
DINKEL, GEORGE W. (early 20TH C)	100-300	L
DINNERSTEIN, HARVEY (1928 -)	*200-900	I
DITEMAN, HALL (20TH C)	400-1800	X (L)
DITTMANN, JOHAN (- 1847)	100-600	F
DIX, CHARLES TEMPLE (1838 - 1872)	100-600	L,M,A
DIXON, FRANCIS STILLWELL (1879 - 1962)	200-1200	L
DIXON, L. MAYNARD	*300-10000	
DIXON, L. MAYNARD (1875 - 1946)	750-50000	L,F,I
DOBKIN, ALEXANDER (1908 - 1975)	100-600	X
DODDS, PEGGY (1900 -)	*100-400	X (G)
DODGE, CHESTER L. (1880 -)	150-750	L
DODGE, WILLIAM DE LEFTWICH (1867 - 1935)	600-7500	L,S
DODSON, RICHARD WHATCOAT (1812 - 1867)	*350-750	F
DODSON, SARAH BALL (1847 - 1906)	600-3000	L,G,F
DOFFLEMEYER, ? (19TH - 20TH C)	300-900	X (L)
DOHANOS, STEVAN (1907 -)	800-10000	I
DOLE, WILLIAM (1917 -)	*1000-6000	A
DOLICE, LEON (20TH C)	*100-500	L
DOLPH, JOHN HENRY (1835 - 1903)	750-8500	W,G,F
DONAGHY, JOHN (1838 - 1931)	500-4000	S,L
DONATI, ENRICO (1909 -)	500-5000	A
DONLY, EVA BROOK (1867 -)	100-600	L,M
DONNELL, JOHN (early 20TH C)	150-650	F
DONNELLY, THOMAS J. (1893 -)	100-400	X
DONOHO, GAINES RUGER (1857 - 1916)	500-12000	L
DORIAN, C.S. (19TH - 20TH C)	300-1200	X (G)
DORIANI, WILLIAM (1891 - 1966)	200-800	G
DORINZ, D. (19TH -20TH C)	*400-1000	X (I)
DORNE, ALBERT (1904 - 1965)	*250-1200	I
DOUGHERTY, PARKE CUSTIS (1867 -)	400-6500	L
DOUGHERTY, PAUL (1877 - 1947)	300-15000	M,L
DOUGHTY , THOMAS (1793 - 1856)	2500-25000	L,M
DOUGLAS, CHESTER (1902 -)	300-1500	X
DOUGLAS, LUTHER (20TH C)	100-400	X
DOUGLAS, WALTER (1864 -)	350-2000	W,L
DOVE, ARTHUR GARFIELD	*2500-150000	
DOVE, ARTHUR GARFIELD (1880 - 1946)	20000-180000	A,I
DOW, ARTHUR WESLEY (1857 - 1922)	400-1200	L
DOW, NELL PIERCE (20TH C)	200-750	L
DOW, OLIN (19TH C ?)	*350-900	L

* -Denotes Mixed Media,Watercolors,Gouaches,Pastels,and/or Drawings

```
DOWNES, P.S. (late 19TH C)                      *600-1800      P
DOWNING, THOMAS (1928 -      )                   250-1500      A
DRAGO, GABRIELLE (20TH C)                        100-600       X (M)
DRAKE, CHARLES E. (1865 - 1918)                  150-650       F,L
DRAKE, WILLIAM HENRY (1856 - 1926)               200-700       W,I
DRAPER, EDITH (early 20TH C)                     100-400       X (F)
DRAPER, WILLIAM FRANKLIN (1912 -      )          350-1200      X (L)
DRAVER, ORRIN (20TH C)                           100-650       L
DRAYTON, JOHN (1766 - 1822)                     *250-800       X (I)
DREIER, KATHERINE S. (1877 - 1952)              *200-750       A
DREW, CLEMENT (1806 - 1889)                      500-5000      M
DREW, GEORGE W. (1875 -      )                   300-2500      L
DREW BEAR, JESSIE (20TH C)                       100-650       G,M,S
DREWES, WERNER (1899 -      )                     700-5000     A
DRIGGS, ELSIE                                   *300-2500
DRIGGS, ELSIE (1898 -      )                     1500-15000    A
DRYDEN, HELEN (1887 -      )                    *200-1200      I
DRYSDALE, ALEXANDER JOHN (1870 - 1934)         *250-1800      L
DUBE, MATHIE (1861 -      )                       350-1500     G,F
DUBOIS, CHARLES E. (1847 - 1885)                 200-1000      L
DUBOIS, GUY PENE (1884 - 1958)                   3000-60000    G,F
DUBREUIL, VICTOR (19TH - 20TH C)                 3500-18000    S
DUCKETT, V.F. (20TH C)                          *100-500       L
DUDLEY, FRANK VIRGIL (1868 -      )              250-750       L
DUESSEL, HENRY A. (19TH C)                       100-1000      L
DUFNER, EDWARD                                  *500-10000
DUFNER, EDWARD (1872 - 1957)                     750-18000     L,F
DUGMORE, A. RADCLYFFE (20TH C)                   100-400       X (W)
DUGMORE, EDWARD (1915 -      )                    700-2500     A
DULL, JOHN J. (1862 -      )                    *100-500       L
DUMLER, MARTIN GEORGE (1868 - 1934)              150-650       F,S
DUMMER, H. BOYLSTON (1878 -      )               100-600       I
DUMMER, JOSEPH OWEN ( ? )                        250-900       L
DUMOND, FRANK VINCENT (1865 - 1951)              500-4500      I,L
DUMONT, PAUL (20TH C)                            150-700       X (M)
DUMONT, JO (19TH - 20TH C)                       400-1000      G,F
DUNBAR, HAROLD (1882 -      )                    150-2000      L,F,I,S
DUNBAR, LILI (20TH C)                            450-1200      X (G)
DUNBAR, PATRICK (20TH C)                         450-1500      M
DUNBIER, AUGUSTUS WILLIAM (1888 - 1977)          600-1800      L
DUNCANSON, ROBERT SCOTT (1821 - 1872)            2000-25000    L
DUNLAP, MARY STEWART (20TH C)                    100-450       L
DUNLAP, WILLIAM (1766 - 1839)                    500-3000      F
DUNLOP, DAN (20TH C)                             100-400       X (G)
DUNN, HARVEY T. (1884 - 1952)                    2000-65000    I
DUNN, JULIA E. (1850 -      )                   *200-700       F
DUNNING, ROBERT SPEAR (1829 - 1905)              3000-65000+   S
DUNSMORE, JOHN WARD (1856 - 1945)                700-3500      G,F
DUNTON, WILLIAM HERBERT (1878 - 1936)            2500-50000    G,L,I
DURAN, BOB (ROBERT)(1938 -      )                500-3000      A
DURAND, ASHER BROWN (1796 - 1886)                3000-100000   L
DURAND, JOHN (18TH C)                            500-3500      P
DUREAU, GEORGE (20TH C)                          500-5000      F
DUREN, KARL (19TH - 20TH C)                      500-2500      L
DURRIE, GEORGE HENRY (1820 - 1863)               5000-100000   L,F
```

* -Denotes Mixed Media,Watercolors,Gouaches,Pastels,and/or Drawings

DUTANT, CHARLES (1908 -)	150-700	L
DUVENECK, FRANK (1848 - 1919)	3000-85000	F,L
DUYCKINCK, GERARDUS (1695 - 1742)	8000-35000	P
DWIGHT, JULIA S. (1870 -)	800-5500	F,L
DWYER, A. (19TH C)	*150-750	I,G
DYE, CHARLIE (1906 - 1973)	15000-70000	L
DYE, CLARKSON (1869 - 1945)	250-1000	L
DYER, C.L. (19TH C)	150-800	X (L)
DYER, CHARLES GIFFORD (1846 - 1912)	*300-1200	L
DYER, ELIZABETH GRIFFIN (19TH C)	100-600	L
DYER, H. ANTHONY (1872 - 1943)	*200-1500	L,M
DYER, NANCY A. (1903 -)	*100-600	X (I)
DYER, URIAH N. (19TH C)	350-1200	X (S)
DYKE, SAMUEL P. (active 1855-70)	500-4000	L,G
DYNINGER, F. (20TH C)	100-400	L
DZIGURSKI, ALEX (1911 -)	350-2000	M
DZUBAS, FRIEDEL (1915 -)	5000-25000	A

E

EAKINS, SUSAN MACDOWELL (1851 - 1938)	450-6500	F,G
EAKINS, THOMAS	*7500-550000	
EAKINS, THOMAS (1844 - 1916)	8000-1000000	G,F,M
EARHART, JOHN FRANKLIN (1853 - 1938)	300-1200	L
EARL, JAMES (1761 - 1796)	2000-8000	F
EARL, RALPH (1751 - 1801)	800-20000	P
EARLE, EYVIND (1916 -)	500-3500	L
EARLE, LAWRENCE CARMICHAEL	*250-3000	
EARLE, LAWRENCE CARMICHAEL (1845 - 1921)	400-4500	F,S
EARLE, RALPH (1751 - 1801)	800-25000	P
EARLY, MILES T. (1886 -)	200-750	X (G)
EASTMAN, EMILY (early 19TH C)	*1000-6000	F
EASTMAN, WILLIAM JOSEPH (1888 - 1950)	100-600	L,S
EATON, CHARLES HARRY (1850 - 1901)	400-2500	L
EATON, CHARLES WARREN (1857 - 1934)	500-7000	L
EATON, JOSEPH ORIEL (1829 - 1875)	350-3500	G,F
EATON, VALOY (20TH C)	1000-8000	X
EATON, WYATT (1849 - 1896)	500-3000	F
EBERT, CHARLES H. (1873 - 1959)	500-7500	L,M
EBERT, MARY ROBERTS (1873 -)	*200-1200	L,M
EBY, KERR (1889 - 1946)	*200-1200	I
EDDY, HENRY STEPHENS (1878 - 1944)	300-2500	L

* -Denotes Mixed Media,Watercolors,Gouaches,Pastels,and/or Drawings

```
EDDY, OLIVER TARBELL (1799 - 1868)             400-1500      X (F)
EDE, FREDERIC (1865 -      )                    400-2800      G,L
EDGERLY, BEATRICE (20TH C)                      100-300       X (F)
EDLICH, STEPHEN (1944 -      )                 1000-10000     A
EDMONDS, FRANCIS WILLIAM (1806 - 1863)         1500-30000     G,L
EDMONDSON, WILLIAM J. (1868 -      )            400-2500      F,L
EDWARD, CHARLES (1797 - 1868)                   200-800       L
EDWARDS, ALICE (19TH C)                         200-800       X (L)
EDWARDS, GEORGE WHARTON (1869 - 1950)           200-1000      G,F,L
EDWARDS, T.F. (20TH C ?)                        200-800       X (G)
EDWARDS, THOMAS (active 1820-55)                500-2500      F,L
EFFIE, WILLIAM (active 1835-50)                 700-2000      F
EGAN, ELOISE (20TH C)                           300-1000      X (G)
EGGENHOFER, NICK                               *450-20000
EGGENHOFER, NICK (1897 -      )                6000-50000     G,F,I
EGGLESTON, BENJAMIN OSRO (1867 - 1937)          250-5500      G,F,L
EGLAU,MAX (1825 -      )                         750-3500      L,S
EHNINGER, JOHN WHETTON (1827 - 1889)           1500-30000     G
EICHELBERGER, ROBERT A. (19TH C)                500-3200      G
EICHOLTZ, JACOB (1776 - 1842)                  1500-25000     F
EILSHEMIUS, LOUIS MICHEL (1864 - 1941)          300-5000      A,F,L
EISELE, C. (19TH - 20TH C)                      250-850       L
EISENLOHR, EDWARD G. (1872 - 1961)              200-900       L
ELDER, JOHN ADAMS (1833 - 1895)                 500-5000      G,F
ELDRED, LEMUEL D. (1848 - 1921)                 500-5000      M
ELK, ALBERT LOOKING (20TH C)                    400-3500      L
ELKINS, HENRY ARTHUR (1847 - 1884)              250-2500      L
ELLINGER, DAVID (20TH C)                       *300-3000      P
ELLIOT, LIDIE (19TH C)                          100-450       X (F)
ELLIOTT, CHARLES LORING (1812 - 1868)           350-5000      F
ELLIS, A. (active 1830-35)                     1000-4500      P
ELLIS, CLYDE GARFIELD (1879 -      )            100-300       X (L)
ELLIS, FREMONT F. (1897 -      )                800-7500      L
ELLSWORTH, CLARENCE ARTHUR (1885 - 1961)       *350-1800      F,G
ELLSWORTH, JAMES SANFORD (1802 - 1874)          400-2500      F
ELTING, N.D. (19TH C)                           350-1500      X (S)
ELWELL, D. JEROME (1857 - 1912)                 750-2500      X (L)
ELWELL, ROBERT FARRINGTON (1874 - 1962)         400-4000      G,F
ELWELL, W.H. ( ? )                              100-500       M
EMBRY, NORRIS (1921 - 1981)                    *500-2500      A
EMERSON, CHARLES CHASE (1874 - 1922)            350-2000      I
EMERSON, W.C. (20TH C)                          200-700       X (F)
EMERY, JAMES (active 1865-75)                   750-3500      M
EMMET, LYDIA FIELD (1866 - 1952)                800-7500      F,I
EMMONS, ALEXANDER HAMILTON (1816 - 1879)        300-1500      F
EMMONS, CHANSONETTA STANLEY (1858 - 1937)       350-1200      F,G,S
EMMONS, DOROTHY STANLEY (1891 -      )          350-2000      L
EMPEL, JAN VAN (20TH C)                         700-2000      X
ENDERS, FRANK (20TH C)                          500-2500      X (F)
ENDERS, OSCAR (19TH C ?)                        100-500       L
ENGEL, NISSAN (20TH C)                          500-2000      G
ENGELHARDT, WALTER (20TH C)                     100-500       L
ENGLE, HARRY L. (1870 -      )                  200-2500      L
ENGLEHARDT, JOSEPH J. (19TH C)                  100-1500      L
ENGLISH, FRANK F. (1854 - 1922)                *200-2500      L,G
```

* -Denotes Mixed Media,Watercolors,Gouaches,Pastels,and/or Drawings

```
ENNEKING, JOHN JOSEPH (1841 - 1916)      500-35000+    L
ENNIS, GEORGE PEARCE                      *200-800
ENNIS, GEORGE PEARCE (1884 - 1936)        400-2200      M
ERDELEY, FRANCIS DE (1904 - 1959)         200-2500      G,F
ERICSON, DAVID (1873 - 1946)              250-1500      M,L
ERNST, JIMMY (1920 -    )                 *500-4000
ERNST, JIMMY (1920 -    )                 800-7500      A
ERTZ, EDWARD F.                           *150-600
ERTZ, EDWARD F. (1862 -    )              350-1800      L,F,I
ESNAULT, MAURICE (20TH C)                 100-400       L
ESPOY, ANGEL DE SERVICE (20TH C)          150-1500      M,L
ESSIG, GEORGE EMERICK                     *150-850
ESSIG, GEORGE EMERICK (1838 -    )        450-3500      M,I
ESTES, RICHARD (1936 -    )               2000-45000    A
ETHERIDGE, C.B. (19TH C)                  800-2500      X (S)
ETNIER, STEPHEN MORGAN (1903 -    )       200-2500      M
ETTING, EMLEN (1905 -    )                200-1000      X
EVANS, BRUCE (20TH C)                     800-3500      A
EVANS, DE SCOTT (S.S.DAVID)(1847 - 1898)  1000-30000    S,G,F
EVANS, JAMES GUY                          *750-7500     P
EVANS, JAMES GUY (mid 19TH C)             8000-40000    P
EVANS, JESSIE BENTON (1866 - 1954)        250-1000      L,F
EVANS, RUDULPH (1878 - 1960)              200-600       F
EVERETT, E. DEARBURN (19TH C)             *100-400      L
EVERGOOD, PHILIP HOWARD FRANCIS           *150-7500
EVERGOOD, PHILIP HOWARD FRANCIS (1901-1973) 1800-15000  A
EVERINGHAM, MILLARD (1912 -    )          100-500       X
EVERS, JOHN (1797 - 1884)                 400-2500      L
EVETT, KENNETH WARNOCK (1913 -    )       100-300       X (F)
EYDEN, WILLIAM ARNOLD JR (1893 -    )     *200-850      L
EYTINGE, SOLOMON (JR) (1833 - 1905)       700-4500      X (G,I)
```

F

```
FABER, JOHN (    - 1906)                  100-400       L
FABER, LUDWIG E. (1855 - 1913)            500-2000      L
FAGAN, JAMES (1864 -    )                 100-600       F
FAHNESTOCK, HENRY REIGERT (1830 - 1909)   600-3800      L
FAHNESTOCK, WALLACE WEIR (1877 -    )     250-4000      L
FAIRCHILD (LOW), MARY (1858 - 1946)       *200-800      F
FAIRMAN, JAMES (1826 -1904)               500-5000      L
FALCONER, JOHN M. (1820 - 1903)           1000-6500     L
```

* -Denotes Mixed Media,Watercolors,Gouaches,Pastels,and/or Drawings

```
FALES, P. (late 19TH C)                                100-750       X (G)
FALKNER, HENRY (20TH C)                                100-700       X
FALTER, JOHN PHILIP (1910 - 1982)                      500-15000     I
FANGOR, WOJCIECH (1922 -    )                           900-3500      A
FARIS, J.A. (late 19TH C)                              *350-1200      F
FARLEY, RICHARD BLOSSOM (1875 -    )                    500-3500      L
FARNDON, WALTER (1876 - 1964)                          250-2500      M,L
FARNES, W.M. (19TH C)                                  100-750       X (M)
FARNSWORTH, ALFRED VILLIERS (1858 - 1908)              *200-850      X (G)
FARNSWORTH, JERRY (1895 -    )                          400-2500      I,F
FARNUM, HERBERT CYRUS (1886 -    )                      150-850       M
FARNY, HENRY F.                                        *2000-225000
FARNY, HENRY F. (1847 - 1916)                          10000-500000  I,G,L
FARRE, HENRI (1871 - 1934)                             600-4500      L
FARRER, HENRY (1843 - 1903)                            *300-5000     L
FARRINGTON, MRS ARCH (19TH - 20TH C)                   500-3000      G
FATTON, GEORGE (19TH C)                                150-650       X (F)
FAULKNER, HERBERT W. (1860 - 1940)                     300-1800      L,G,I
FAURE, MARIE (19TH C)                                  250-850       W,S
FAUSETT, WILLIAM DEAN (1913 -    )                      100-750       L
FAWCETT, ROBERT (1903 - 1967)                          *250-4000     I
FAY, WILLIAM E. (1882 - 1967)                          *200-900      X (G)
FECHIN, NICOLAI (1881 - 1955)                          4500-65000+   G,F
FEELEY, PAUL (1913 - 1966)                             1500-5000     A
FEININGER, LYONEL                                      *1000-30000
FEININGER, LYONEL (1871 - 1956)                        20000-275000  A,I
FEINSTEIN, SAMUEL (20TH C)                             *100-300      X (G)
FEKE, ROBERT (1724 - 1769)                             800-5000      F
FELINGER, JEAN PAUL (late 19TH C)                      200-900       X (F)
FELL, J.R. (20TH C)                                    100-400       L
FELLOWS, FRANK WAYLAND (1833 - 1900)                   200-1000      X (L)
FELLOWS, FRED (1934 -    )                              2000-18000    X (L)
FENIMORE, T.J. (19TH C)                                300-1200      X (L)
FENN, HARRY (1845 - 1911)                              *250-1500     I
FENSON, R. (19TH - 20TH C)                             200-700       L
FENTON, CHARLES L. (1808 - 1877)                       600-2000      X (F)
FENTON, HALLIE CHAMPLIN (1880 - 1935)                  100-500       L
FEO, CHARLES DE (1892 - 1978)                          *100-500      X (F)
FERBER, HERBERT                                        *6000-15000
FERBER, HERBERT (1906 -    )                            15000-50000   A
FERGUSON, ELEANOR M. (1876 -    )                       100-500       X (S)
FERGUSON, HENRY A. (1842 - 1911)                       500-4500      L
FERREN, JOHN                                           *300-2500
FERREN, JOHN (1905 - 1970)                             850-3500      A
FERRIS, JEAN LEON JEROME (1863 - 1930)                 1000-7500     G
FERY, JOHN (1865 - 1934)                               600-5500      L,W
FEUDEL, ARTHUR (1857 -    )                             *150-600      L
FEVRET DE ST MEMIN, CHARLES (1770 - 1852)              2500-8000     F
FIELD, EDWARD LOYAL (1856 - 1914)                      250-2000      L
FIELD, ERATUS SALISBURY (1805 - 1900)                  3000-35000    P
FIENE, ERNEST (1894 - 1965)                            400-6500      L,S,F
FILCER, LUIS (20TH C)                                  100-700       L
FILLEAU, EMERY A (active 1890-1910)                    500-4500      G,L,F
FILMUS, TULLY (1908 -    )                              *100-700      X (G,F)
FINCH, KEITH (1920 -    )                               150-800       A
```

* —Denotes Mixed Media,Watercolors,Gouaches,Pastels,and/or Drawings

```
FINCH, RUBY DEVOL (19TH C)                      1000-4000    F
FINCK, HAZEL (1894 - 1977)                       200-850     L
FINCKEN, JAMES H. (1860 - 1943)                  150-650     L
FINK, FREDERICK (1817 - 1849)                    500-2500    G,F
FINKELGREEN, DAVID (1888 - 1931)                 650-2800    G,F
FINSTER, REVEREND HOWARD (1916 -      )          200-2000    P
FIRENZE, PAUL (20TH C)                          *1500-3500   X
FISCHER, ANTON OTTO (1882 - 1962)                650-5000    M,G,I
FISH, GEORGE G. (1849 -      )                  *100-600     X (I,M)
FISH, JANET (1938 -      )                       3500-15000  A
FISHER, ALVAN (1792 - 1863)                      1500-15000  L,G,F,M
FISHER, ANNE S. (      - 1942)                  *300-900     X (L)
FISHER, D.A. (19TH C)                            100-500     L,M
FISHER, GEORGE H. (19TH C ?)                    *400-1500    L
FISHER, HARRISON (1875 - 1934)                  *400-5000    I
FISHER, HUGO ANTOINE (1867 - 1917)              *250-1500    L,W
FISHER, HUGO MELVILLE (1876 - 1946)              100-850     L,M
FISHER, MAC S. (20TH C)                         *100-600     L
FISHER, MARK (WILLIAM MARK)(1841 - 1923)         650-7500    L,F
FISK, HARRY T. (20TH C)                          500-1200    X
FISKE, GERTRUDE (1879 - 1961)                    350-1200    F,L
FITLER  WILLIAM CROTHERS (1897 - 1926)           250-3000    L
FITZ, ALLEE C. (19TH - 20TH C)                   300-900     X (S)
FITZ, BENJAMIN RUTHERFORD (1855 - 1891)          400-2500    X (G)
FITZGERALD, HARRINGTON (1847 - 1930)             300-1500    M,L
FLAGG, H. PEABODY (1859 -      )                 100-750     L,G
FLAGG, JAMES MONTGOMERY                         *150-2000
FLAGG, JAMES MONTGOMERY (1877 - 1960)            800-8000    X
FLAGG, MONTAGUE (1842 - 1915)                    400-1200    X (S)
FLAHERTY, THORPE (19TH - 20TH C)                 300-750     L
FLANNAGAN, JOHN B. (1898 - 1942)                *450-1200    X (F)
FLANNERY, VAUGHN (20TH C)                        250-1000    X (G)
FLAVELLE, GEOFF H. (19TH - 20TH C)              *150-650     L,M
FLAVIN, DAN (1933 -      )                      *750-6500    A
FLECK, JOSEPH A. (1892 - 1977)                   1000-7000   L,F
FLEISCHBEIN, FRANCOIS (1804 - 1862)              350-3500    F
FLETCHER, CALVIN (1882 -      )                  200-850     L,M
FLOCH, JOSEPH (JOSEF) (1894 - 1977)              200-750     F
FLOETER, KENT (1937 -      )                    *300-700     A
FLORIAN, WALTER (1878 - 1909)                    600-1500    L,F
FLORIMONT, AUSTIN (active 1775-95)              *800-1800    F
FLORSHEIM, RICHARD ABERLE (1916 - 1979)          150-650     X
FOGARTY, THOMAS (1873 - 1938)                   *450-2500    I
FOLAWN, THOMAS JEFFERSON (1876 - 1934)          *100-500     X (F)
FOLINSBEE, JOHN FULTON (1892 - 1972)             500-5000    L
FOLLETT, FOSTER O. (1872 -      )                500-1800    S
FOOTE, JACK (20TH C)                             250-900     X
FOOTE, WILL HOWE (1874 - 1965)                   300-5000    F,L
FORBES, CHARLES S. (1860 -      )                250-2500    L,F,I
FORBES, EDWIN (1839 - 1895)                      750-4500    L,W,M
FORD, HENRY CHAPMAN (1828 - 1894)                200-700     L
FORD, LOREN (1891 -      )                       350-1200    X (G)
FORD, NEILSON (      - 1931)                     200-800     X (F)
FOREST, LOCKWOOD DE (1850 - 1932)                150-850     L,M
FOREST, WESNER LA (20TH C)                       700-4000    F
```

✦ -Denotes Mixed Media,Watercolors,Gouaches,Pastels,and/or Drawings

FORESTER, ? (19TH C)	100-400	X (S)
FORESTORR, ? (20TH C)	*100-600	X (G)
FORRESTAL, F.J. (20TH C)	250-1200	L
FORSTER, GEORGE (19TH C)	2500-8000	S
FORSYTHE, VICTOR CLYDE (1885 -)	200-1500	L,G
FORTUNE, E. CHARLTON (1885 -)	600-4000	X (L)
FOSBURGH, JAMES WHITNEY (1910 -)	400-2800	X
FOSS, OLIVIER (1920 -)	200-900	L
FOSS, PETER OLIVER (1865 - 1932)	450-3000	P
FOSTER, ALAN (1892 - 1934)	700-3500	I
FOSTER, BEN	*200-800	
FOSTER, BEN (1852 - 1926)	350-5000	L,S
FOSTER, CHARLES (1850 - 1931)	300-1800	L
FOSTER, G.S. (20TH C)	200-750	L
FOSTER, H.K. (19TH C)	400-1800	L
FOSTER, JOHN (1648 - 1681)	*500-950	F,I,L
FOSTER, WILL (1882 -)	150-500	F,S
FOUJIOKA, NOBOM (20TH C)	100-600	L
FOULKE, CAPTAIN B.F. (19TH - 20TH C)	100-400	X (M)
FOULKES, LLYN (1934 -)	1000-5000	A
FOURNIER, ALEXIS JEAN (1865 - 1948)	500-2800	L
FOWLER, FRANK (1852 - 1910)	200-750	F
FOWLER, O.K. (early 19TH C)	900-4500	F
FOWLER, TREVER THOMAS (1830 - 1871)	400-2000	G,F
FOX, ROBERT ATKINSON (1860 - 1927)	350-2000	L,G,I
FRANCA, MANUEL JOACHIM DE (1808 - 1865)	450-7500	F,G
FRANCE, EURILDA LOOMIS (1865 - 1931)	150-4500	L,I
FRANCE, JESSE LEACH (1862 -)	100-600	X (L)
FRANCIS, J.J. (20TH C)	*100-500	L
FRANCIS, JOHN F. (1808 - 1886)	1500-65000	S,F
FRANCIS, MRS. JYRA (19TH C)	200-700	X (M)
FRANCIS, SAM	*2000-75000	
FRANCIS, SAM (1923 -)	15000-775000	A
FRANCISCO, J. BOND (1863 - 1931)	400-3000	L
FRANK, CHARLES L. (19TH - 20TH C)	100-600	L
FRANK, GERALD A. (1888 -)	100-500	X (G)
FRANK, MARY (1933 -)	*200-1500	A
FRANKENSTEIN, GODFREY (1820 - 1873)	500-3000	L
FRANKENTHALER, HELEN (1928 -)	2500-100000	A
FRANSIOLI, THOMAS ADRIAN (1906 -)	800-5500	A
FRANZEN, AUGUST (1863 - 1938)	3500-8500	G,F
FRASCONI, ANTONIO M. (1919 -)	*100-600	I
FRASER, CHARLES A. (1782 - 1860)	600-4500	L,F
FRAZER, WILLIAM (18TH - 19TH C)	400-900	M
FRAZIER, KENNETH (1867 - 1949)	500-3500	X (F)
FREDERICK, FRANK FOREST (1866 -)	250-1000	L
FREDERICKS, ALFRED (19TH C)	150-800	I
FREDERICKS, ERNEST (1877 -)	100-500	L
FREEDLANDER, ARTHUR R. (1875 - 1940)	100-450	L,F
FREEDLEY, DURR (1888 -1938)	500-5000	X (F)
FREEDMAN, MAURICE (1904 -)	300-1000	X (S)
FREELAND, ANNA C. (1837 - 1911)	100-500	F,G,S
FREEMAN, DON (1908 -)	400-2000	X (G)
FREEMAN, JAMES EDWARD (1808 - 1884)	500-2000	F,G
FREEMAN, STEWART (20TH C)	100-400	X

* -Denotes Mixed Media,Watercolors,Gouaches,Pastels,and/or Drawings

```
FREEMAN, WILLIAM (1925 -      )              500-2000    X (W)
FREEZOR, W.H.M. (20TH C)                     100-600     X (F)
FREILICHER, JANE (1924 -      )              200-1000    L
FREITAG, CONRAD (active 1875-95)             300-1200    M
FRELINGHUYSEN, SUZY (20TH C)                 2500-18000  A
FRENCH, FRANK (1850 - 1933)                  300-1200    A (G)
FRERICHS, WILLIAM C. A. (1829 - 1905)        500-5000    L,M
FRESQUIS, PEDRO ANTONIO (active 1810-40)     100-600     X (G)
FREY, JOSEPH (1892 -      )                  200-1500    L
FRIEDENTHAL, DAVID (20TH C)                  *200-850    X (L)
FRIEDMAN, ARNOLD (1879 - 1946)               850-10000   L,F,S
FRIEDMAN, MARTIN (1896 -      )              100-300     M
FRIEND, WASHINGTON F. (1820 - 1881)          *300-1800   L
FRIES, CHARLES ARTHUR (1854 - 1940)          300-2500    L,I
FRIESEKE,FREDERICK CARL (1874 - 1939)        4000-85000  F,L
FROHER, ROWLAND (20TH C)                     *100-600    X (G)
FROMKES, MAURICE (1872 - 1931)               100-900     F
FROMUTH, CHARLES HENRY (1861 - 1937)         *350-1000   X
FROST, ARTHUR BURDETT                        *300-18000
FROST, ARTHUR BURDETT (1851 - 1928)          2000-18000  I
FROST, F.S. (19TH C)                         300-1200    X (L)
FROST, GEORGE ALBERT (1843 -      )          400-2800    L,G
FROST, JOHN (1890 -      )                    100-600     L
FROST, JOHN ORNE (1852 - 1928)               500-18000   P,M
FROTHINGHAM, JAMES (1786 - 1864)             700-4000    F
FRY, JOHN HEMMING (1860 - 1946 )             400-1800    L
FRYMIRE, JACOB (1770 - 1822)                 5000-15000  P
FUCHS, ERNEST (20TH C)                       100-600     X (F)
FUECHSEL, HERMANN (1833 - 1915)              500-12000   L,M
FUERTES, LOUIS AGASSIZ (1874 - 1927)         *500-8000   W
FUGLISTER, FRITZ (20TH C)                    350-900     X (F)
FUHR, ERNEST (1874 - 1933)                   *200-850    I
FULDE, EDWARD (19TH - 20TH C)                600-2000    X (G)
FULLER, ARTHUR D. (1889 - 1966)              *200-1000   I
FULLER, G.F. (19TH C)                        150-700     X (L)
FULLER, GEORGE (1822 - 1884)                 500-2000    L,F
FULLER, LEONARD (1822 - 1871)                300-1500    X
FULLER, S.W. (19TH C)                        100-750     L
FULLICK, E. (early 20TH C)                   100-600     L,F
FULOP, KAROLY (1898 -      )                 *250-1200   X (G)
FULTON, FITCH (20TH C)                       100-700     L
FURLMAN, FREDERICK (1874 -      )            100-600     L
FURLONG, CHARLES WELLINGTON (1874 -      )   1000-7500   I
FUSSEL, CHARLES LEWIS (1840 - 1905)          800-15000   X (M)
```

* -Denotes Mixed Media,Watercolors,Gouaches,Pastels,and/or Drawings

G

GAENNSLEN, OTTO ROBERT (1876 -)	150-1000	X
GAERTNER, CARL F. (1898 - 1952)	200-1200	L,I
GAG, WANDA HAZEL (1893 - 1946)	*200-1000	L,G,I
GAGE, GEORGE WILLIAM (1887 - 1957)	200-1500	I
GALLAGHER, SEARS (1869 - 1955)	*100-1500	L,M,F
GALLATIN, ALBERT EUGENE (1882 - 1952)	1000-8500	A
GALLISON, HENRY HAMMOND (1850 - 1910)	300-4500	L
GALLO, FRANK (1933 -)	*100-850	F
GAMBIER, M. (19TH C)	100-750	L
GAMBLE, EDNA (19TH - 20TH C)	*100-450	X (S)
GAMBLE, JOHN MARSHALL (1863 - 1957)	450-3500	L
GAMBLE, ROY C. (1887 -)	150-1500	G,F,L
GAMMELL, ROBERT HALE IVES (1893 -)	400-2500	F,G
GANNAM, JOHN (1897 - 1965)	*300-1500	I
GANSO, EMIL	*350-2500	
GANSO, EMIL (1895 - 1941)	400-5000	F,L
GARBER, DANIEL (1880 - 1958)	3500-85000	L
GARDENER, ROBERT (early 19TH C)	*1000-3000	X (L)
GARDINER, DONALD (20TH C)	150-750	X (G)
GARDNER, ARCHIBALD S. (1904 -)	200-800	M
GARDNER, SHEILA (20TH C)	*500-2000	L
GARRATT, J.H.(19TH - 20TH C)	*100-500	X (L)
GARRETT, EDMUND HENRY	*150-1000	
GARRETT, EDMUND HENRY (1853 - 1929)	200-1500	I,L
GARSON, ETTA CORBETT (1898 - 1968)	200-900	L
GASKE, F.J. (19TH - 20TH C)	*200-850	X (L)
GASPARD, LEON (1882 - 1964)	1000-50000	L
GASSER, HENRY MARTIN (1909 - 1981)	*150-900	L
GASSETTE, GRACE (19TH - 20TH C)	100-700	X (M)
GASSIM, MARY W. (19TH C)	150-750	L
GATCH, LEE (1902 - 1968)	700-12000	A
GAUEN, M. (early 20TH C)	100-600	F
GAUGENGIGL, IGNAZ MARCEL (1855 - 1932)	500-3500	F
GAUL, ARRAH LEE (20TH C)	200-850	X (M)
GAUL, GILBERT (WILLIAM GILBERT)(1855-1919)	1000-25000	G,F,L
GAULEY, ROBERT DAVID (1875 - 1943)	350-1500	F
GAULT, MARY D. (early 19TH C)	500-4750	X (L)
GAVENCKY, FRANK J. (1888 -)	250-1000	X (L)
GAW, WILLIAM A. (1891 - 1973)	100-600	X
GAY, AUGUST (20TH C)	100-500	X (W)
GAY, EDWARD (1837 - 1928)	200-3500	L
GAY, GEORGE HOWELL (1858 - 1931)	*100-3000	M,L
GAY, WALTER (1856 - 1937)	750-14000	G,L
GAY, WINCKWORTH ALLAN (1821 - 1910)	350-1500	L,M
GAYER, A. (19TH C)	200-1000	L
GAYLOR, SAMUEL WOOD (1883 -)	*100-400	I
GAZE, HAROLD (20TH C)	*450-1500	I
GECHTOFF, LEONID (20TH C)	100-400	X (L)
GEDEOHN, PAUL (20TH C)	250-900	X (G)

*Denotes Mixed Media,Watercolors,Gouaches,Pastels, and/or Drawings

GEHRY, P. (19TH C)	100-700	X (S)
GENTH, LILLIAN MATHILDE (1876 - 1953)	350-4000	F
GEOFFROI, HARRY (19TH - 20TH C)	250-1200	X
GEORGE, A. (late 19TH C)	100-500	L
GEORGES, PAUL (1923 -)	5000-35000	A
GERBI, CLAUDIO (20TH C)	100-600	X (S)
GERBINO, ROSARIO U. (19TH - 20TH C)	200-900	L
GERRY, SAMUEL LANCASTER (1813 - 1891)	400-5000	L
GETMAN, WILLIAM (1917 - 1972)	*100-400	X (S)
GEYER, HERMAN (19TH C)	150-2000	L
GIBBS, E.T. (19TH C)	*100-400	L
GIBBS, GEORGE (1870 - 1942)	*100-600	I
GIBBS, H. (20TH C)	100-500	A
GIBBS, MARY ANN (19TH C)	*400-1800	F
GIBSON, CHARLES DANA	*300-3500	
GIBSON, CHARLES DANA (1867 - 1944)	500-6000	I,F
GIBSON, WILLIAM HAMILTON (1850 - 1896)	*100-600	L,I
GIDDINGS, FRANK A. (1882 -)	*100-500	X
GIES, JOSEPH W. (1860 - 1935)	100-6000	F,L
GIFFORD, CHARLES HENRY	*150-1500	
GIFFORD, CHARLES HENRY (1839 - 1904)	400-3500	L
GIFFORD, EDWARD C. (20TH C)	100-400	L
GIFFORD, PAULINE (19TH - 20TH C)	200-900	X (S)
GIFFORD, ROBERT GREGORY (1895 -)	*100-500	I
GIFFORD, ROBERT SWAIN (1840 - 1905)	450-7500	L
GIFFORD, SANFORD ROBINSON (1823 - 1880)	1500-200000	L
GIGNOUX, REGIS FRANCOIS (1816 - 1882)	1500-25000	L
GIHON, ALBERT DAKIN (1866 -)	200-700	L
GIHON, CLARENCE MONTFORD (1871 - 1929)	800-7500	L
GIKOW, RUTH (1913 - 1983)	200-1200	X (F)
GILBERT, A. (19TH C)	100-500	L
GILBERT, ARTHUR HILL (1894 -)	300-1000	L,G
GILBERT, C. IVAR (20TH C)	*100-300	X
GILCHRIST, WILLIAM WALLACE (1879 - 1926)	1000-12000	F
GILDER, ROBERT F. (1856 - 1946)	200-900	L
GILES, HORACE P. (19TH C)	*100-800	L
GILL, ANN (early 19TH C)	*100-800	X
GILL, DELANCEY (1859 -)	200-700	L
GILL, JAMES (1934 -)	500-2500	A,F
GILL, MARIQUITA (20TH C)	500-3000	X (L)
GILL, TOM (1899 -)	*200-700	L
GILLIAM, SAM JR. (1933 -)	3500-15000	A
GILSON, ROGER E. (20TH C)	100-500	X (L)
GIOBBI, EDWARD (1926 -)	*200-1500	X
GIOVANNI, N. (20TH C)	100-600	L
GIRARDIN, FRANK J. (1856 -)	250-1000	L
GISEVIUS, GERHARD (20TH C)	100-400	L
GISIKE, IDA (20TH C)	150-650	X (L)
GISSON, ANDRE (?)	350-4500	F,L
GIURGOLA, ROMALDO (19TH - 20TH C)	*200-800	I
GLACKENS, WILLIAM JAMES	*150-25000	
GLACKENS, WILLIAM JAMES (1870 - 1938)	2500-350000	F,L,I
GLARNER, FRITZ (1899 - 1972)	8000-75000	A
GLASER, ELIZABETH (active 1830-40)	*500-7500	P
GLASS, F.R. (20TH C)	*100-500	X

*Denotes Mixed Media,Watercolors,Gouaches,Pastels, and/or Drawings

GLASS, JAMES WILLIAM (1825 - 1855)	450-1800	G,F
GLEASON, JOE DUNCAN (1881 - 1959)	200-1800	I
GLEW, EDWARD LEES (1817 - 1870)	1000-10000	L,F
GLINTENCAMP, HENRY (1887 - 1946)	150-2500	I,L
GLWELL, FARRINGTON (1874 - 1962)	300-1500	X (G)
GODARD, GABRIEL (1933 -)	100-600	X
GODFREY, E. (19TH C)	100-400	L
GOEBEL, ROD (20TH C)	500-2800	L
GOETSCH, GUSTAV F. (1877 - 1969)	100-600	F,L
GOETZ, HENRI (1909 -)	*100-650	A
GOINGS, F. (19TH C)	100-600	L
GOINGS, RALPH (1928 -)	2000-25000	A
GOLD, ALBERT (1916 -)	100-500	I
GOLDBERG, MICHAEL (1924 -)	750-8500	A
GOLDBERG, RUBE (20TH C)	*250-2000	I
GOLDEN, ROLLAND (1931 -)	*200-850	X (L)
GOLDING, WILLIAM O. (1874 - 1943)	*600-2500	P
GOLDINGHAM, J.B. (19TH C)	100-400	L
GOLDSTEIN, HYMAN (20TH C)	*100-500	L
GOLDTHWAITE, ANNE (1875 - 1944)	*100-700	L,F
GOLLINGS, WILLIAM ELLING	*400-5000	
GOLLINGS, WILLIAM ELLING (1878 - 1932)	700-30000	G,F
GOLUB, LEON ALBERT (1922 -)	700-7500	A
GONSKE, WALT (20TH C)	200-900	X
GOODE, JOE (1937 -)	*500-2500	A
GOODES, EDWARD A. (active 1855-85)	500-2500	X (M)
GOODNOUGH, ROBERT (1917 -)	500-8000	A
GOODWIN, ARTHUR C.	*400-6500	
GOODWIN, ARTHUR C. (1864 - 1929)	500-30000	L
GOODWIN, BELLE (19TH C)	800-3500	X (S)
GOODWIN, EDWIN WEYBURN (1800 - 1845)	100-600	X (F)
GOODWIN, PHILIP RUSSELL (1882 - 1935)	400-8500	G,L,I
GOODWIN, RICHARD LABARRE (1840 - 1910)	400-6000	S,W,L
GOODYEAR, C. (19TH C)	*100-500	X (S)
GORBINO, ROSARIO (20TH C)	100-800	X
GORCHOV, RON (1930 -)	800-6000	A
GORDER, LUTHER EMERSON VAN (1861 - 1931)	150-750	G,L
GORKY, ARSHILE	*800-150000	
GORKY, ARSHILE (1905 - 1948)	5000-65000	A
GORLICH, SOPHIE (1855 - 1893)	1000-9000	G
GORMAN, R.C. (1933 -)	*400-1800	X (F)
GORSON, AARON HENRY (1872 - 1933)	700-14000	L
GOTLIEB, JULES (1897 -)	200-3500	I
GOTTLIEB, ADOLPH	*1500-25000	
GOTTLIEB, ADOLPH (1903 - 1974)	5000-225000	A
GOTTLIEB, LEOPOLD (?)	*350-1200	X
GOTTWALD, FREDERIC C. (1860 - 1941)	600-2000	L
GOULD, WALTER (1829 - 1893)	4000-25000	G
GOURNSEY, C. (19TH C)	*250-1200	X (L)
GRABACH, JOHN R. (1886 -)	100-600	F,G,L
GRACE, GERALD (1918 -)	100-500	X (G)
GRAHAM, GEORGE (19TH - 20TH C)	*100-400	X (G)
GRAHAM, JOHN D. (1881 - 1961)	1000-25000	A
GRAHAM, RALPH W. (1901 -)	*100-800	G
GRAHAM, ROBERT ALEXANDER (1873 - 1946)	500-8000	X (L,F)

*Denotes Mixed Media,Watercolors,Gouaches,Pastels, and/or Drawings

```
GRAHAM, WILLIAM (1841 - 1910)                    400-2000      L
GRAILLY, VICTOR DE (1804 - 1889)                 400-8500      L,F
GRAMATKY, HARDIE (1907 -      )                  *250-1200      I
GRAND, HENRY LE (19TH C)                          600-4500      L
GRANDEE, JOE RUIZ (1929 -      )                  400-2800      F
GRANER Y ARUFFI, LUIS (1867 - 1929)              300-4000      F,G,L
GRANT, CHARLES HENRY (1866 - 1938)               250-2500      M
GRANT, CLEMENT ROLLINS (1849 - 1893)             300-7000      L,F
GRANT, DWINELL (20TH C)                           500-3800      X (A?)
GRANT, FREDERIC M. (1886 -      )                 800-7500      I
GRANT, GORDAN HOPE                               *300-1800
GRANT, GORDON HOPE (1875 - 1962)                  500-5500      M,I
GRANT, J. JEFFREY (1883 - 1960)                   300-2000      L
GRANT, JAMES (1924 -      )                      *300-1000      A
GRANT, WILLIAM (mid 19TH C)                      *1000-3000      P
GRANVILLE-SMITH, WALTER                          *150-3000
GRANVILLE-SMITH, WALTER (1870 - 1938)            350-30000     L,F,I
GRAVES, ABBOTT FULLER (1859 - 1936)              500-25000     L,G,F,S
GRAVES. MORRIS COLE                              *600-10000
GRAVES, MORRIS COLE (1910 -      )               1000-25000     A
GRAVES, NANCY                                    *6000-15000
GRAVES, NANCY (1940 -      )                     15000-50000     A
GRAVES, O.E.L. (1912 -      )                     150-700      X (W)
GRAY, CHARLES A. (1857 -      )                   200-1000      F
GRAY, CLEVE (1918 -      )                        500-4500      A
GRAY, FREDERICK G. (20TH C)                       100-600      X (G)
GRAY, HENRY PERCY (1869 - 1952)                  *450-9500      L
GRAY, HENRY PETERS (1819 - 1877)                  300-2500      L
GRAY, M. MAY (20TH C)                             100-350      X (F)
GRAY, PERCY"(See GRAY, HENRY PERCY)"
GRAY, URBAN (20TH C ?)                            150-650      X (L)
GRAY, WILLIAM F. (1866 -      )                   150-750      X (M)
GRAZIA, TED DE                                   *250-800
GRAZIA, TED DE (1909 -      )                     300-2500      W
GRAZIANI, SANTE (1920 -      )                    800-3000      A
GREACEN, EDMUND WILLIAM (1877 - 1949)            1000-15000     F,L
GREASON, WILLIAM (1884 -      )                   200-800      L
GREATOREX, KATHLEEN HONORA (1851 -      )         600-2000      S,I
GREEN, CHARLES EDWIN LEWIS (1844 -      )         500-2500      M
GREEN, EDITH JACKSON (1876 - 1934)               100-600      X (L)
GREEN, FRANK RUSSELL (1856 - 1940)               350-3000      S,L
GREEN, WILLIAM BRADFORD (1871 - 1945)            100-600      L
GREENBAUM, JOSEPH (1864 -      )                  250-950      L
GREENE, BALCOMB (1904 -      )                    500-3500      A
GREENE, STEPHEN (1918 -      )                    800-3500      A
GREENE, WALTER L. (late 19TH C)                  *100-650      X (L)
GREENLEAF, JACOB I. (1887 -      )                100-400      X (L)
GREENWOOD, ETHAN ALLEN (1779 - 1856)             750-8500      F
GREENWOOD, JOHN (1727 - 1792)                    400-2000      P
GREENWOOD, JOSEPH H. (1857 - 1927)               150-2500      L
GREENWOOD, MARION (1909 - 1970)                  500-2500      G
GREER, JAMES EMERY (19TH C)                       100-900      L
GREGOR, HAROLD (1929 -      )                     900-9500      A
GREGORY, ELIOT (1854 - 1915)                      100-600      F
GRELL, LOUIS FREDERICK (1887 -      )            *100-600      X
```

*Denotes Mixed Media,Watercolors,Gouaches,Pastels, and/or Drawings

GREMKE, DICK (19TH - 20TH C)	200-1000	L
GREMKE, M.D. (20TH C)	400-1500	L
GRIFFIN, THOMAS BAILEY (active c.1865-80)	300-2000	L
GRIFFIN, WALTER (1861 - 1935)	750-6500	L
GRIFFIN, WILLIAM (1861 -)	600-5000	L
GRIFFIN, WORTH DICKMAN (1892 -)	100-600	X (M)
GRIFFITH, BILL (20TH C)	*100-600	X
GRIFFITH, JULIE SULZER (- 1945)	100-400	M
GRIFFITH, LOUIS K. (20TH C)	*100-600	X (G)
GRIFFITH, LOUIS OSCAR (1875 -)	100-600	L,F
GRIGGS, SAMUEL W. (1827 - 1898)	400-2800	L,S
GRILLEY, ROBERT (1920 -)	200-850	X
GRILLO, JOHN (1917 -)	600-1200	A
GRIMM, PAUL (20TH C)	400-2500	L
GRINNELL, GEORGE VICTOR (- 1934)	100-1000	L
GRIOMARE, EDWARD T. (20TH C)	300-1200	X
GROESBECK, DANIEL SAYRE (20TH C)	*100-600	F
GROLL, ALBERT LOREY (1866 - 1952)	200-2500	L
GROOMS, MIMI (20TH C)	*100-500	X
GROOMS, RED (1937 -)	*600-15000	A
GROPPER, WILLIAM	*250-5000	
GROPPER, WILLIAM (1897 - 1977)	600-15000	G,F,I
GROS, D. (early 19TH C)	300-1200	L
GROSE, D.C. (active 1865-90)	150-1800	L
GROSE, HARRIET ESTELLE (- 1914)	400-2000	X (S)
GROSS, CHAIM (1904 -)	*150-1000	A
GROSS, G. (20TH C)	200-800	G,F
GROSS, JULIET WHITE (1882 - 1934)	400-1800	X
GROSS, OSKAR (1871 - 1963)	500-1800	X (A?)
GROSS, PETER ALFRED (1849 - 1914)	150-1500	L,G
GROSSENHEIDER, RICHARD PHILIP (1911-1975)	*800-4500	X
GROSSMAN, EDWIN BOOTH (1887 - 1957)	100-700	L,M
GROSZ, GEORGE (1893 - 1959)	*1200-25000	A
GROTH, JOHN (1908 -)	*200-1200	I
GROVER, OLIVER DENNET (1861 - 1927)	250-1200	L,G
GRUELLE, RICHARD BUCKNER (1851 - 1915)	200-1200	L,S
GRUGER, FREDERIC RODRIGO (1871 - 1953)	*200-1200	I
GRUNER, CARL (active 1850-65)	700-2000	F
GRUPPE, CHARLES PAUL (1860 - 1940)	300-9500	L,M
GRUPPE, EMILE ALBERT (1896 - 1978)	300-7500	L,M
GUE, DAVID JOHN (1836 - 1917)	300-4000	L,M,F
GUERELSON, A.M. (20TH C ?)	700-4000	X
GUERIN, JOSEPH (1889 -)	300-1500	L,M
GUERIN, JULES (1866 - 1946)	*400-3000	F,I
GUERRERO, JULES (1914 -)	800-6500	X (A?)
GUGLIELMI, O. LOUIS (1906 - 1956)	3000-25000	A
GUIFON, LEON (19TH C)	400-2000	X (L)
GUILLAUME, L. (19TH C)	*150-750	L,F
GUION, MOLLY (1810 -)	100-500	G
GULAGER, CHARLES (active 1860-80)	250-1200	X (M)
GUMPEL, HUGH (20TH C)	*100-400	L
GURGIN, W. (19TH C)	350-1200	X (W)
GUSSOW, BERNARD (1881 - 1957)	100-500	L,F
GUSTAVSON, HENRY (1864 - 1912)	250-800	L
GUSTEMER, G. (19TH C)	4000-25000	F

*Denotes Mixed Media,Watercolors,Gouaches,Pastels, and/or Drawings

```
GUSTON, PHILIP (1913 - 1980)                  10000-250000 A
GUY, FRANCIS (1760 - 1820)                    5000-60000   L
GUY ,SEYMOUR JOSEPH (1824  -  1910)           3000-125000  G,F
GWATHMEY, ROBERT                              *600-3000
GWATHMEY, ROBERT (1903 -      )               1000-7500    G,F
GYBERSON, INDIANA (19TH - 20TH C)             500-1800     F
```

H

```
HAAPPANEN, JOHN N. (1891 -      )                  300-2000     L
HAAS, MAURITZ FREDERIK HENDRIK DE (1832-95) 500-10000    M
HABERLE, JOHN (1856 - 1933)                      *300-1500
HABERLE, JOHN (1856 - 1933)                       800-7500     F,S
HADDOCK, ARTHUR (20TH C)                          700-2000     L
HAELEN, JOHN A. (19TH - 20TH C)                   100-500      F
HAERST, G. (19TH C) - 1887)                       100-850      L
HAES JANVIER, FRANCES DE (1775 - 1824)            450-2000     F
HAESELER, ALICE P. SMITH (19TH - 20TH C)         *200-700      M,L
HAGAMAN, JAMES (20TH C)                           150-900      G,L
HAGBERG, C.J. (19TH C)                            100-400      M
HAGERBRUNNER, DAVID (20TH C)                     *400-2800     X (W)
HAGERUP, NELS (1864 - 1922)                       250-3000     M
HAGNY, J. (19TH C)                                100-400      P
HAHN, KARL WILHELM (1829 - 1887)                  4000-60000   G
HAINES, RICHARD (1906 -      )                    100-800      X (L)
HALBERG, CHARLES EDWARD (1855 -      )            100-800      M
HALE, ELLEN DAY (1855 - 1940)                     1000-15000   F,L
HALE, LILIAN WESTCOTT (1881 - 1953)               800-7500     F
HALE, MARY POWELL HELME (1862 - 1934)             100-500      X (L)
HALE, PHILIP LESLIE (1865 - 1931)                 700-30000    F
HALL, ANNE (1792 - 1863)                          700-4500     F
HALL, FREDERICK GARRISON (1879 - 1946)           150-800      X (G)
HALL, GEORGE HENRY (1825 - 1913)                  500-18000    G,S,F
HALL, HENRY BRYAN (1808 - 1884)                   500-3500     F,S
HALL, HOWARD HILL (1887 - 1933)                   500-10000    X (G)
HALL, PETER (1828 - 1895)                        *100-500      F
HALL, THOMAS VICTOR (20TH C)                     *100-600      X (G)
HALL, E. W. (19TH C)                              300-1200     L
HALL, WILLIAM SMITH (19TH C)                      800-4500     F
HALLETT, HENDRICKS A. (1847 - 1921)              *200-900      M,L
HALLOWAY, GEORGE (20TH C)                         100-600      X (L)
HALLOWELL, GEORGE HAWLEY (1871 - 1926)           500-3000     L
HALLOWELL, ROBERT (1886 - 1939)                  *100-900      X (M,S)
```

*Denotes Mixed Media,Watercolors,Gouaches,Pastels, and/or Drawings

Name	Price	Media
HALLWIG, OSCAR (1858 - 1880)	300-900	X (F)
HALOWAY, EDWARD STRATTON (- 1939)	100-800	X (M)
HALPERT, SAMUEL T.	*200-800	
HALPERT, SAMUEL T. (1884 - 1930)	350-7500	L,F
HALSALL, WILLIAM FORMBY (1841 - 1919)	300-3000	M
HALTON, MINNIE HOLLIS (20TH C)	100-750	X (G)
HAMBLETT, THEORA (1895 -)	250-1200	P
HAMBLIN, STURTEVANT J. (active 1835-55)	3000-45000	P
HAMBRIDGE, JAY (1867 - 1924)	350-1800	X (I,S)
HAMILTON, EDGAR SCUDDER (1869 - 1903)	400-2000	X (G)
HAMILTON, EDWARD WILBUR DEAN (1862 -)	500-3500	L,F
HAMILTON, HAMILTON (1847 - 1928)	500-12000	L,F
HAMILTON, HELEN (19TH - 20TH C)	300-1500	L
HAMILTON, JAMES (1819 - 1878)	500-8500	M,L
HAMILTON, JOHN MCLURE (1853 - 1936)	200-1800	I,F,S
HAMILTON, ROBERT (1877 - 1954)	250-1500	G,L,F
HAMILTON, WILLIAM R. (or M.)(1810 -)	900-4000	F
HAMMER, JOHN J. (1842 - 1906)	350-1800	G,L
HAMMERSTAD, JOHN H. (19TH C)	100-700	X (M,L)
HAMMOND, ARTHUR J. (1875 - 1947)	100-500	X (M,L)
HANARTY, ALICE E. (late 19TH C)	100-500	X (L)
HANAU, JEAN (1899 - 1966)	*300-1000	X (I)
HANDWRIGHT, GEORGE (1873 - 1951)	*200-1000	X
HANE, ROGER (1938 - 1974)	200-1500	I
HANKS, JERVIS F. (1799 -)	500-2000	P
HANKS, LON (19TH - 20TH C)	200-850	X (M)
HANLEY, J.B. (active 1870-85)	800-3500	G
HANSEN, ARMIN CARL (1886 - 1957)	900-25000	L,F
HANSEN, EJNER (1884 - 1965)	700-8500	F
HANSEN, HANS PETER (1881 - 1967)	100-1500	G,F
HANSEN, HAROLD (20TH C)	*100-400	L
HANSEN, HERMAN WENDELBORG (1854 - 1924)	*6000-45000	G
HANSON, R. (19TH C)	100-600	X (S)
HARDENGERGH, GERARD RUTGERS (1856 - 1915)	*100-600	L
HARDING, CHESTER (1792 - 1866)	300-2500	F
HARDING, GEORGE MATTHEWS	*250-1500	
HARDING, GEORGE MATTHEWS (1882 - 1959)	450-4000	I
HARDING, H.H. (late 19TH C)	200-1200	M
HARDING, JOHN L. (1835 - 1882)	500-3500	F
HARDWICK, MELBOURNE H.	*300-750	
HARDWICK, MELBOURNE H. (1857 - 1916)	400-4000	M,L,G
HARDY, ANNA ELIZABETH (1839 - 1934)	300-1800	S
HARDY, JEREMIAH P.(1800 - 1888)	350-1500	F
HARDY, WALTER MANLEY (1877 -)	*150-900	L,I
HARDY, WILLIAM F. (19TH - 20TH C)	150-900	L
HARE, JOHN KNOWLES (1882 - 1947)	*100-800	I,M
HARE, WILLIAM (active 1820-50)	3000-15000	M,F
HARGENS, CHARLES (1893 -)	100-800	G
HARLOW, LOUIS KENNY (1850 - 1913)	*100-500	L,M
HARMAN, FRED (1902 -)	*500-4500	I
HARMER, ALEXANDER F. (1857 - 1925)	400-2500	G
HARMON, CHARLES (- 1936)	100-1200	L
HARMON, W.S. (19TH C)	400-1500	L
HARNETT, WILLIAM MICHAEL (1848 - 1892)	1000-300000	S
HARNEY, PAUL E. (1850 - 1915)	350-1500	W,L,F

*Denotes Mixed Media,Watercolors,Gouaches,Pastels, and/or Drawings

79

```
HARRA, M.A. (19TH C)                              300-1500      X (S)
HARRINGTON, OLIVER W. (1913 -      )             100-400       X (L)
HARRINGTON, RUFUS (20TH C)                       100-600       X (M)
HARRIS, CHARLES X. (1856 -      )                700-8500      F
HARRIS, MARIAN D. (1904 -      )                 100-600       X (L)
HARRIS, ROBERT GEORGE (1911 -      )             400-2000      I,F
HARRIS, SAM HYDE (20TH C)                        200-1200      L
HARRIS, W. (19TH C)                              100-500       L
HARRISON, ALEXANDER (1853 - 1930)                450-6000      M,L
HARRISON, BIRGE (1854 - 1929)                    500-30000     L
HARRISON, MARK ROBERT (1819 - 1894)              500-5000      L,G
HARRISON, THOMAS ALEXANDER (1853 - 1930)         300-5500      M,L,G,F
HART, GEORGE O. ("POP" HART)(1868 - 1933)        *250-3500     L,G
HART, JAMES MCDOUGAL (1828 - 1901)               500-25000     L
HART, SALOMON ALEXANDER (1806 - 1881)            600-12000     G
HART, T.H. (19TH C ?)                            100-850       L
HART, WILLIAM HOWARD (1863 -      )              400-4500      L
HART, WILLIAM M. (1823 - 1894)                   800-18000     L,W
HARTIGAN, GRACE (1922 -      )                   1500-12000    A
HARTLEY, MARSDEN                                 *300-10000
HARTLEY, MARSDEN (1878 - 1943)                   700-80000     A,S
HARTLEY, RACHEL (1884 -      )                   100-650       G,I
HARTMAN, BERTRAM                                 *200-1200
HARTMAN, BERTRAM (1882 - 1960)                   400-2500      L
HARTMAN, SYDNEY K. (1863 -      )                *100-450      I,L
HARTMANN, GEORG (      - 1934)                   100-500       X (F)
HARTRATH, LUCIE (19TH - 20TH C)                  *100-750      L
HARTSON, WALTER C. (1866 -      )                *200-800      L
HARTWICH, HERMAN (1853 - 1926)                   250-3500      L,W,F
HARTWICK, GEORGE GUNTHER (active 1845-60)        600-7500      L
HARVEY, ELI (1860 - 1957)                        450-1800      L,F
HARVEY, GEORGE (1800 - 1878)                     900-10000     L,F
HARVEY, GEORGE (1835 - 1920)                     1000-12000    L,F
HARVEY, GERALD (1933 -      )                    10000-75000   L,G
HARVEY, HENRY T. (19TH C)                        250-1500      L,F
HASBROUCK, DU BOIS FENELON                       *100-600
HASBROUCK, DU BOIS FENELON (1860 - 1934)         500-2500      L
HASELTINE, CHARLES FIELD (1840 -      )          100-900       L
HASELTINE, WILLIAM STANLEY (1835 - 1900)         350-15000     L
HASENFUS, RICHARD C. (20TH C)                    500-4000      X (M)
HASKELL, ERNEST (1876 - 1925)                    *250-900      L
HASKELL, IDA C. (1861 - 1932)                    500-3500      G
HASKELL, JOSEPH ALLEN (1808 - 1894)              200-2500      P
HASKELL, T.R. (late 19TH C)                      100-500       L
HASKINS, GAYLE PORTER (1887 - 1962)              500-3000      X (G)
HASSAM, FREDERICK CHILDE                         *2500-125000
HASSAM, FREDERICK CHILDE (1859 - 1935)           4500-225000   L,F
HASSELBUSH, LOUIS (1863 -      )                 600-1500      X (F)
HASTINGS, HOWARD L. (20TH C)                     100-700       L
HASTINGS, MATTHEW (1834 - 1919)                  250-1500      F,G
HATFIELD, PAULINE (early 20TH C)                 100-500       X (S)
HATHAWAY, GEORGE M. (1852 - 1903)                200-2800      M
HATHAWAY, RUFUS (1770 - 1822)                     5000-85000    P
HAUGH, N. (19TH C)                               *100-800      X (S)
HAUPT, ERIK GUIDE (1891 -      )                 800-6500      L,F
```

*Denotes Mixed Media,Watercolors,Gouaches,Pastels, and/or Drawings

HAUPT, THEODORE G. (20TH C)	200-950	A
HAUSER, JOHN	*1000-15000	
HAUSER, JOHN (1858 - 1913)	1000-15000	L,F
HAUSHALTER, GEORGE M. (1862 -)	100-750	G
HAUSMAN, CHAUNCEY (19TH C)	100-700	F
HAVARD, JAMES PICKNEY (1937 -)	5000-30000	A
HAVELL, ROBERT JR (1793 - 1878)	1500-35000	L
HAVEN, FRANKLIN DE (1856 - 1934)	450-3000	L
HAWKINS, JOHN (20TH C)	200-700	X (M)
HAWLEY, HUGHSON (1850 - 1936)	*300-2500	X (L,I)
HAWTHORNE, CHARLES WEBSTER (1872 - 1930)	1000-95000	F
HAYDEN, CHARLES HENRY (1856 - 1901)	300-1500	L
HAYDEN, EDWARD PARKER (- 1922)	300-1500	L
HAYDEN, ELLA FRANCES (1860 -)	*100-750	L
HAYES, BARTON S. (19TH C ?)	700-3500	X (S)
HAYNIE, WILBUR (1929 -)	100-400	A
HAYS, GEORGE A. (1854 -)	250-2500	L,W
HAYS, WILLIAM JACOB SR (1830 - 1875)	800-6000	W,S
HAYS, WILLIAM JACOB JR (1872 - 1954)	700-4500	L,G
HAYTER, CHARLES (1761 - 1835)	*700-2000	F
HAYWARD, FRANK (1867 -)	250-1200	L
HAYWARD, ROGER (1899 - 1979)	*150-650	A
HAZARD, ARTHUR MERTON (1872 - 1930)	300-3500	L,F,I
HAZELL, S.N. (19TH C)	400-1500	G
HAZELTON, MARY BREWSTER (early 20TH C)	400-1200	F
HEAD, J. (19TH C)	100-600	L
HEADE, MARTIN JOHNSON (1819 - 1904)	4000-190000	L,S,F
HEALY, GEORGE PETER ALEXANDER (1813 - 1894)	300-12000	F
HEATH, FRANK L. (19HT - 20TH C)	500-4500	L
HEATH, W.A. (late 19TH C)	150-750	X (L)
HEATON,AUGUSTUS GEORGE GOODYEAR (1844-1931)	500-5000	F,G
HEATON OF ALBANY, JOHN (18TH C)	1000-6500	P
HEBERER, C. (early 20TH C)	150-700	L
HEDGES, ROBERT D. (1878 -)	100-600	M
HEDINGER, ELISE (1854 -)	800-4000	X (S)
HEFFRON, M. (19TH C)	400-1800	X
HEICHER, FORD (late 19TH C)	100-500	G
HEIL, CHARLES EMILE (1870 -)	*150-400	I
HEITH, V. (20TH C ?)	100-750	L
HEITZEL, GEORGE (1826 - 1906)	*100-400	L
HEKKING, JOSEPH ANTONIO (active 1860-80)	500-3500	L
HELCK, CLARENCE PETER (1893 -)	*200-2500	I
HELD, AL (1928 -)	2500-35000	A
HELD, JOHN (JR) (1889 - 1958)	*300-3500	I
HELDNER, KNUTE (1884 - 1952)	400-3500	X (G)
HELIKER, JOHN EDWARD (1909 -)	400-3500	I,L
HELLER, E. (20TH C)	200-1000	L
HELLER, JOHN M. (20TH C)	350-2500	X (I)
HELLER, S. (20TH C)	100-600	X
HELMICK, HOWARD (1845 - 1907)	400-4500	I
HENDERSON, WILLIAM PENHALLOW (1877-1943)	*400-2500	F,G
HENNESSY, TIMOTHY (1925 -)	200-750	A
HENNESSY, WILLIAM JOHN (1839 - 1917)	500-25000	G,L,I
HENNINGS, ERNEST MARTIN (1886 - 1956)	1000-75000	G,L
HENRI, ROBERT	*350-12000	

*Denotes Mixed Media,Watercolors,Gouaches,Pastels, and/or Drawings

HENRI, ROBERT (1865 - 1929)	500-65000	F,G
HENRICI, JOHN H. (19TH -20TH C)	250-4000	G,F
HENRY, EDWARD LAMSOM	*400-12000	
HENRY, EDWARD LAMSON (1841 - 1919)	700-175000+	G,L,F
HENSHAW, GLENN COOPER (1881 - 1946)	200-700	L,M
HERBST, FRANK C. (20TH C)	200-850	I
HERGENRODER, EMILE (19TH - 20TH C)	100-700	X (F)
HERGESHEIMER, ELLA S. (1873 - 1943)	250-1200	F,S
HERGET, H. (19TH - 20TH C)	200-1500	X (G)
HERING, HARRY (1887 -)	100-800	G
HERKOMER, HERMAN G. (1863 -)	500-2500	G,F
HERRERA, VELINO SHIJE (1902 - 1973)	*250-1200	X (L)
HERRICK, HENRY W. (1824 - 1906)	*250-1200	L,F
HERRICK, MARGARET COX (1865 -)	*200-1200	L,F,S
HERRMANN, FRANK S. (1866 - 1942)	*600-2000	L
HERRMANN, NORBERT (1891 - 1966)	100-600	L
HERSCH, LEE F. (20TH C)	500-3000	X (F)
HERTER, ADELE (1869 - 1946)	300-2500	X (S)
HERTER, ALBERT (1871 - 1950)	*900-4500	F,G,L
HERZEL, PAUL (1876 -)	100-750	I
HERZOG, HERMANN (1832 - 1932)	800-30000	L,M
HERZOG, LOUIS (1868 -)	150-850	L
HERZOG, MAX (19TH - 20TH C)	200-1000	X (S)
HESS, J.N. (late 19TH C)	400-2000	X (G)
HESS, SARA M. (1880 -)	500-3500	L
HESSE, EVA (1936 - 1970)	*2500-15000	A
HESSELIUS, JOHN (1728 - 1778)	2500-25000	F
HETHERINGTON, CHARLES (20TH C)	100-700	M
HETZEL, GEORGE (1826 - 1906)	450-15000	S,L,F
HEUEL, BOB (20TH C)	100-500	X (F)
HEUSTIS, LOUISE LYONS (19TH C)	350-1500	F
HEWETT, EDWARD (1874 -)	150-650	X (A)
HEWINS, AMASA (1785 - 1855)	1000-6500	G,F,L
HIBBARD, ALDRO THOMPSON (1886 - 1972)	650-10000	L
HIBBARD, MARY (19TH - 20TH C)	100-600	F,G
HIBEL, EDNA (1917 -)	400-4500	F
HICKOK, CONDE WILSON (19TH -20TH C)	400-1800	L
HICKS, EDWARD (1770 - 1849)	15000-300000	P
HICKS, GEORGE (20TH C)	200-1000	X (L)
HICKS, SIDNEY S. (19TH C)	*150-750	X (M)
HICKS, THOMAS (1823 - 1890)	500-6500	F,L,G
HIDLEY, JOSEPH H. (1830 - 1872)	5000-75000	P
HIGGINS, CARLETON (1848 - 1932)	350-1800	L,G
HIGGINS, EUGENE	*100-900	
HIGGINS, EUGENE (1874 - 1958)	300-3500	G,F,L
HIGGINS, GEORGE FRANK (active 1855-85)	350-2500	L
HIGGINS, WILLIAM VICTOR	*1500-12000	
HIGGINS, WILLIAM VICTOR (1884 - 1949)	2000-40000	L,F
HIGHWOOD, CHARLES (19TH - 20TH C)	500-2000	L
HIKKIMG, J.A. (19TH C)	700-4000	X (L)
HILDA, E. BAILY (19TH - 20TH C)	400-1800	X
HILDEBRANDT, HOWARD LOGAN (1872 - 1958)	500-6000	F,G
HILDEBRANT, CORNELIA E. (20TH C)	100-600	F
HILER, HILAIRE (1898 -)	100-650	L,G
HILL, ANDREW P. (19TH C)	350-1800	L,G

*Denotes Mixed Media,Watercolors,Gouaches,Pastels, and/or Drawings

```
HILL, ANNA GILMAN (20TH C)                              350-1500      L
HILL, ARTHUR TRUMBULL (1868 -       )                   500-2500      L,F
HILL, EDWARD RUFUS (1852 - 1908)                        400-3500      L
HILL, HOWARD (19TH C)                                   600-5000      W
HILL, JOHN HENRY (1839 - 1922)                         *200-7500      L
HILL, JOHN WILLIAM                                     *800-50000
HILL, JOHN WILLIAM (1812 - 1879)                       1000-30000     L
HILL, THOMAS (1829 - 1908)                              500-60000     L,F,S
HILLERN, BERTHA VON (19TH C)                            150-900       X (L)
HILLIARD, F. JOHN (1886 -      )                        400-2000      F
HILLIARD, WILLIAM HENRY (1836 - 1905)                   300-3500      L,F
HILLINGS, JOHN (      - 1894)                           5000-35000    P
HILLS, ANNA ALTHEA (1882 - 1930)                        400-1200      L,F
HILLS, LAURA COMBS (1859 - 1952)                       *300-1800      S
HILLYER, WILLIAM (JR.) (early 19TH C)                   500-2000      F
HILTON, JOHN WILLIAM (1904 -      )                     400-1200      L
HILTON, ROY (19TH - 20TH C)                             500-4000      X
HINCKLEY, THOMAS HEWES (1813 - 1896)                    350-6500      W,L,S
HIND,WILLIAM GEORGE RICHARDSON (1833-1888)             *100-750       L
HINES, PAUL (19TH - 20TH C)                             300-1500      L,F
HINKLE, CLARENCE KEISER (1880 - 1960)                   200-1000      S,L
HINMAN, CHARLES (1932 -      )                          2000-15000    A
HINTERMEISTER, HENRY (1897 -      )                     400-6000      I
HINTON, W.H. (20TH C)                                   200-900       I
HIRSCH, JOSEPH (1920 - 1981)                            2500-25000    A,G,F,I
HIRSCH, STEFAN (1899 -      )                           800-6500      A
HIRSCHBERG, CARL (1854 - 1923)                          150-1500      L,M,F
HIRSCHFELD, ALBERT (1903 -      )                      *300-2000      I
HIRSH, ALICE (1888 - 1935)                              150-600       X
HIRSHFIELD, MORRIS (1872 - 1946)                        5000-45000    P
HIRST, CLAUDE RAGUET                                   *200-4500
HIRST, CLAUDE RAGUET (1855 - 1942)                      300-12000     S
HITCHCOCK, DAVID HOWARD (1861 - 1943)                   350-1500      L,I
HITCHCOCK, GEORGE                                      *250-3000
HITCHCOCK, GEORGE (1850 - 1913)                         700-35000     F,L,M
HITCHCOCK, LUCIUS WOLCOTT (1868 - 1942)                 350-4500      I
HITCHINS, JOSEPH (19TH C)                               400-2000      X (L)
HOBART, CLARK (1880 -      )                            200-2500      L
HOBBS, GEORGE THOMPSON (1846 -      )                   300-1500      L
HOBBS, MORRIS HENRY (1892 -      )                     *200-900       X
HODGDON, SYLVESTER PHELPS (1830 - 1906)                 300-3000      L,F
HODGKINS, A.W. (19TH - 20TH C)                         *100-600       L
HODGKINS, S. (19TH - 20TH C)                            100-600       L
HOEBER, ARTHUR (1854 - 1915)                            300-4500      L,F
HOEGGER, AUGUSTUS (1848 - 1908)                         100-850       X (S)
HOEN, L. (20TH C)                                      *100-350       L
HOERMAN, CARL (1885 -      )                            100-600       L
HOFF, MARGO (1912 -      )                             *200-1200      X
HOFFBAUER, CHARLES C. J. (1875 - 1957)                  200-6500      M,F,G
HOFFMAN, ARNOLD (1886 -      )                          250-1800      L
HOFFMAN, FRANK B. (1888 - 1958)                         600-3500      I
HOFMANN, CHARLES C. (1821 - 1882)                       10000-100000  P(L)
HOFMANN, HANS                                          *500-20000
HOFMANN, HANS (1880 - 1966)                             4500-275000   A
HOFSTETTER, WILLIAM A. (1884 -      )                  *100-400       L
```

*Denotes Mixed Media,Watercolors,Gouaches,Pastels, and/or Drawings

HOGAN, JEAN (20TH C)	100-600	X
HOGG, A.W. (early 20TH C)	100-700	L
HOGNER, NILS (1893 -)	300-1500	G
HOIT, ALBERT GALLATIN (1809 - 1856)	500-9000	F,L
HOKINSON, HELEN E. (20TH C)	*150-700	I
HOLBROOK, L.T. (19TH C)	200-900	L
HOLDING, JOHN (late 19TH C)	*100-400	X (I?)
HOLDREDGE, RANSOME GILLETTE (1836 - 1899)	900-8000	L
HOLLAND, A. (20TH C)	100-600	X (F)
HOLLOWAY, EDWARD STRATTON (- 1939)	250-1800	L,I
HOLMES, RALPH (1876 -)	250-1200	L,I
HOLMES, WILLIAM HENRY (1846 - 1933)	*200-1000	L,F
HOLT, NELL (20TH C)	*200-800	G
HOLTY, CARL ROBERT	*350-2500	
HOLTY, CARL ROBERT (1900 - 1973)	800-4000	A
HOMER, WINSLOW	*3500-550000	
HOMER, WINSLOW (1836 - 1910)	10000-2000000	M,G,L,I
HONDIUS, GERRIT (1891 -)	200-1500	F
HONDO, K. (20TH C)	*100-400	F
HOPE, JAMES (1818 - 1892)	900-15000	L,G,F
HOPE, THOMAS H. (- 1926)	750-5000	S,L
HOPKIN, ROBERT (1832 - 1909)	300-3500	M,L
HOPKINS, BUDD (1931 -)	400-3500	A
HOPKINS, C.E. (1886 -)	*100-600	L
HOPKINS, W. (19TH C)	*100-700	P
HOPKINSON, CHARLES SYDNEY (1869 - 1962)	600-8500	F
HOPPER, EDWARD	*900-85000	
HOPPER, EDWARD (1882 - 1967)	4500-330000	G,L
HOPPIN, THOMAS FREDERICK (1816 - 1872)	400-2500	G,I
HOROWITZ, LOUISE MCMAHON (20TH C)	100-500	G,M
HORTER, EARL (1881 - 1940)	*200-1200	S,L
HORTON, ELIZABETH S. (1902 -)	200-1000	G,L
HORTON, WILLIAM SAMUEL	*300-4500	
HORTON, WILLIAM SAMUEL (1865 - 1936)	600-40000	G,L,F,S
HOSKINS, GAYLE PORTER (1887 - 1962)	100-1200	I
HOUSTON, FRANCES C. (1867 - 1906)	400-2500	F
HOVENDEN, THOMAS (1840 - 1895)	800-20000	G,F
HOW, KENNETH G. (1883 -)	150-900	L,G
HOWARD, B.K. (19TH - 20TH C)	150-1000	L
HOWARD, CHARLES (1899 -)	300-900	X
HOWARD, HENRY MOWBRAY (1873 -)	100-1200	M,L
HOWE, E.R. (19TH C)	100-800	L
HOWE, H.H. (20TH C)	100-600	M,L
HOWE, R.O. (19TH C)	100-800	L
HOWE, WILLIAM HENRY (1846 - 1929)	250-3000	L,G
HOWELL, FELICIE WALDO (1897 -)	500-6500	L,F
HOWELL, WILLIAM H. (1860 - 1925)	400-3000	L
HOWITT, JOHN NEWTON (1885 - 1958)	100-1500	I
HOWLAND, ALFRED CORNELIUS (1838 - 1909)	400-5000	G,L
HOWLAND, GEORGE (1865 - 1928)	*100-800	L
HOWLAND, ISABELLA (1895 -)	*100-400	X
HOWLAND, JOHN DARE (19TH - 20TH C)	500-4500	W,L
HOYLE, RAPHAEL (1804 - 1838)	600-5000	L
HUBARD, WILLIAM JAMES (1807 - 1862)	3500-15000	F
HUBBARD, F.M.B. (1869 - 1930)	200-1000	X (S)

*Denotes Mixed Media,Watercolors,Gouaches,Pastels, and/or Drawings

HUBBARD, RICHARD WILLIAM (1816 - 1888)	500-5000	L,M,F
HUBBELL, CHARLES H. (20TH C)	100-750	X
HUBBELL, HENRY SALEM (1870 - 1949)	700-35000	F
HUDDLE, REBA E. (20TH C)	100-400	G,F
HUDSON, CHARLES BRADFORD (1865 -)	200-1000	X (L)
HUDSON, CHARLES WILLIAM (1871 - 1943)	*150-750	L,F
HUDSON, ERIC ELMER FOREST (1862 -)	*100-600	X (G)
HUDSON, GRACE CARPENTER (1865 - 1937)	750-35000	F,L
HUDSON, JOHN BRADLEY JR (1832 - 1903)	400-3500	L
HUFFINGTON, JOHN C. (1864 - 1929)	*200-1000	M,L
HUGE, JURGEN FREDERICK (1809 - 1878)	1000-8500	P
HUGGINS, M.W. (20TH C)	100-500	L,S
HUGHES, DAISY MARGUERITTE (1883 - 1968)	100-900	L
HUGHES, GEORGE (1907 -)	100-1500	I
HULBERT, KATHERINE ALLMOND (- 1961)	200-1000	X
HULDAH, (20TH C)	350-2000	F
HULISTON, J.D. (early 20TH C)	100-500	L
HULLENKREMER, ODON (20TH C)	350-1200	X
HULTBERG, JOHN (1922 -)	*100-1500	A
HUMMELL, ANTHONY (20TH C)	*150-1000	X
HUMPHREY, RALPH (1932 -)	1000-6500	A
HUMPHREY, WALTER BEACH (1892 -)	300-3500	I
HUNT, CHARLES D. (1840 - 1914)	250-1500	L
HUNT, HENRY P. (19TH C)	500-3500	L,G
HUNT, LYNNE BOGUE (1878 - 1960)	700-2500	W,G,I
HUNT, SAMUEL VALENTINE (1803 - 1893)	500-3500	L,S
HUNT, THOMAS L. (1882 - 1938)	400-1800	L
HUNT, WILLIAM MORRIS (1824 - 1879)	800-50000	F,L
HUNTER, CLEMENTINE (1880 -)	250-1200	P
HUNTER, FRED LEO (19TH - 20TH C)	100-1000	M,L
HUNTER, JOHN YOUNG (1874 - 1955)	500-3500	X (G)
HUNTER, MAX (19TH - 20HT C)	100-400	L
HUNTINGTON, C. LYMAN (19TH C)	200-850	X (F)
HUNTINGTON, D.W. (19TH - 20TH C)	*100-700	W,G
HUNTINGTON, DANIEL (1816 - 1906)	800-6000	F,G
HUNTINGTON, JIM (1941 -)	600-4500	A
HURD, PETER (1904 - 1984)	*300-6500	L,I,G
HURDLE, GEORGE LINTON (1868 - 1922)	*100-600	L
HURLEY, WILSON (1924 -)	500-20000	L
HURTING, J.D. (19TH - 20TH C)	*100-400	L
HURTT, ARTHUR R. (1861 -)	250-1500	L,I
HUSTON, WILLIAM (late 19TH C)	500-3000	L
HUTCHENS, FRANK TOWNSEND (1869 - 1937)	350-6500	F,L
HUTCHINS, A. (20TH C)	100-400	X
HUTCHINSON, D.C. (20TH C)	100-850	I
HUTCHINSON, FREDERICK WILLIAM (1874-1953)	200-1500	L
HUTTY, ALFRED HEBER (1877 - 1954)	*400-2500	G,L
HYDE, WILLIAM HENRY (1858 - 1943)	200-1800	F
HYNEMAN, HERMAN N. (1859 - 1907)	600-4500	F,S
HYNEMAN, JULIA (19TH - 20TH C)	250-1000	L

*Denotes Mixed Media,Watercolors,Gouaches,Pastels, and/or Drawings

I

IDELL, MARGARET C. (20TH C)	*100-400	X (L)
ILSLEY, FREDERICK JULIAN (1855 - 1933)	200-900	L,M
ILYIN, PETER (1887 - 1950)	200-900	L,M
IMHOF, JOSEPH A. (1871 - 1955)	*800-6500	F,G
INDIANA, ROBERT (1928 -)	4500-35000	A
INGALLS, WALTER J. (1805 - 1874)	250-1500	F,S,G
INGEN, HENRY A. VAN (1833 - 1898)	500-4000	L,W
INGERLE, RUDOLPH F. (1879 - 1950)	350-1200	L,G
INGHAM, CHARLES CROMWELL (1796 - 1863)	600-2000	F
INGHAM, WILLIAM (active 1855-1860)	700-4000	F,S
INMAN, HENRY (1801 - 1846)	350-10000	F,L,G
INMAN, JOHN O'BRIEN (1828 - 1896)	500-7500	G,L,F
INNESS, GEORGE (1825 - 1894)	800-225000	L
INSLEY, ALBERT B. (1842 - 1937)	350-5000	L
INUKAI, KYOHEI (1934 -)	400-3500	A
IPCAR, DAHLOV (1917 -)	*100-400	X
IPSEN, ERNEST LUDWIG (1869 - 1951)	200-800	F
IRELAND, LEROY (1889 -)	400-2500	G,S
IRVINE, WILSON HENRY (1869 - 1936)	600-12000	L,F
IRVING, JOHN BEAUFAIN (1825 - 1877)	600-3500	F,G
IRWIN, ROBERT (1928 -)	5000-30000	A
ISHAM, SAMUEL (1855 - 1914)	400-3000	F
IVES, FREDERICK EUGENE (1856 - 1937)	250-1000	F
IVES, PERCY (1864 -)	350-4000	G,F

J

JACKSON, CHARLES AKERMAN (1857 -)	100-600	L
JACKSON, ELBERT McGRAN (1896 -)	300-3000	I
JACKSON, ELIZABETH LESLEY (1867 - 1934)	*100-600	M,L
JACKSON, HERBERT W. (late 19TH C)	200-900	F
JACKSON, LUCY ATKINS (19TH - 20TH C)	300-1500	X (G)
JACKSON, ROBERT L. (20TH C)	100-450	X
JACKSON, WILLIAM FRANKLIN (1850 - 1936)	300-2000	L
JACKSON, WILLIAM H. (1832 -)	*150-750	L
JACOB, MICHEL (1877 -)	700-3500	F,S

*Denotes Mixed Media,Watercolors,Gouaches,Pastels, and/or Drawings

JACOB, NED	*900-4500	
JACOB, NED (1938 -)	5000-30000	G,F
JACOBS, MILNE (early 20TH C)	100-600	L
JACOBSEN, ANTONIO	*800-4000	
JACOBSEN, ANTONIO (1850 - 1921)	1200-20000+	M
JACOBSON, OSCAR BROUSSE (1882 - 1934)	150-900	M,L,G
JAHAM, M.DE (20TH C)	100-600	G
JAHNKE, WILLIAM (1937 -)	100-300	X (L)
JAMBOR, LOUIS (1884 - 1954)	150-700	G,F
JAMES, FREDERICK (1845 - 1907)	500-4500	X
JAMES, H. (19TH C)	*300-1500	X
JAMESON, JOHN (1842 - 1864)	500-5500	L
JAMISON, PHILIP (1925 -)	*300-4000	L,S
JANSEN, LEO (20TH C)	100-400	X (F)
JANSSON, ALFRED (1863 - 1931)	300-2500	L
JARVIS, JOHN WESLEY (1780 - 1840)	1500-35000	F
JECT-KEY, D. WU (20TH C)	100-500	X (L)
JEFFERSON, JOSEPH IV (1829 - 1905)	250-2000	L
JEN, PANG (20TH C)	100-400	F
JENKINS, CHARLES WALDO (1820 -)	600-1500	F
JENKINS, GEORGE WASHINGTON (1816 - 1907)	250-2500	G,F,L
JENKINS, J. LeBRUN (1876 - 1951)	150-600	L,G
JENKINS, JOHN ELLIOT (1868 -)	100-600	L
JENKINS, PAUL	*300-4500	
JENKINS, PAUL (1923 -)	1000-65000	A
JENNIN, JONATHAN (active 1830-40)	*1500-5500	P
JENNYS, WILLIAM (active 1780-1810)	1500-20000	P
JENNINGS, RICHARD (19TH C)	800-3500	F
JENSEN, ALFRED (1903 - 1981).	3500-35000	A
JENSEN, GEORGE (1878 -)	200-2000	L
JENSEN, THOMAS M. (1831 - 1916)	300-1800	X (F,M)
JEX, GARNET W. (1895 - 1979)	150-700	L,G
JICHA, JOE (20TH C ?)	100-500	L
JOHANSEN, JOHN CHRISTIEN (1876 - 1966)	250-2500	L,G
JOHNS, JASPER (1930 -)	*10000-350000	A
JOHNS, JOSEPH W. (1833 - 1877)	2500-12000	L,G
JOHNSON, ARTHUR (1874 - 1954)	700-6000	F,L
JOHNSON, BEN (1902 -)	900-2500	A
JOHNSON, CONTENT (- 1949)	200-900	L,G
JOHNSON, DAVID (1827 - 1908)	750-30000	L
JOHNSON, EASTMAN (1824 - 1906)	750-375000	G,F
JOHNSON, FRANCIS NORTON (1878 - 1931)	200-1000	X
JOHNSON, FRANK TENNEY (1874 - 1939)	1000-125000	F,G,I
JOHNSON, GUY (1927 -)	500-2500	A
JOHNSON, HARVEY (1920 -)	8500-25000	G
JOHNSON, LESTER	*500-5000	
JOHNSON, LESTER (1919 -)	1000-20000	A
JOHNSON, LUCAS (1940 -)	300-1200	A
JOHNSON, MARSHALL (1850 - 1921)	500-3500	M
JOHNSON, PAUL (20TH C)	*100-600	X
JOHNSON, RAY (1927 -)	*500-5000	A
JOHNSTON, JOHN (1753 - 1818)	650-1800	F
JOHNSTON, JOHN HUMPHREYS (1857 -)	400-3000	L
JOHNSTON, JOHN R. (active 1850-75)	800-3500	F,L
JOHNSTON, REUBEN LE GRANDE (1850 - 1914)	250-950	L

*Denotes Mixed Media,Watercolors,Gouaches,Pastels, and/or Drawings

```
JOHNSTON, RICHARD T. (20TH C)               100-650      L
JOHNSTON, ROBERT E. (1885 - 1933)           300-2500     I
JOINER, HARVEY (1852 - 1932)                400-2500     L
JOLLEY, GWILT (1859 -       )               100-500      X (F)
JONES, F. EASTMAN (19TH C)                  350-1500     L
JONES, FRANCIS COATES (1857 - 1932)         750-20000    F
JONES, HUGH BOLTON (1848 - 1907)            350-20000    L
JONES, JOE (or JOSEPH JOHN) (1909 - 1963)   400-4500     G,F
JONES, LEON FOSTER (1871 - 1940)            300-2500     L
JONES, MARY E.H. (mid 19TH C)               *300-1200    P
JONES, PAUL (1860 -       )                 450-1500     W,F
JONES, ROBERT EDMOND (1887 -       )        *400-4500    I
JONES, SETH C. (1853 - 1930)                *300-1000    I
JONES, SUSAN (1897 -       )                250-1200     X (I,S)
JONES, WILLIAM F. (19TH C)                  1200-7500    W,G
JONNEVOLD, CARL HENRIK (1856 - 1930)        250-1800     L
JONTINEL, J.H.R. (19TH C)                   500-3000     X (L)
JORDAN, GUS (19TH - 20TH C)                 350-1800     X (M)
JORDAN, MARGUERITE (20TH C)                 *100-900     X (F)
JORGENSEN, CHRISTIAN                        *150-1500
JORGENSEN, CHRISTIAN (1860 - 1935)          400-4500     L
JORGENSON, WILLIAM (20TH C)                 400-1800     X (G)
JOSEPH, RICHARD (20TH C)                    800-4500     A
JOSEPHI, ISAAC (19TH - 20TH C)              450-1800     L,F
JOUETT, F.S. (19TH C)                       350-2500     X (M)
JOUETT, MATTHEW HARRIS (1787 - 1827)        400-4000     F
JOULLIN, AMEDEE (1862 - 1917)               350-5500     F,G
JOYLES, C.S. (19TH C)                       300-1200     X (M)
JUDD, DONALD (1928 -       )                *600-4000    A
JUDSON, C. CHAPEL (1864 -       )           100-500      L
JUDSON, MINNIE LEE (1865 - 1939)            100-650      L
JUDSON, WILLIAM LEES                        *200-1200
JUDSON, WILLIAM LEES (1842 - 1928)          400-3500     L,G,F
JUERGENS, ALFRED (1866 - 1934)              300-1200     X
```

K

```
KACERE, JOHN C. (1920 -       )             5000-20000   A
KAELIN, CHARLES SALIS                       *300-5000
KAELIN, CHARLES SALIS (1858 - 1929)         750-7500     M,L
KAHILL, JOSEPH B. (1882 - 1957)             300-900      F
KAHN, WOLF (1927 -       )                  *250-1200    X
KALBFUS, GEORGE (19TH C)                    1000-6500    G,F
```

*Denotes Mixed Media,Watercolors,Gouaches,Pastels, and/or Drawings

KALI, MRS. HENRYK WEYNEROWSKI (20TH C)	200-1200	X (F)
KALIN, VICTOR (1919 -)	250-1500	I
KALLEM, HENRY (1912 -)	100-600	X
KALMENOFF, MATTHEW (1905 -)	250-1200	L
KANE, JOHN (1860 - 1934)	1500-25000	G,F,L
KANTOR, MORRIS	*150-600	
KANTOR, MORRIS (1896 - 1974)	200-1800	A
KAPPES, ALFRED (1850 - 1894)	500-10000	X (G)
KARFIOL, BERNARD (1886 - 1952)	250-4000	L,F
KAROLY-SZANTO, ? (20TH C)	*100-400	X
KATZ, ALEX	*800-6500	
KATZ, ALEX (1927 -)	1000-45000	A
KAUFFMANN, GEORGE F. (19TH C)	*100-400	X (F)
KAUFFMANN, ROBERT (1893 -)	200-1500	I
KAUFMANN, THEODORE (1814 - 1887/90)	5000-45000	G
KAULA, LEE LUFKIN (19TH - 20TH C)	300-5500	F,L
KAULA, WILLIAM JURIAN (1871 - 1953)	350-7500	L
KAUTZKY, TED (20TH C)	*200-1000	L
KAYN, HILDE BAND (1906 - 1950)	200-1200	X (G)
KEEP, A.L. (20TH C)	100-400	X (L)
KEFFER, FRANCES (1881 - 1954)	100-500	X
KEIFFER, EDWIN L. (1921 -)	300-1500	X (L)
KEINHOLZ, EDWARD (20TH C)	100-600	A
KEITH, CASTLE (19TH - 20TH C)	300-1500	L
KEITH, ELIZABETH (1887 -)	500-4000	X (S)
KEITH, WILLIAM (1839 - 1911)	350-30000	L,F
KELLER, ARTHUR IGNATIUS (1866 - 1924)	*200-3500	I
KELLER, CHARLES FREDERICK (19TH - 20TH C)	200-1000	L
KELLER, CLYDE LEON (1872 - 1941)	200-1800	L
KELLER, HENRY GEORGE (1870 - 1949)	300-1200	X (G)
KELLEY, RAMON (20TH C)	*400-2000	X
KELLOGG, HARRY J. (19TH C)	200-1000	X
KELLOGG, MARY KILBORNE (1814 - 1889)	150-650	X (L)
KELLY, CLAY (19TH - 20TH C)	100-400	X (F)
KELLY, ELLSWORTH	*4000-15000	
KELLY, ELLSWORTH (1923 -)	10000-95000	A
KELLY, FRANCIS ROBERT (1927 -)	200-900	X
KELLY, J. REDDING (1868 - 1939)	150-700	F,L
KELPE, PAUL (1902 -)	4000-15000	A
KEMP, OLIVER (1887 - 1934)	400-2500	I
KEMPER, HENRY W. (19TH C)	600-4500	L,F
KENDALL, WILLIAM SERGEANT (1869 - 1938)	300-1000	X (F)
KENDRICK, DANIEL (20TH C)	100-500	X
KENNEDY, WILLIAM W. (1817 -)	700-5000	F
KENNON, C.H. (19TH C)	100-600	L
KENSETT, JOHN FREDERICK (1818 - 1872)	800-120000+	M,L
KENSIL, WILLIAM H. (19TH C)	400-1500	X (S)
KENT, ROCKWELL	*200-3500	
KENT, ROCKWELL (1882 -)	500-40000	L,F,I
KEPPLER, JOSEPH (1838 - 1894)	*100-850	I
KERKAM, EARL (1890 - 1965)	300-2000	A,F
KERNAN, JOSEPH F. (1878 - 1958)	500-2800	I
KESTER, LENARD (1917 -)	100-600	X (L)
KETT, EMILE (1828 - 1880)	400-3500	L,S
KEY, JOHN ROSS (1837 - 1920)	350-12000	L

*Denotes Mixed Media,Watercolors,Gouaches,Pastels, and/or Drawings

```
KIENBUSCH, WILLIAM (1914 -      )        300-1000      X
KIENHOLZ, EDWARD                         *200-1200
KIENHOLZ, EDWARD (1927 -     )           1500-6000     A
KIESALAK, J. (19TH C)                    300-1000      X (L)
KIHN, WILFRED LANGDON (1898 - 1957)      1500-12000    L,F
KILLGORE, CHARLES P. (20TH C)            200-1000      X (L)
KILVERT, B. CORY (1881 - 1946)           *100-1000     I,M
KIMBALL, CHARLES FREDERICK (1831 - 1903) 200-1000      L,M
KIMBEL, RICHARD M. (20TH C)              250-1200      L
KING, ALBERT F. (1854 - 1934)            300-20000     S,L
KING, CHARLES BIRD                       *300-5000
KING, CHARLES BIRD (1785 - 1862)         500-30000     F,G
KING, EMMA B. (20TH C)                   300-1500      X (G)
KING, HAMILTON (1871 - 1952)             *100-800      I
KING, JOE (20TH C)                       400-1800      F
KING, PAUL (1867 - 1947)                 500-10000     L
KINGMAN, DONG M. (1911 -     )           *200-6000     L,I
KINGSBURY, EDWARD R. (    - 1940)        200-1800      L,M
KINGSTEIN, JONAH (1923 -     )           100-400       X
KINGWOOD, CHARLES (20TH C)               *100-500      X (L)
KINNARD, H. (19TH - 20TH C)              100-500       X (M)
KINSELLA, JAMES (1857 - 1923)            100-850       L
KINSEY, ALBERTA (1875 - 1955)            100-300       X (F)
KINSTLER, EVERITT RAYMOND (1926 -    )   *400-3500     I
KIPNESS, ROBERT (20TH C ?)               100-600       X (A?)
KIRK, RICHARD (20TH C)                   100-400       X
KIRKPATRICK, FRANK LE BRUN (1853 - 1917) 1000-3500     F(I?)
KIRMSE, MARGUERITE (1885 - 1954)         *200-700      I
KISSACK, R.A. (1878 -     )              *100-500      F
KISSEL, ELEANORA (1891 - 1966)           250-1500      L,S
KITAJ, RONALD B. (1932 -     )           800-40000     A
KITCHEL, HUDSON M. (20TH C)              100-1000      L
KITCHELL, JOSEPH GRAY (1862 -     )      150-1200      L
KITTELL, NICHOLAS BIDDLE (1822 - 1894)   200-1200      L,F
KIVETT, B. CORY (20TH C)                 200-900       X
KLACKNER, C. (19TH C)                    400-2500      X (G)
KLAGSTAD, ARNOLD (1898 -     )           100-500       X (L)
KLEEMAN (KLEMANN?), RON (1937 -     )    1000-12000    A
KLEIN, M.J. (20TH C)                     100-300       X (L)
KLEMPNER, ERNEST S. (1867 - 1962)        500-3500      F,I
KLINE, FRANZ                             *600-35000
KLINE, FRANZ (1910 - 1962)               4500-900000   A
KLITGAARD, GEORGINA (1893 -     )        *150-800      S,L
KLOTZ, EDWARD (20TH C)                   100-400       L
KLUMPP, GUSTAV (1902 -1980)              1000-7500     P
KNAPER, G.H. (20TH C ?)                  100-500       X (L)
KNAPP, CHARLES W. (1823 - 1900)          450-5000      L
KNATHS, KARL                             *150-1200
KNATHS, KARL (1891 - 1971)               450-10000     A
KNEEDLER, J. (20TH  C)                   100-500       X
KNIGHT, CHARLES ROBERT (1874 - 1953)     *200-4500     W,L
KNIGHT, CLAYTON (1891 - 1969)            *100-700      I
KNIGHT, DANIEL RIDGWAY                   *600-3500
KNIGHT, DANIEL RIDGWAY (1839 - 1924)     1200-35000    F,G
KNIGHT, JOHN A. (1825 -     )            100-750       M,L
```

*Denotes Mixed Media,Watercolors,Gouaches,Pastels, and/or Drawings

```
KNIGHT, LOUIS ASTON (1873 -1948)              300-12000    L
KNOPF, NELLIE AUGUSTA (1875 - 1962)           100-850      M,L
KNOWLES, FARQUHAR MCGILLVRAY (1860 - 1932)    350-5000     M,L,I
KNOWLES, JOE (20TH C)                         *100-500     X (G)
KNOX, SUSAN RICKER (1874 - 1960)              150-2500     F
KOCH, JOHN (1909 - 1978)                      1200-50000   F,S,G
KOCH, PYKE (20TH C)                           2500-20000   X
KOCH, SAMUEL (1887 -      )                    100-500      X (S)
KOCHER, MARY (20TH C)                         100-400      X (L)
KOCK, GERD (1929 -      )                     100-400      X (L)
KOEHLER, PAUL R. (1866 - 1909)               200-1000     L
KOENIGER, WALTER (1881 -      )               400-6500     L
KOERNER, HENRY (1915 -      )                 600-4000     A
KOERNER, P.K. (19TH C)                        100-500      X (L)
KOERNER, WILLIAM HENRY DETHLEF (1878-1938)    1000-45000   I
KOHLER, WILLIAM EIFFE V.R. (19TH C)           300-1500     X (L)
KOLLNER, AUGUSTUS (1813 - 1870)               *300-2000    M,L
KOLLOCK, MARY (1840 - 1911)                   500-3500     L,F,S
KOONING, ELAINE DE (1920 -      )             600-5000     A
KOONING, WILLEM DE                            *3000-250000+
KOONING, WILLEM DE (1904 -      )             5000-2000000 A
KOOPMAN, AUGUSTUS (1869 - 1914)               300-1500     X (L)
KOOPMAN, JOHN R. (1881 - 1949)                *150-650     X (L)
KOPF, MAXIM (20TH C)                          100-500      X
KOPMAN, BENJAMIN D. (1887 - 1965)             200-1200     F,G
KORAB, KARL (1937 -      )                    2500-20000   A
KORSAKOFF, S. DE (20TH C)                     100-400      X (M)
KOSA, EMIL (1903 - 1968)                      300-2500     X
KOSKI, ?    (20TH C)                          *100-400     X (F)
KOST, FREDERICK WILLIAM (1861 - 1923)         200-1200     L,G
KOTIN, ALBERT (1907 -      )                  200-1000     A
KRAFFT, CARL RUDOLPH (1884 - 1938)            200-6000     L,G
KRASNER, LEE (1911 -      )                   8000-75000   A
KRASNOW, PETER (1890 - 1979)                  500-3500     X
KREHBIEL, ALBERT H. (1875 - 1945)             150-1500     G,L
KREPP, FRIEDRICH (19TH C)                     200-700      X (F)
KRETZINGER, CLARA JOSEPHINE (1883 -      )    100-500      X (G)
KREUTER, WERNER (20TH C)                      *100-400     X (F)
KRIMMEL, JOHN LEWIS (1789 - 1821)             10000-150000 G,F
KROGH, PER LASSON (1889 -      )              200-2000     F
KROLL, ABRAHAM (1919 -      )                 400-3200     F,G
KROLL, LEON                                   *100-2500
KROLL, LEON (1884 - 1974)                     1500-14000   F,L
KRONBERG, LOUIS                               *100-5000
KRONBERG, LOUIS (1872 - 1964)                 400-5500     F,G
KROTTER, R. (20TH C)                          100-400      L
KRUEGER, E. (19TH - 20TH C)                   150-750      X (G)
KRUGER, RICHARD (20TH C)                      150-600      L
KRUIF, HENRI GILBERT DE (1882 - 1944)         200-1000     X
KRUSHENICK, NICHOLAS (1929 -      )           800-4500     A
KUBIK, KAMIE (20TH C)                         *200-1200    X (L)
KUEHNE, MAX (1880 - 1968)                     400-3500     S,L
KUENSTLER, G. (20TH C)                        100-400      X (L)
KUHLMANN, G. EDWARD (1882 - 1934)             100-700      L,F
KUHN, WALT                                    *300-2500
```

*Denotes Mixed Media,Watercolors,Gouaches,Pastels, and/or Drawings

```
KUHN, WALT (1877 - 1949)                    900-35000      A,F,L,S
KULICKE, ROBERT (1924 -      )              200-1000       X
KULLOCK, M. (19TH C)                        100-500        X (L)
KUNDERT, B. (19TH - 20TH C)                 300-1200       L
KUNIYOSHI, YASUO                            *200-5000
KUNIYOSHI, YASUO (1893 - 1953)              2000-40000     A,F,L
KUNSTLER, MORT (1931 -      )               300-8500       I,F
KUNTZ, KARL (18TH - 19TH C)                 350-1500       X (G)
KURLANDER, H.W. (20TH C)                    150-650        X (F)
KYLE, JOSEPH (1815 - 1863)                  300-1200       F,G,S
```

L

```
LA CHANCE, GEORGE (1888 -      )            200-900        L,F
LA FARGE, JOHN                              *750-45000
LA FARGE, JOHN (1835 - 1910)                3000-75000     S,F
LA FARGE, JULES (19TH C)                    150-850        L
LABRIE, ROSE (1916 -      )                 1000-5000      P
LACHMAN, HARRY B. (1886 - 1974)             250-1500       L
LACROIX, PAUL (active 1855-70)              1000-15000     S
LAER, ALEXANDER T. VAN (1857 - 1929)        300-1500       L
LAGATTA, JOHN (1894 - 1977)                 500-3500       I
LAGERBERG, DON (1938 -      )               400-1500       A
LAHEY, RICHARD FRANCIS (1893 - 1979)        *200-800       G,F
LAING, GERALD (20TH C)                      500-4500       A
LAMASURE, EDWIN (      - 1916)              *100-600       L
LAMB, F. MORTIMER (1861 - 1936)             400-3500       L,F,W
LAMB, KATE B. (20TH C)                      100-500        X (L)
LAMBDIN, GEORGE COCHRAN (1830 - 1896)       1200-45000     S,F,G
LAMBDIN, JAMES REID (1807 - 1889)           700-15000      F
LAMBERT, TED R. (1905 - 1960)               3000-15000     X (L)
LANCASTER, MARK (1938 -      )              400-3000       A
LANCKEN, FRANK VON DER (1872 - 1950)        350-3000       F,G
LAND, ERNEST ALBERT (20TH C)                150-850        X
LANDERYOU, R. (late 19TH C)                 100-750        L
LANE, EMMA (late 19TH C)                    100-400        X (S)
LANE, ERNEST (19TH C)                       100-700        X (L)
LANE, FITZ HUGH (1804 - 1865)               20000-325000   L,M
LANG, LOUIS (1814 - 1893)                   750-60000      F,G,L
LANGLEY, EDWARD (20TH C)                    500-2500       L
LANGWORTHY, WILLIAM H. (late 19TH C)        300-1200       G,L
LANMAN, CHARLES (1819 - 1895)               350-4500       L
```

*Denotes Mixed Media,Watercolors,Gouaches,Pastels, and/or Drawings

Name	Price	Code
LANSIL, WALTER FRANKLIN (1846 - 1925)	300-3500	M,L
LARENCE, R.J. (19TH - 20TH C)	*100-500	L
LARSEN, MIKE (20TH C)	*100-500	X (F)
LARSON, EDWARD (1931 -)	1000-8500	P
LARSSON, MARCUS (1825 - 1864)	400-2000	X (L)
LASCARI, SALVATORE (1884 -)	100-800	X (F)
LATHROP, WILLIAM LANGSON (1859 - 1938)	500-6500	L
LATIMER, LORENZO PALMER	*150-1000	
LATIMER, LORENZO PALMER (1857 - 1941)	300-2500	L
LATOIX, GASPARD (19TH - 20TH C)	*1000-5000	F
LAUFMAN, SYDNEY (20TH C)	100-400	X (F)
LAUGHLIN, EDWARD (20TH C)	100-650	X
LAURENCE, SIDNEY M. (1865 - 1940)	500-35000	L
LAURENT, JOHN (20TH C)	250-1000	F
LAURENT, ROBERT (1890 - 1970)	*100-750	X (W)
LAURITZ, PAUL (1889 - 1975)	400-3500	L
LAUTERER, ARCH (20TH C)	*200-600	I
LAUX, AUGUST (1847 -1921)	400-5000	S,W
LAVALLE, JOHN	*100-400	
LAVALLE, JOHN (1896 -)	600-4000	G,F
LAVALLEY, JONAS JOSEPH (1858 - 1930)	500-2000	S
LAVIGNE, AUDREY RAE (19TH C)	*100-400	X
LAWLESS, CARL (1896 - 1934)	300-5000	L
LAWLOR, GEORGE W. (1848 -)	300-5500	F
LAWMAN, JASPER HOLMAN (1825 - 1906)	700-6500	L,F
LAWRENCE, JACOB (1917 -)	*1000-25000	A
LAWRENCE, VAIL EUGENE (1856 - 1934)	2000	
LAWRIE, ALEXANDER (1828 - 1917)	600-3500	F,L
LAWSON, ERNEST (1873 - 1939)	1000-100000	L
LAWSON, MARK (20TH C)	650-2500	I
LAZARUS, JACOB HART (1822 - 1891)	200-1000	F
LAZZARIO, PIETRO (1898 -)	*300-1000	A
LAZZELL, BLANCHE (- 1956)	600-9000	A,L,M
LEA, TOM (1907 -)	800-4000	I
LEAKE, GERALD (1885 -)	400-1800	X (F)
LEAR, LAVIN (20TH C)	*100-400	X (F)
LEAVITT, EDWARD CHALMERS (1842 - 1904)	400-12000	S,L
LEAVITT, JOHN FAUNCE (1905 - 1974)	*250-2000	M
LEAVITT, R.C. (20TH C ?)	200-900	X (M)
LEAVITT, SHELDON (JR) (19TH C ?)	500-3500	X
LEBDUSKA, LAWRENCE H. (1894 - 1966)	300-5000	P
LEBRUN, RICO	*200-1000	
LEBRUN, RICO (1900 - 1964)	300-2500	A
LECHAY, MYRON (1898 -)	150-950	L,F
LECLEAR, THOMAS (1818 - 1882)	300-5000	G,F
LEE, BERTHA STRINGER (1873 - 1937)	100-1000	L
LEE, CHEE CHIN S. CHEUNG (20TH C)	100-400	X
LEE, DORIS EMRICK (1905 -)	300-4000	L,G
LEE, SAMUEL M. (- 1841)	300-1500	L,F
LEEDY, LAURA A. (1881 -)	150-600	X (L)
LEETEG, EDGAR (20TH C)	400-1500	F
LEGANGER, NICOLAY TYSLAND (1832 - 1894)	100-800	L,M
LEGRAND, HENRY (active 1855-85)	400-5000	L,F
LEHR, ADAM (1853 - 1924)	150-1000	X (S)
LEIGH, WILLIAM ROBINSON (1866 - 1955)	2000-150000	I,F

*Denotes Mixed Media,Watercolors,Gouaches,Pastels, and/or Drawings

```
LEIGHTON, KATHERINE WOODMAN (1876 - 1952)    400-3000        F
LEIGHTON, NICHOLAS WINFIELD (1847 - 1898)    500-4500        X (F)
LEIGHTON, SCOTT (1849 - 1898)                400-30000       W,F
LEIKER, W. (19TH C)                          150-600         X (L)
LEISSER, MARTIN B. (1845 -      )            500-3000        L
LEITH-ROSS, HARRY (1886 -      )             400-4500        L,S
LEITNER, LEANDER (1873 -       )             100-1200        X (L)
LELAND, HENRY (1850 - 1877)                  600-5000        G,F
LEMAIRE, CHARLES (20TH C)                    *200-1000       X (I)
LESLIE, ALFRED (1927 -        )              2500-20000      A
LESLIE, FRANK (see HENRY CARTER)
LESLIE, G. (late 19TH C)                     300-1200        L
LEU, AUGUST WILHELM (1819 - 1887)            1000-7500       L
LEUTZE, EMANUEL GOTTLIEB (1816 - 1868)       600-30000       F,G,M
LEVER, RICHARD HAYLEY                        *100-2500
LEVER, RICHARD HAYLEY (1876 - 1958)          300-35000       M,L
LEVI, JULIAN (1874 -       )                 250-3000        F,M,G
LEVIER, CHARLES (1920 -       )              250-1800        L,M,S
LEVINE, DAVID (1926 -       )                *150-850        I
LEVINE, JACK                                 *150-5000
LEVINE, JACK (1915 -       )                 800-40000       A,G,F
LEVY, ALEXANDER OSCAR (1881 - 1947)          200-1800        L,F,I
LEVY, NAT (20TH C)                           *100-700        X (L)
LEVY, WILLIAM AUERBACH (1889 - 1964)         200-900         X (F,L)
LEWANDOWSKI, EDMUND D. (1914 -      )        800-4500        X
LEWIS, C.H.                                  *100-650
LEWIS, C.H. (19TH C)                         400-2500        F,M
LEWIS, EDMUND DARCH                          *250-4000
LEWIS, EDMUND DARCH (1835 - 1910)            400-8500        M,L
LEWIS, EMERSON (20TH C)                      *100-500        I
LEWIS, GEORGE JEFFREY (20TH C)               150-700         X (L,F)
LEWIS, MARTIN (1883 - 1962)                  *500-5000       G,L
LEWITT, SOL (1928 -       )                  *200-3000       A
LEYENDECKER, FRANCIS X. (1877 - 1924)        500-7500        I
LEYENDECKER, JOSEPH CHRISTIAN (1874 - 1951)  700-30000       I
LIBBY, FRANCIS ORVILLE (1884 -      )        100-1000        X (L)
LIBERMAN, ALEXANDER (1912 -      )           800-6500        A
LIBERTE, JEAN (20TH C)                       100-400         X (L,F)
LICHTENSTEIN, ROY                            *3000-575000
LICHTENSTEIN, ROY (1923 -      )             7000-450000     A
LIE, JONAS (1880 - 1940)                     650-30000       M,L
LINCOLN, EPHRAIM F. (19TH C)                 800-4500        M
LINDENMUTH, TOD (1885 -      )               300-1000        L,G,M
LINDER, HENRY (1854 - 1910)                  100-700         L
LINDGREN, MARJORIE REED (20TH C)             300-1500        X
LINDHOLM, W. (19TH C)                        300-1000        X (M)
LINDIN, CARL OLAF ERIC (1869 - 1942)         100-750         X (M)
LINDNER, E. (20TH C)                         *100-500        X (L)
LINDNER, RICHARD                             *800-30000
LINDNER, RICHARD (1901 - 1978)               1500-300000     A
LINDNEUX, ROBERT OTTOKAR (1871 - 1970)       100-1200        F,L
LINDSAY, THOMAS CORWIN (1845 - 1907)         300-2000        L,F
LINFORD, CHARLES (1846 - 1897)               400-2000        L
LINSON, CORWIN KNAPP (1864 - 1934)           800-3500        X (I)
LINTON, FRANK BENTON ASHLEY (1871 - 1944)    300-700         X (F)
```

*Denotes Mixed Media,Watercolors,Gouaches,Pastels, and/or Drawings

LINTOTT, EDWARD BERNARD (1875 - 1951)	*150-600	F,L
LIPPINCOTT, WILLIAM HENRY (1849 - 1920)	400-14000	F,L,I
LIPSKY, PAT (1941 -)	500-2500	X
LITTLE, A.P. (19TH C)	100-1000	X (S)
LITTLE, JOHN WESLEY (1867 - 1923)	*100-600	L,M
LITTLE, NATHANIEL STANTON (1893 -)	500-3500	X (M)
LITTLE, PHILIP	*100-850	
LITTLE, PHILIP (1857 - 1942)	400-4500	M,L
LITTLEFIELD, WILLIAM HORACE (1902 -)	100-300	A
LITTLEWOOD, JOHN (19TH C)	100-600	X (G)
LLOYD, SARA (20TH C)	450-3500	L,F
LOCHRIE, ELIZABETH DAVEY (1890 - 1976)	350-1500	X (F,G)
LOCK, F.W. (mid 19TH C)	*400-2500	L,F
LOCKWOOD, JOHN WARD (1894 - 1963)	*100-1200	L
LOCKWOOD, WILTON (ROBERT) (1862 - 1914)	300-3000	F,S
LOEB, LOUIS (1866 - 1909)	200-2000	F,G,I
LOEBERS, ADRIAN (20TH C)	100-850	X (L)
LOEMANS, ALEXANDER FRANCOIS (19TH C)	400-3500	L
LOFTEN, RICHARD (20TH C)	100-600	X
LOGAN, MAURICE (1886 -)	*300-900	X (M)
LOGAN, ROBERT FULTON (1889 - 1959)	500-4500	G,L
LOGAN, ROBERT HENRY (1874 - 1942)	500-5500	F
LONE WOLF,	*600-3500	
LONE WOLF, (1882 - 1970)	1000-18000	X (F)
LONG, STANLEY M. (1892 - 1972)	*100-850	X (G)
LONGFELLOW, ERNEST WADSWORTH (1845 - 1921)	300-2000	L
LONGFELLOW, MARY KING (19TH - 20TH C)	*400-1500	L,M
LONGO, ROBERT (1923 -)	*800-2500	A
LONGPRE, PAUL DE (1855 - 1911)	*600-3200	S
LOOMIS, ANDREW (WILLIAM ANDREW)(1892-1959)	250-2500	I
LOOMIS, CHARLES RUSSELL (- 1883)	*100-1000	M,L,S
LOOMIS, CHESTER R. (1852 - 1924)	400-3500	L,F
LOOMIS, JESSIE PARROTT (?)	*100-700	X (L?)
LOOMIS, P.L. (early 20TH C)	100-300	X (S)
LOOMIS, W.H. (early 20TH C)	*300-1200	X (F)
LOOP, HENRY AUGUSTUS (1831 - 1895)	100-800	F,L
LOOP, JEANETTE SHEPPERD H. (1840-1909)	100-1000	F
LOOP, JENNIE (19TH C)	400-1200	X (F)
LOPEZ, CARLOS (20TH C)	150-1200	X (F)
LOPEZ-LOZA, LUIS (1939 -)	700-2800	A
LORENZ, RICHARD (1858 - 1915)	500-30000	G,F,L
LORING, FRANCIS WILLIAM (1838 - 1905)	300-1200	G,L
LOTHROP, GEORGE EDWIN (20TH C)	600-3000	X (A?)
LOTICHIUS, ERNEST (late 19TH C)	400-2500	G,L,W
LOTT, E. (19TH C)	100-400	X (L)
LOUDERBACK, WALT (1887 - 1941)	100-2000	I
LOUGHEED, ROBERT ELMER (1910 - 1982)	800-35000	L,G,W,I
LOUIS, MORRIS (1912 - 1962)	7500-450000	A
LOVEJOY, RUPERT (20TH C)	350-3000	L
LOVELL, KATHERINE ADAMS (19TH - 20TH C)	250-1200	L,F,S
LOVELL, TOM (1909 -)	1500-100000	I,F,G
LOVEN, FRANK W. (1869 - 1941)	200-3500	L,I
LOVERIDGE, CHARLES (19TH C)	300-1800	L
LOVERIDGE, CLINTON (1824 - 1902)	300-1800	L
LOW, LAWRENCE GORDON (1912 -)	150-3500	F,S,I

*Denotes Mixed Media,Watercolors,Gouaches,Pastels, and/or Drawings

```
LOW, WILL HICOCK (1853 - 1932)               400-12000     I
LOW, WILLIAM GILMAN (19TH - 20TH C)          500-3000      X (L,W)
LOWE, R. (19TH - 20TH C)                      100-400       X
LOWELL, MILTON H. (1848 - 1927)              200-1200      L
LOWELL, ORSON BYRON                          *200-1000
LOWELL, ORSON BYRON (1871 - 1956)            400-3000      I
LOWES, H.C. (19TH C)                          200-800       X (W)
LOWNES, ANNA (19TH C)                         400-2500      X (S)
LOWRY, WILLIAM  J. (19TH C)                   100-700       L
LUCAS, ALBERT PIKE (1862 - 1945)             250-1500      L
LUCE, MOLLY (1896 -     )                     500-5000      G,F,L
LUCE, PERCIVAL DE (1847 - 1914)              250-1000      X (L)
LUCIONI, LUIGI (1900 -     )                  500-7500      S,L
LUKS, GEORGE BENJAMIN                        *200-5000
LUKS, GEORGE BENJAMIN (1867 - 1933)          1500-250000   G,F,L
LUMIS, HARRIET RANDALL (1870 - 1953)         500-20000     L,M
LUMLEY, ARTHUR (1837 - 1912)                 300-2000      F,I
LUNDBERG, AUGUST FREDERICK (early 20TH C)    1000-40000    X (G)
LUNDBORG, FLORENCE (1871 - 1949)             *150-850      X (I)
LUNDEAN, J. LOUIS (20TH C)                    300-2000      X (W)
LUNDEBERG, HELEN (1908 -     )                200-3500      M,G,F
LUNGREN, FERNAND HARVEY (1857 - 1932)        *500-4500     L,I
LURIE, NAN (20TH C)                           100-700       X
LUTZ, DAN (1906 - 1978)                       100-1000      A
LUYTIES, JAN VAN (19TH C)                     100-800       L
LYFORD, PHILIP (1887 - 1950)                  200-2000      F,L,I
LYMAN, JOSEPH (JR) (1843 - 1913)             500-3500      L
LYONNEL, A. (19TH - 20TH C)                   100-700       L
```

M

```
MAAR, DORA (20TH C)                          250-1200      X (L)
MACALLISTER, CARRIE R. (19TH - 20TH C)       400-4000      L
MACAULIFFE, JAMES J. (1848 - 1921)           500-9500      G,L
MACCORD, CHARLES WILLIAM (1852 - 1923)       300-1200      L
MACCORD, ELIZABETH (19TH - 20TH C)           100-600       X
MACCORD, MARY NICHOLENA (20TH C)             500-6500      X (L)
MACDONALD, HAROLD L. (1861 -     )           100-900       G,F
MACDONALD, JAMES EDWARD HERVEY (1873-1932)   2000-65000    L
MACDONALD-WRIGHT, STANTON                    *500-8500
MACDONALD-WRIGHT, STANTON (1890 - 1973)      600-30000     A,F,S
MACEWEN, WALTER                              *200-4000
```

*Denotes Mixed Media,Watercolors,Gouaches,Pastels, and/or Drawings

MACEWEN, WALTER (1860 - 1943)	350-7500	G,F,L
MACGILVARY, NORWOOD HODGE (1874 - 1950)	800-6000	X (L)
MACGINNIS, HENRY R. (1875 - 1962)	700-4500	F
MACHEN, WILLIAM HENRY (1832 - 1911)	500-2500	W,S
MACHESNEY, CLARA TAGGART (1860 -)	150-850	X (L)
MACINNIS, CHARLES (19TH C)	300-1200	G,F
MACIVER, LOREN (1909 -)	1000-12000	A
MACKENDRICK, LILIAN (1906 -)	300-2500	X (F)
MACKNIGHT, DODGE (1860 - 1934)	*200-1200	L
MACKUBIN, FLORENCE (1866 - 1918)	*100-500	F,W
MACLAUGHLIN, CHARLES J. (20TH C)	150-900	X (L)
MACLAUGHLIN, GERALD (20TH C)	200-1000	X
MACLEOD, WILLIAM (active 1840-65)	800-6500	L
MACNEAL, FREDERICK A. (early 20TH C)	*100-500	L
MACOMBER, MARY LIZZIE (1861 - 1916)	550-9500	F
MACRAE, ELMER LIVINGSTON	*100-2500	
MACRAE, ELMER LIVINGSTON (1875 - 1952)	500-25000	L,G,F,S
MACRUM, GEORGE H. (20TH C)	100-950	X
MACSOUD, NICHOLAS S. (1884 -)	100-850	L,F
MACY, WENDELL FERDINAND (20TH C)	250-2000	L
MACY, WILLIAM STARBUCK (1853 - 1916)	400-5500	L,G
MADER, LOUIS (1842 - 1892)	2500-25000	L,G,
MAENTEL, JACOB (1763 - 1863)	*500-20000	F
MAGEE, JAMES C. (1846 - 1924)	250-5000	L
MAHAFFEY, NOEL (1944 -)	1500-12000	X
MAILLOT, VICTORIA (early 20TH C)	300-1500	X (S)
MAJOR, B. (19TH - 20TH C)	100-800	L
MAJOR, ERNEST LEE (1864 - 1950)	400-3000	F,L,S
MAKO, B. (1890 -)	100-1200	X
MALCOM, ELIZABETH (20TH C)	*100-500	X (F)
MALHERBE, WILLIAM (20TH C)	200-5500	L,F,S
MAN-RAY,	*300-55000	
MAN-RAY, (Emmanuel Radinski) (1890 - 1976)	500-175000+	A
MANGOLD, ROBERT	*400-12000	
MANGOLD, ROBERT (1937 -)	3500-35000	A
MANGRAVITE, PEPPINO (1896 -)	*400-3000	A
MANIGAULT, EDWARD MIDDLETON (1887 - 1922)	500-2000	X (L)
MANLEY, THOMAS R. (1853 -)	100-650	L
MANN, PARKER (1852 - 1918)	100-750	L
MANNHEIM, JEAN (1863 -1945)	300-4000	L,F
MANNING, RUSSEL G. (- 1982)	*100-600	X (G)
MARATTA, HARDESTY GILLMORE (1864 -)	*200-1000	X (L,W)
MARBLE, JOHN NELSON (1855 - 1918)	100-650	L,F
MARCA-RELLI, CONRAD (1913 -)	*600-7000	A
MARCHAND, JOHN NORVAL (1875 - 1921)	*300-2500	I
MARCHANT, EDWARD DALTON (1806 - 1887)	700-2000	F
MARCIUS-SIMONS, PINCKNEY (1867 - 1909)	500-7500	G,F
MARCY, WILLIAM (20TH C)	*100-300	X
MARDEN, BRICE (1938 -)	*2000-20000	A
MARGO, BORIS (1902 -)	300-3000	A
MARGULIES, JOSEPH	*200-900	G,F,L
MARGUILES, JOSEPH (1896 -)	400-3000	G,F,L
MARIA, WALTER DE (1935 -)	*1000-10000	A
MARIN, JOHN	*500-50000	
MARIN, JOHN (1870 - 1953)	10000-35000	A,M,L

*Denotes Mixed Media,Watercolors,Gouaches,Pastels, and/or Drawings

```
MARIS, WALTER DE (1877 -      )               300-2000      X
MARK, GEORGE WASHINGTON (1795 - 1879)         800-10000     P
MARK, LOUIS (1867 - 1942)                     300-1000      F
MARKHAM, CHARLES C. (1837 - 1907)             1000-10000    G,S
MARKOS, S. (20TH C)                           500-3000      X (G)
MARLATT, H. IRVING (     - 1929)             250-1200      M,L
MARPLE, WILLIAM L. (1827 - 1910)              500-4000      L
MARSDEN, THEODORE (19TH C)                    400-2000      X (W)
MARSH, FELICIA MEYER (20TH C)                 100-500       F,L
MARSH, FREDERICK DANA (1872 - 1961)           200-1500      F,G
MARSH, REGINALD                               *300-40000
MARSH, REGINALD (1898 - 1954)                 600-45000     G,F,I
MARSHALL, CLARK S. (19TH - 20TH C)            100-450       L
MARSHALL, FRANK HOWARD (1866 -      )         100-600       M,L
MARSHALL, THOMAS W. (1850 - 1874)             500-4000      G,L
MARSHALL, WILLIAM EDGAR (1837 - 1906)         500-6500      F
MARTENET, MARJORIE D. (19TH - 20TH C)         100-500       X
MARTIN, A. (19TH C)                           100-400       L
MARTIN, AGNES (1912 -      )                  *1000-100000  A
MARTIN, FLETCHER                              *250-4000
MARTIN, FLETCHER (1904 - 1979)                600-5000      G,F
MARTIN, HELEN DOAK (19TH - 20TH C)            100-600       L
MARTIN, HOMER DODGE (1836 - 1897)             500-20000     L
MARTIN, J.H. (19TH C)                         150-950       X (L)
MARTIN, KNOX (1923 -      )                   400-5000      A
MARTIN, L.B. (19TH C)                         400-2500      X (M)
MARTINEZ, XAVIER                              *200-1200
MARTINEZ, XAVIER (1874 - 1943)                800-8500      X (L,F)
MARTINI, JOSEPH DE (1896 -      )            *100-400       G,L
MARTINO, ANTONIO PIETRO (1902 -      )        200-1200      L
MASON, ALICE TRUMBULL (1904 - 1971)           500-4500      X
MASON, FRANK H. (1921 -      )                100-800       X (L)
MASON, GEORGE CHAMPLIN (1820 - 1894)          300-1200      L
MASON, MAUD MARY (1867 - 1956)                100-750       X (L,S)
MASON, ROY MARTELL (1886 -      )            *100-500       X (G)
MASON, SANFORD (1798 - 1862)                  500-2500      F
MASON, WILLIAM SANFORD (1824 - 1864)          800-6500      G,F
MATHEUS, A. (19TH - 20TH C)                   100-700       L
MATHEWS, ARTHUR FRANK                         *500-4500
MATHEWS, ARTHUR FRANK (1860 - 1945)           850-30000     F,G,L
MATHEWS, J. (early 19TH C)                    2500-12000    P
MATHEWSON, FRANK CONVERS (1862 - 1941)        150-1800      F,L,S
MATTESON, TOMPKINS HARRISON (1813 - 1884)     600-7500      G,F
MATTHEWS, W.T. (19TH - 20TH C)                100-500       X (F,S)
MATTSON, HENRY ELLIS (1887 - 1971)            100-700       X (F,L)
MATULKA, JAN                                  *400-5000
MATULKA, JAN (1890 - 1972)                    800-8000      A
MATZAL, LEOPOLD C. (1890 -      )             150-850       F
MAURER, ALFRED HENRY                          *600-7500
MAURER, ALFRED HENRY (1868 - 1932)            700-185000    A,F,L
MAURER, LOUIS (1832 - 1932)                   2500-65000    G,F,W
MAXFIELD, CLARA (19TH - 20TH C)               *100-700      X (S)
MAXFIELD, JAMES E. (1848 -      )             100-500       X
MAXWELL, PAUL (20TH C)                        *100-500      L
MAYER, CONSTANT (1829 - 1911)                 300-6000      G,F
```

*Denotes Mixed Media,Watercolors,Gouaches,Pastels, and/or Drawings

98

MAYER, FRANK BLACKWELL (1827 - 1899)	400-25000	G,F
MAYER, PETER BELA (1888 -)	500-20000	L,M
MAYFIELD, ROBERT B. (1869 - 1935)	100-600	X
MAYNARD, GEORGE WILLOUGHBY (1843 - 1923)	*300-3500	X (M,F)
MAYNARD, RICHARD FIELD (1875 -)	500-3500	X (F)
MAZZONOVICH, LAWRENCE (1872 -)	400-4000	L
MCAULIFFE, JAMES J. (1848 - 1921)	300-10000	G,M,L
MCCALL, CHARLES (20TH C)	200-1200	X (F)
MCCARTER, HENRY (1865 - 1943)	*100-700	I
MCCARTHY, FRANK (1924 -)	750-55000	I
MCCARTHY, HELEN K. (1884 -)	100-300	X (M)
MCCHESNEY, CLARA T. (early 20TH C)	*100-500	F,L
MCCLELLAND, BARCLAY (1891 - 1943)	*100-500	X
MCCLOSKEY, J. BURNS (20TH C)	200-1500	X (G)
MCCOLLUM, ALLAN (20TH C)	400-1200	A
MCCOMAS, FRANCIS JOHN	*600-7000	
MCCOMAS, FRANCIS JOHN (1874 - 1938)	750-20000	L
MCCOMAS, GENE (20TH C)	*100-300	F
MCCONNELL, GEORGE (1852 - 1929)	100-850	M,L
MCCORD, GEORGE HERBERT	*250-750	
MCCORD, GEORGE HERBERT (1848 - 1909)	400-4500	L
MCCOY, LAWRENCE R. (1888 -)	150-850	X (F)
MCCRACKEN, JOHN HARVEY (1934 -)	400-4500	A
MCCREA, SAMUEL HARKNESS (1867 -)	500-3500	L
MCCULLEN, A. (19TH C)	*350-2500	X (L)
MCCUTCHEON, JOHN T. (1870 -)	*100-500	I
MCDERMOTT, J.R. (1919 - 1977)	100-1000	I
MCDOUGALL, J.A. JR (1843 -)	500-2500	X (G)
MCENTEE, JERVIS (1828 - 1891)	700-55000	L
MCEVOY, EUGENIE (20TH C)	100-600	X (L)
MCEWEN, WALTER	*450-6500	
MCEWEN, WALTER (1860 - 1943)	500-6000	F,L
MCFARLANE, DAVID (19TH C)	1000-25000	M
MCFEE, HENRY LEE	*200-3000	
MCFEE, HENRY LEE (1886 - 1953)	500-7000	F,L,S
MCGARREL, JAMES (1930 -)	800-10000	A
MCGRATH, CLARENCE (1938 -)	3000-12000	X
MCGRATH, JOHN (1880 - 1940)	100-700	X
MCGREW, RALPH BROWNELL (1916 -)	10000-50000	X (F)
MCGUINNESS, C.W. (early 19TH C)	*1000-5000	P
MCILHENNEY, CHARLES (1858 - 1904)	300-1200	L
MCILWORTH, THOMAS (actice 1755-65)	400-1500	F
MCINTOSH, ROBERT J. (20TH C)	100-800	X (F)
MCKAY, M.R. (19TH C)	150-1000	L
MCKENNEY, HENRIETTA FOXHALL (1825 - 1877)	400-2500	L
MCKEY, EDWARD MICHAEL (1877 - 1918)	100-600	X
MCLAUGHLIN, JOHN (1898 - 1976)	5000-20000	A
MCLEAN, HOWARD (19TH - 20TH C)	1200-15000	G,F
MCLEAN, RICHARD (1934 -)	5000-40000	A
MCLOUGHLIN, GREGORY (20TH C)	100-700	X (S)
MCMANUS, GEORGE (1884 -)	*200-1000	I
MCMANUS, JAMES GOODWIN (1882 -)	*100-400	F
MCMEIN, NEYSA (1890 - 1949)	*200-2000	I
MCNETT, W. BROWN (19TH - 20TH C)	100-700	L
MEADE, WILLIAM (20TH C)	200-1000	X

*Denotes Mixed Media,Watercolors,Gouaches,Pastels, and/or Drawings

```
MEAKIN, LEWIS HENRY (1853 - 1917)              400-2500      L
MECHAU, FRANK (1904 - 1946)                    500-3500      G,W,L
MEEKER, JOSEPH RUSLING (1827 - 1887)           800-8000      L
MEEKS, EUGENE (1843 -      )                    350-4500      G
MEESER, LILIAN B. (1864 -      )                100-600       X (S)
MEGARGEE, LON (1883 - 1960)                     350-1500      F,L
MELBY, G. (19TH C)                             300-1200      X (M)
MELCHERS, JULIUS GARI (1860 - 1932)            1000-35000    F
MELEGA, FRANK (1906 -      )                    100-500       X
MELLEN, MARY (19TH C)                          500-7500      L,M
MELLON, ELEANOR (1894 -      )                  200-1000      F,L
MELROSE, ANDREW W. (1836 - 1901)               700-20000+    L,M
MELTSNER, PAUL R. (1905 -      )                100-800       X (F)
MELTZER, ARTHUR (1893 -      )                  400-12000     L,F
MENDENHALL, JACK (1937 -      )                 5000-15000    A
MENKES, SIGMUND (1896 -      )                  300-2500      F,S
MENTE, CHARLES (19TH - 20TH C)                 200-2000      X (I)
MENZLER-PEYTON, BERTHA S. (1874 -      )        400-3000      X (L)
MERKIN, RICHARD (1938 -      )                  *200-1500     A
MERRILD, KNUD (1894 - 1954)                    150-800       X (A)
MERRILL, FRANK THAYER (1848 -      )            *200-1500     I
MERRITT, ANNA LEA (1844 - 1930)                500-2000      F
MESSER, EDMUND CLARENCE (1842 -      )          300-1500      L,F
MESTROVIC, IVAN (1883 - 1962)                  *100-600      F
METCALF, ELIAB (1785 - 1834)                   800-3500      F
METCALF, WILLARD LEROY                         *400-4500
METCALF, WILLARD LEROY (1858 - 1925)           600-150000    L
METEYARD, THOMAS BRADFORD (1865 - 1928)        300-1800      L
METHVEN, H. WALLACE (1875 -      )              400-2800      X (L)
MEURER, CHARLES ALFRED (1865 - 1955)           250-4500      F,S,L
MEUTTMAN, WILLIAM (19TH - 20TH C)              *500-3500      X (L)
MEYER, CHRISTIAN (1838 - 1907)                 500-4000      L,F
MEYER, ERNEST (1863 - 1961)                    300-2000      L
MEYER, HERBERT (1882 - 1960)                   500-3000      G,L,S
MEYER, RICHARD MAX (late 19TH C)               400-3200      G,L
MEYER-KASSEL, HANS (20TH C)                    *100-500      F
MEYEROWITZ, WILLIAM (1898 -      )              200-1500      L,S,F
MEYERS, HARRY MORSE (1886 - 1961)              400-2000      I
MEYERS, RALPH (1885 - 1948)                    500-3500      L,F
MEZA, ENRIQUE (20TH C)                         100-600       X (L)
MICEU, VIRGINIA (19TH C)                       400-2000      L
MICHAELIS, H. VON (20TH C)                     300-1000      X
MIDDLETON, STANLEY GRANT (1852 -      )         400-3000      F,L
MIELATZ, CHARLES F. W. (1864 - 1919)           200-1200      M
MIELZINER, JO (1901 - 1976)                    *100-1500      I
MIERUM, GEORGE H. (20TH C)                     800-4500      X (L)
MIFFLIN, JOHN HOUSTON (1807 - 1888)            400-1500      F
MIFFLIN, LLYOD (1846 - 1921)                   400-3500      L
MIGNOT, LOUIS REMY (1831 - 1870)               600-30000     L
MIKUS, ELEANORE (1927 -      )                  100-800       A
MILBURN, JOHN (19TH C)                         500-4500      P
MILDER, JAY (1934 -      )                      200-2500      A
MILDWOFF, BEN (20TH C)                         *100-500      X (L)
MILLAR, ADDISON THOMAS (1860 - 1913)           300-7500      F,G,L,S
MILLAR, JAMES (18TH C)                         500-25000     F
```

*Denotes Mixed Media,Watercolors,Gouaches,Pastels, and/or Drawings

MILLER, A.R. (20TH C)	100-500	A
MILLER, ALFRED JACOB)	*3000-125000	
MILLER, ALFRED JACOB (1810 - 1874)	15000-200000	L,F
MILLER, BARSE (1904 -)	*100-800	L
MILLER, CHARLES HENRY (1842 - 1922)	200-4500	M,L
MILLER, F.H. (19TH C)	600-4500	X (S)
MILLER, FRANCIS (1855 - 1930)	100-700	L,F
MILLER, HENRY (20TH C)	*300-2000	X (I?)
MILLER, J.C. (20TH C)	100-600	L
MILLER, KENNETH HAYES (1876 - 1952)	300-12000	F,G,S,L
MILLER, MELVIN (1937 -)	250-1500	L,G
MILLER, RALPH DAVISON (1858 - 1945)	200-3500	L
MILLER, RICHARD E. (1875 - 1943)	400-275000	F,S,L
MILLER, WILLIAM RICKARBY	*600-3000	
MILLER, WILLIAM RICKARBY (1818 - 1893)	600-10000	L,F,M,S
MILLESON, ROYAL HILL (1849 -)	100-800	L
MILLET, CLARENCE (1897 - 1959)	600-6500	L
MILLET, FRANCIS DAVID (1846 - 1912)	1500-65000	F,I
MILONE, G. (19TH C)	300-2500	X (F)
MINAMOTO, KANAME (20TH C)	100-800	F
MINNEGERODE, MARIETTA (19TH C)	*100-800	X (F)
MINNELLI, VINCENTE (1910 -)	*300-1500	I
MINOR, ANNE ROGERS (1864 -)	150-1200	L
MINOR, ROBERT CRANNELL (1839 - 1904)	300-4000	L
MIRA, ALFRED S. (20TH C)	300-1800	X (L)
MITCHELL, ARTHUR (1864 -)	150-1200	L
MITCHELL, C.T. (19TH - 20TH C)	100-400	L
MITCHELL, E.T. (19TH C)	200-1200	L
MITCHELL, GEORGE BERTRAND (1872 - 1966)	200-1500	L,F
MITCHELL, JOAN (1926 -)	1000-50000	A
MITCHELL, JOHN CAMPBELL (1862 - 1922)	250-1500	L
MITCHELL, THOMAS JOHN (1875 -)	200-1500	X (L)
MIZEN, FREDERICK KIMBALL (1888 - 1964)	400-1800	I,F
MOCHARANAK, MARY (20TH C)	100-500	X (F)
MODRA, THEODORE B. (1873 - 1930)	*100-700	X (W)
MOELLER, LOUIS CHARLES (1855 - 1930)	1000-35000	G,F
MAHOLY-NAGY, LAZLO	*600-25000	
MOHOLY-NAGY, LAZLO (1895 - 1946)	10000-95000	A
MOHRMANN, JOHN HENRY (1857 - 1916)	1000-4500	M
MOLARSKY, A. (1883 - 1951)	100-500	X (L)
MOLARSKY, MAURICE (1885 - 1950)	100-600	S,F
MOLINA, VALENTIN (1880 -)	400-1500	X
MOLINARY, ANDREAS (1847 - 1915)	700-5000	X (L)
MONEGAR, CLARENCE BOYCE (20TH C)	*100-500	L,G
MONKS, JOHN AUSTIN SANDS (1850 - 1917)	250-1200	W,L
MONSEN, G. (19TH C)	100-600	X (M)
MONTALANT, JULIUS O. (active 1850-60)	300-2000	L
MONTGOMERY, ALFRED (1857 - 1922)	400-3000	G,S,L
MOON, CARL (1878 - 1948)	400-1500	X (F)
MOORE, ABEL BUEL (19TH C)	400-1500	F
MOORE, BENSON BOND (1882 -)	200-700	L
MOORE, EDWIN AUGUSTUS (1858 - 1925)	1000-6500	X (S)
MOORE, FRANK MONTAGUE (1887 - 1967)	250-800	L
MOORE, GUERNSEY (1874 - 1925)	*500-3500	X (F)
MOORE, HARRY HUMPHREY	*150-1800	

*Denotes Mixed Media,Watercolors,Gouaches,Pastels, and/or Drawings

MOORE, HARRY HUMPHREY (1844 - 1926)	1500-10000	F,M
MOORE, JACOB BAILY (1815 - 1893)	*500-2500	F
MOORE, JAMES HENRY (1854 - 1913)	*100-600	X (L)
MOORE, NELSON AUGUSTUS (1824 - 1902)	250-2500	L,F
MOORE, W.J. (19TH C)	250-1000	X (M)
MORA, FRANCIS LUIS	*100-2000	
MORA, FRANCIS LUIS (1874 - 1940)	500-12000	F,L
MORALES, ARMANDO	*1500-6000	
MORALES, ARMANDO (1927 -)	600-10000	A
MORAN, EDWARD (1829 - 1901)	800-25000	M,G,F
MORAN, EDWARD PERCY (1862 - 1935)	250-12000	F,G,L
MORAN, H. (19TH C)	400-1800	L
MORAN, LEON (JOHN LEON) (1864 - 1941)	450-8500	F,G,L
MORAN, PAUL NIMMO (1864 - 1907)	500-6000	F,G
MORAN, PETER (1841 - 1914)	700-35000	W,L
MORAN, THOMAS	*1000-175000	
MORAN, THOMAS (1837 - 1926)	1500-700000	L,M
MORATZ, FRANK (20TH C)	100-500	X (F)
MORGAN, JANE (1832 - 1898)	300-2000	G
MORGAN, MARY DE NEALE (19TH - 20TH C)	*200-1000	L
MORGAN, PATRICK (1904 -)	100-800	X (S)
MORGAN, RANDALL (1920 -)	300-1000	L,F
MORGAN, SISTER GERTRUDE (1900 - 1980)	200-3500	P
MORGAN, THEODORE J. (1872 -)	300-1500	L,S
MORGAN, WALLACE (1873 - 1948)	*100-900	I
MORGAN, WILLIAM (1826 - 1900)	400-5500	F,G
MORLEY, MALCOLM	*700-3500	
MORLEY, MALCOLM (1931 -)	3000-35000	A
MORO, PAUL (20TH C)	300-1800	L,S
MORONI, F. (early 20TH C)	100-750	F
MORRELL, WAYNE BEAM (1923 -)	150-1200	L,M
MORRIS, A. (19TH - 20TH C)	200-900	L
MORRIS, ANDREW (active 1845-55)	400-1500	F
MORRIS, C.D. (19TH - 20TH C)	350-2000	L
MORRIS, GEORGE FORD (20TH C)	600-3000	X (F)
MORRIS, GEORGE L.K. (1905 - 1975)	1500-15000	A
MORRIS, KYLE (1918 - 1979)	600-3000	A
MORRIS, NATHALIE (19TH - 20TH C)	300-900	X (F)
MORRIS, ROBERT (1931 -)	*500-4000	A
MORRISON, DAVID (1885 - 1934)	*100-600	X (M,S)
MORSE, EDWARD LIND (1857 - 1923)	400-1500	X (L,G)
MORSE, GEORGE FREDERICK (1834 -)	200-2000	L,M
MORSE, GEORGE R. (19TH C)	100-600	L
MORSE, HENRY DUTTON (1826 - 1888)	400-3000	W
MORSE, I.B. (20TH C)	200-800	L
MORSE, J.B. (active 1875 - 1890)	100-1000	L
MORSE, SAMUEL F.B. (1791 - 1872)	800-35000	F,M
MORSE, VERNON JAY (1898 - 1965)	250-1000	X (L)
MORTON, WILLIAM E. (1843 - 1916)	500-5000	L
MORVILLER, JOSEPH (active 1855-70)	450-10000	L
MOSER, JAMES HENRY (1854 - 1913)	400-4000	L
MOSERT, ZOE (20TH C)	*400-1500	X (F)
MOSES, ("GRANDMA") (1860 - 1961)	1500-125000	P
MOSES, ED (1926 -)	*700-3000	A
MOSES, FORREST K. (1893 - 1974)	300-3000	X (L)

*Denotes Mixed Media,Watercolors,Gouaches,Pastels, and/or Drawings

MOSES, THOMAS G. (1856 - 1934)	100-750	L
MOSES, THOMAS PALMER (19TH C)	*100-700	X (L)
MOSES, WALTER FARRINGTON (1874 -)	100-600	L
MOSLER, HENRY (1841 - 1920)	300-12000	F,G
MOSLER, JOHN HENRY (19TH C)	*100-800	X (L)
MOSS, R.F. (1898 - 1954)	300-1500	L
MOSTEL, ZERO (20TH C)	100-1200	X (F)
MOTE, MARCUS (1817 - 1890)	2000-20000	F,L
MOTHERWELL, ROBERT	*600-50000	
MOTHERWELL, ROBERT (1915 -)	3000-250000	A
MOTTET, JEANIE GALLUP (1884 - 1934)	400-2500	X (F)
MOUNT, EVILINA (19TH C)	500-2500	L
MOUNT, SHEPARD ALONZO (1804 - 1868)	750-15000	F,L,W
MOUNT, WILLIAM SIDNEY (1807 - 1868)	4000-850000	G,F,L,S
MOUNTFORT, ARNOLD (1873 - 1942)	300-12000	F
MOWBRAY, HENRY SIDDONS (1858 - 1928)	1000-45000	F
MOYLAN, LLOYD (1893 -)	500-3500	F,L
MUELLER, ALEXANDER (1872 - 1935)	300-1800	F,L
MUHLENFELD, (active 1895-1905)	500-1500	M
MULERTT, CAREL EUGENE	*250-1500	
MULERTT, CAREL EUGENE (1869 - 1915)	700-3500	F,L
MULHAUPT, FREDERICK JOHN (1871 - 1938)	250-4500	M,L,F
MULLER, HEINRICH (1823 - 1853)	700-4500	L
MULLER-URY, ADOLF FELIX (1862 -)	100-1000	F,L,S
MULLICAN, LEE (1919 -)	*100-600	X
MUMFORD, R.T. (19TH - 20TH C)	100-400	L
MUNGER, GILBERT (1837 - 1903)	600-4000	L
MUNROE, ALBERT F. (19TH - 20TH C)	300-1500	X (S)
MUNSON, H. (19TH C)	100-800	L
MUNSON, KNUTE (20TH C)	*150-750	F,L
MURA, FRANK (1861 -)	300-3000	X (L)
MURCH, WALTER TANDY (1907 - 1967)	2000-25000	A
MURPHY, ADAH CLIFFORD (early 20TH C)	200-1000	X (F,I)
MURPHY, C.A. (early 20TH C)	100-300	L
MURPHY, CHRISTOPHER JR (1902 -)	300-1500	X (F,G)
MURPHY, HERMAN DUDLEY (1867 - 1945)	250-7500	L
MURPHY, JOHN FRANCIS	*200-3000	
MURPHY, JOHN FRANCIS (1853 - 1921)	500-7500	L
MURRAY, ELIZABETH (1940 -)	500-2500	A
MURRAY, GEORGE (1822 -)	200-1000	L
MURRY, J.E. (19TH C)	200-900	X (S)
MUSS-ARNOLT, GUSTAV (1858 - 1927)	500-6500	W
MYERS, JEROME	*400-6500	
MYERS, JEROME (1867 - 1940)	600-35000	G,F

*Denotes Mixed Media,Watercolors,Gouaches,Pastels, and/or Drawings

N

NADELMAN, ELIE (1882 - 1946)	*500-5000	A,F
NAGEL, HERMAN F. (1876 -)	350-1500	X (W)
NAGLER, EDITH KROGER VAN (1895 - 1978)	100-2500	F,I
NAGLER, FRED A. (1891 - 1934)	*100-400	X (F)
NAHL, CHARLES CHRISTIAN (1818 - 1878)	1500-100000	G,F,L,W
NAILOR, GEROLD (1917 - 1952)	*100-800	X (F)
NAKIAN, REUBEN (1897 -)	*500-2500	A
NANGERONI, CARLO (1922 -)	250-1000	A
NARJOT, ERNEST (1827 - 1898)	600-20000	L,F
NASH, WILLARD AYER (1898 - 1943)	*100-1500	F,L,S
NAST, THOMAS	*200-4500	
NAST, THOMAS (1840 - 1902)	1800-60000	I
NATKIN, ROBERT (1930 -)	500-20000	A
NAUMAN, BRUCE (1941 -)	*600-2500	A
NEAGLE, JOHN (1796 - 1866)	500-7500	F
NEAL, DAVID DALHOFF (1838 - 1915)	1000-4500	F
NEALE, A. (19TH - 20TH C)	100-500	X (M)
NEEL, ALICE (1901 -)	500-3500	A,S,F
NEHLIG, VICTOR (1830 - 1910)	700-6500	F,G,L
NEILSON, RAYMOND PERRY RODGERS (1881-1964)	600-20000	G,F
NEIMAN, LEROY	*350-12000	
NEIMAN, LEROY (1926 -)	750-40000	A
NELAN, CHARLES (1859 - 1904)	*100-750	X (I)
NELL, MISS TONY (20TH C)	*100-850	X (I)
NELLE, ANTHONY (19TH - 20TH C)	*1200-3500	I
NELSON, EDWARD D. (- 1871)	1200-6500	L
NELSON, GEORGE LAURENCE (1887 - 1978)	100-4500	F,L
NELSON, J. (late 19TH C)	300-1200	X (G)
NELSON, RALPH LEWIS (1885 -)	100-500	X (L)
NELSON, WILLIAM (1861 - 1920)	*100-4000	F,G,L
NEMETHY, ALBERT (20TH C)	300-3000	G,L,M
NESBITT, LOWELL (1933 -)	500-20000	A
NESBITT, ROBERT H. (20TH C)	200-1500	X
NETTLETON, WALTER (1861 - 1936)	300-2000	L
NEUHAUS, EUGEN (1879 - 1963)	100-800	X (L)
NEUMAN, ROBERT S. (1926 -)	150-850	X (L)
NEVELSON, LOUISE (1900 -)	*600-5000	A,F
NEWBERRY, JOHN STRONG (1822 - 1892)	*100-500	I,F
NEWELL, GEORGE GLENN (1870 - 1947)	300-3000	W,L
NEWELL, HUGH (1830 - 1915)	700-3500+	G,F,L
NEWELL, PETER SHEAF (1862 - 1924)	*100-1000	F
NEWHALL, HARRIOT B. (1874 -)	*300-1000	G
NEWHAM, JOHN DEEING (19TH - 20TH C)	300-1200	X (L)
NEWMAN, BARNETT	*10000-60000	
NEWMAN, BARNETT (1905 - 1970)	20000-275000+	A
NEWMAN, CARL (1858 - 1932)	300-2000	F,L
NEWMAN, GEORGE A. (20TH C)	100-1500	X (L)
NEWMAN, ROBERT LOFTIN (1827 - 1912)	500-3500	X (F)
NEWMAN, WILLIE BETTY (1864 -)	100-700	F,L
NEWTON, GILBERT STUART (1794 - 1835)	300-6000	G,F

*Denotes Mixed Media,Watercolors,Gouaches,Pastels, and/or Drawings

NIBLETT, GARY (1943 -)	5000-35000	L,F
NICHOLAS, GRACE (19TH C)	100-400	P
NICHOLAS, P. (19TH C)	100-500	L,F
NICHOLAS, THOMAS (20TH C)	*300-1500	X (W)
NICHOLLS, RHODA HOLMES (1854 - 1930)	200-1500	X (G)
NICHOLS, BURR H. (1848 - 1915)	250-1800	G,F,L
NICHOLS, CELESTE BRUFF (active 1885-1910)	200-1000	X (S)
NICHOLS, DALE WILLIAM	*500-1800	
NICHOLS, DALE WILLIAM (1904 -)	400-12000	G,F,L
NICHOLS, HENRY HOBART (1869 - 1962)	300-12000	L
NICHOLS, SPENCER BAIRD (1875 - 1950)	400-5000	F,L
NICHOLSON, CHARLES W. (20TH C)	100-1000	X (S)
NICHOLSON, EDWARD HORACE (1901 - 1966)	250-1500	M,F,L
NICHOLSON, GEORGE WASHINGTON (1832 - 1912)	300-12000	L,F
NICOLL, JAMES CRAIG (1846 - 1918)	600-10000	M
NICOLL, NICOL (1923 -)	*200-1200	X (G)
NICOLS, AUDLEY DEAN (20TH C)	400-2000	L
NIEMAYER, JOHN HENRY (1839 - 1932)	400-1800	F
NILES, GEORGE E. (1837 - 1898)	200-1000	X (G)
NIRO, ROBERT DE (1922 -)	400-1800	X (S)
NISBET, ROBERT H.	*100-800	
NISBET, ROBERT H. (1879 - 1961)	250-1500	L
NOBLE, JOHN (1874 - 1935)	750-4000	M,F
NOBLE, THOMAS SATTERWHITE (1835 - 1907)	400-9500	F
NOGUCHI, ISAMU (1904 -)	*500-4500	F
NOLAN, E.B. (19TH - 20TH C)	*100-500	X (L)
NOLAND, KENNETH (1924 -)	5000-300000	A
NOLF, JOHN (1871 -)	100-1200	I
NORDELL, CARL J. (1885 -)	600-6500	S,F
NORDELL, POLLY (19TH - 20TH C)	*100-600	F
NORDFELDT, BROR JULIUS OLSSON	*450-2500	
NORDFELDT, BROR JULIUS OLSSON (1878-1955)	1000-8500	G,F,S
NORDHAUSEN, AUGUST HENRY (1901 -)	150-750	F
NORDSTROM, CARL HAROLD (1876 - 1934)	100-500	L
NORFOLK, WALTER (19TH - 20TH C)	100-500	X
NORMAN, MABEL (20TH C)	100-400	X (G)
NORSE, STANSBURY (19TH C)	150-800	L
NORTH, NOAH (1809 - 1880)	4000-20000	P
NORTHCOTE, JAMES (1822 - 1904)	400-6500	F,L,M
NORTON, L.D. (19TH - 20TH C)	100-900	X (L,M)
NORTON, WILLIAM EDWARD	*200-2000	
NORTON, WILLIAM EDWARD (1843 - 1916)	450-9500	M,L
NORTWICK, EVAN (20TH C)	100-400	X (F,G)
NOTT, RAYMOND (20TH C)	*100-500	L
NOURSE, ELIZABETH	*200-25000	
NOURSE, ELIZABETH (1859 - 1938)	1200-35000	F
NOWAK, FRANZ (19TH C)	*500-3500	S
NOYES, BERTHA (20TH C)	350-850	X (F)
NOYES, GEORGE LOFTUS (1864 - 1951)	350-25000	L
NUDERSCHER, FRANK B. (1880 - 1959)	400-2500	L,I
NUHLER, AUGUSTUS W. (- 1920)	*100-600	X (M)
NURSTRUM, C. (20TH C)	*100-600	X (M)
NUYTTENS, JOSEF PIERRE (1880 -)	*100-700	X (F)
NYE, EDGAR (1879 - 1943)	200-1500	L

*Denotes Mixed Media,Watercolors,Gouaches,Pastels, and/or Drawings

O

O'DONOVAN, WILLIAM RUDOLPH (1844 - 1920)	*150-600	L
O'GRADY, DONN (20TH C) •	300-1200	X
O'HAGEN, JOHN L. (20TH C)	100-500	X
O'HARA, ELIOT (1890 -)	*200-1000	L
O'HIGGINS, PABLO	*600-1500	
O'HIGGINS, PABLO (1904 -)	500-4500	X (F)
O'KEEFFE, GEORGIA	*500-100000	
O'KEEFFE, GEORGIA (1887 -)	4500-325000	A
O'KELLEY, MATTIE LOU (1907 -)	3500-15000	P
O'KELLY, ALOYSIUS (1853 -)	350-3500	F,L
O'LEARY, ANGELA (1879 - 1921)	*200-1500	L
O'LEARY, GALBRAITH (20TH C)	400-1800	L
O'NEIL, ROSE CECIL (1875 - 1944)	*400-1500	I
O'SHEA, JOHN (active 1925-40)	100-800	L
OAKES, WILBUR (1876 -)	150-1000	X (M)
OAKLEY, THORNTON	*250-3000	
OAKLEY, THORNTON (1881 - 1953)	400-6000	I
OAKLEY, VIOLET (1874 - 1961)	*100-1200	F,S,I
OATES, MERRITT L.C. (19TH - 20TH C)	100-300	X (F)
OBATA, CHUIRA (20TH C)	*100-500	X (L)
OBERTEUFFER, GEORGE (1878 - 1937)	800-15000	L,M
OCHTMAN, LEONARD (1854 - 1934)	700-10000	L
OCHTMAN, MINA FUNDA (1862 - 1924)	200-1800	X (L)
ODDIE, WALTER M. (1808 - 1865)	500-6000	L
OF, GEORGE F. (1876 -)	500-3500	X (S)
OGDEN, FREDERICK D. (19TH C)	400-1500	L,I
OGDEN, J. WILLIAM (19TH C)	100-700	L
OGLIVIE, JOHN CLINTON (1838 - 1900)	500-9500	L,M
OGLIVY, CLINTON (1838 - 1900)	400-1500	M
OKADA, KENZO (1902 -)	2000-25000	A
OKAMURA, ARTHUR (1932 -)	500-6500	A
OLDENBURG, CLAES THURE (1929 -)	*1000-30000	A
OLESEN, OLAF (1837 -)	500-4000	L
OLINSKY, IVAN GREGOREVITCH (1878 - 1962)	600-7000	F
OLITSKI, JULES (1922 -)	2000-60000	A
OLIVEIRA, NATHAN	*500-3500	
OLIVEIRA, NATHAN (1928 -)	1000-15000	A
OLIVER, JEAN NUTTING (1883 -)	100-1000	X (F)
OLIVER, THOMAS CLARKSON (1827 - 1893)	400-6500	M
OLSEN, HENRY (1902 -)	200-1000	X (M)
OLSEN, HERB (1905 - 1973)	*100-650	L
OLSON, J. OLAF (1894 - 1979)	*100-500	L,F
ONDERDONK, JULIAN (1882 - 1922)	500-10000	L
ONGLY, W. (19TH C)	150-800	L,F
OPERTI, ALBERT JASPER (1852 - 1922)	*350-2500	M
OPPENHEIM, DENNIS (1938 -)	800-3000	A
OPPER, JOHN (1908 -)	*200-2500	A
ORCULL, A.C. (late 19TH C)	100-500	L

*Denotes Mixed Media,Watercolors,Gouaches,Pastels, and/or Drawings

ORD, JOSEPH BIAYS (1805 - 1865)	2000-15000	F,S
ORGAN, MARJORIE (1886 - 1931)	400-3500	I
ORMSBY, DOROTHY (19TH - 20TH C)	400-1800	L,F
ORR, ALFRED EVERITT (1886 -)	*100-500	L,I
ORR, ELLIOT (1904 -)	100-400	X (F)
OSBURN, SALLY (20TH C)	*100-650	F
OSCAR, CHARLES (20TH C)	200-900	X (F)
OSSORIO, ALFONSO ANGEL (1916 -)	*400-6500	A
OSTHAUS, EDMUND HENRY (1858 - 1928)	500-15000	W
OSTRANDER,WILLIAM CHESEBOURGH (1858 -)	*350-1200	X (L)
OSTROWSKY, SAM (1885 -)	200-1200	F,S
OTIS, BASS (1784 - 1861)	800-3500	F
OTIS, GEORGE DEMONT	*200-1500	
OTIS, GEORGE DEMONT (1877 - 1962)	500-7500	L,M
OTTINGER, GEORGE MORTON (1833 - 1917)	800-12000	G
OUREN, KARL (1882 - 1943)	100-700	L
OVEREND, WILLIAM HEYSMAN (1851 - 1898)	500-6500	M,I
OWEN, BILL (1942 -)	6500-35000	G,F,L
OWEN, FRANK EDWARD (1907 -)	400-2000	A
OWEN, GEORGE (active 1855-75)	400-3500	G,F
OWEN, JOEL (20TH C)	*100-500	L
OWEN, ROBERT EMMETT (1878 - 1959)	400-4000	L

*Denotes Mixed Media,Watercolors,Gouaches,Pastels, and/or Drawings

P

```
PAALEN, ALICE (20TH C)                          *150-750       A
PACE, STEPHEN (1918 -      )                      500-5000      A
PACH, WALTER (1883 - 1958)                        400-2500      X (F)
PACKARD, MABEL (19TH - 20TH C)                    600-2500      X (L)
PADDOCK, ETHEL LOUISE (1887 -      )             *100-600       G,F,M
PAGE, ELIZABETH AMIE (1908 -      )               100-600       L
PAGE, MARIE DANFORTH (1869 - 1940)               900-12000      F
PAGE, WALTER GILMAN (1863 - 1934)                350-4000       F,L,S
PAGE, WILLIAM                                    *300-2000
PAGE, WILLIAM (1811 - 1885)                       500-5000      F,L,G,M
PAGES, JULES EUGENE (1867 - 1946)                700-20000      L,F,G
PAGINTON, (19TH - 20TH C)                         200-1800      L
PAIL, EDOUARD (1851 -      )                      300-2000      L
PAINE, H.H. (19TH C)                             1500-6000      P
PAINE, SUSANNAH (1792 - 1862)                    1000-7500      F,L
PAIRPOINT, NELLIE M. (19TH - 20TH C)              100-750       L,W
PALFRIES, J. (19TH C)                             100-600       X (L)
PALMER, ADELAIDE (19TH - 20TH C)                  150-750       X (S)
PALMER, ERATUS DOW (1817 - 1904)                 *100-300       F
PALMER, PAULINE (1867 - 1938)                     250-3500      L,F
PALMER, SAMUEL (19TH C)                          *100-1200      X (W)
PALMER, WALTER LAUNT                             *500-7000
PALMER, WALTER LAUNT (1854 - 1932)               700-15000      L,F,M
PALMER, WILLIAM C. (1906 -      )                *100-1000      X (L,I)
PANCOAST, MORRIS HALL (1877 -      )              150-1000      L,I
PANSING, FRED (active 1885-1905)                 1000-35000     M,L
PAPPAS, JOHN L. (1898 -      )                    100-300       X (L)
PARADISE, JOHN (1783 - 1833)                      400-1800      P
PARCELL, MALCOLM S. (1896 -      )                500-3500      L,G
PARIS, HAROLD (1925 -      )                      *             A?
PARISEN, WILLIAM DE (1800 - 1832)                 100-850       F
PARISH, JANE (19TH C)                             800-2500      S
PARK, ROSWELL (active 1820's)                    *5000-25000    X (L)
PARKER, CHARLES STEWART (1860 - 1930)             200-2000      L,M,F
PARKER, EDGAR (1840 -      )                       800-6000      L,F
PARKER, JOHN ADAMS (1829 - 1905)                  400-1800      L
PARKER, JOHN F. (1884 -      )                     100-800       X (S)
PARKER, KAY PETERSON (20TH C)                    *100-500       X
PARKER, LAWTON S. (1868 - 1954)                   500-18000     L,F
PARKER, RAYMOND (RAY) (1922 -      )              500-7000      A
PARKHURST, H. (20TH C)                            100-400       X (G)
PARKINGTON, J. (19TH C)                           100-750       L
PARRISH, CLARA WAEVER (      - 1925)             *150-850       L,F
PARRISH, DAVID BUCHANAN (1939 -      )           2000-10000     A
PARRISH, MAXFIELD FREDERICK                      *200-6000
PARRISH, MAXFIELD FREDERICK (1870 - 1966)        1500-75000     I
PARRISH, STEVEN WINDSOR (1846 - 1938)            250-3500       L
PARROT, A. (19TH C)                              100-500        L
PARROTT, WILLIAM SAMUEL (1844 - 1915)            400-6000       L
PARSHALL, DEWITT (1864 - 1956)                   200-1200       L
```

* Denotes Mixed Media,Watercolors,Gouaches,Pastels, and/or Drawings.

Name	Range	Code
PARSHALL, DOUGLAS EWELL (1899 -)	400-2000	L
PARSONS, A. (19TH C)	150-1200	X (L,M)
PARSONS, BETTY B. (20TH C)	*100-650	L
PARSONS, CHARLES (1821 - 1910)	400-3500	M,G
PARSONS, ORRIN SHELDON (1866 - 1943)	300-3800	L
PARSONS, THEOPHILUS (1876 - 1934)	100-500	L,F
PARTINGTON, RICHARD LANGTRY (1868 - 1929)	400-2000	L
PARTON, ARTHUR (1842 - 1914)	450-15000	L
PARTON, ERNEST (1845 - 1933)	400-4000	L
PARTON, HENRY WOODRIDGE (1858 - 1933)	600-4500	F,L
PASCIN, JULES	*400-30000	
PASCIN, JULES (1885 - 1930)	2000-75000	A,F
PASKELL, WILLIAM	*100-500	
PASKELL, WILLIAM (- 1951)	250-1000	L,M
PATECKY, ALBERT (20TH C)	100-800	L,F
PATTERSON, AMBROSE MCCARTHY (1877 - 1930)	400-3500	L
PATTERSON, CHARLES ROBERT (1878 - 1958)	400-4000	M
PATTERSON, HOWARD ASHMAN (1891 -)	100-750	L,F
PATTERSON, MARGARET JORDAN (1887 -)	*150-750	I,L
PATTERSON, ROBERT (1898 - 1981)	100-800	I
PATTISON, JAMES WILLIAM (1844 1915)	600-4500	L,F
PATTON, KATHERINE (19TH - 20TH C)	300-1500	X (M,L)
PATTY, WILLIAM ARTHUR (1889 - 1961)	100-650	X (M)
PAUL, JEREMIAH (- 1830)	2000-65000	G,F
PAULI, RICHARD (1855 - 1892)	300-1500	L
PAULSON, O. (19TH C)	400-4500	L
PAULUS, FRANCIS PETRUS (1862 - 1933)	150-1800	G,L,S
PAUS, HERBERT ANDREW (1880 - 1946)	*200-2500	I
PAVIL, ELIE ANATOLE (1873 - 1948)	300-3500	L,F
PAXSON, EDGAR SAMUEL	*500-35000	
PAXSON, EDGAR SAMUEL (1852 - 1919)	5000-70000	F,G,I
PAXSON, ETHEL (1885 -)	150-900	L,F,I
PAXTON, JOHN (19TH - 20TH C)	500-6000	F
PAXTON, WILLIAM MCGREGOR	*200-15000	
PAXTON, WILLIAM MCGREGOR (1869 - 1941)	2000-80000	F,L,S
PAYNE, EDGAR ALWIN (1882 - 1947)	700-12000	L
PEAKE, CHANNING (1910 -)	*100-700	X (F)
PEALE, CHARLES WILSON (1741 - 1827)	15000-225000	F
PEALE, HARRIET CARY (1800 - 1869)	700-2500	F
PEALE, JAMES (1749 - 1831)	1500-375000	S,F,L,M
PEALE, MARY JANE (1827 - 1902)	700-5000	F,S
PEALE, RAPHAELLE (1774 - 1825)	5000-175000	S,F
PEALE, REMBRANDT (1778 - 1860)	1500-75000	F
PEALE, RUBENS (1784 - 1865)	700-10000	S,W
PEALE, SARAH MIRIAM	*100-900	
PEALE, SARAH MIRIAM (1800 - 1885)	600-3500	F,S
PEALE, TITIAN RAMSEY	*700-15000	
PEALE, TITIAN RAMSEY (1799 - 1885)	1000-25000	I,W,L
PEARCE, CHARLES SPRAGUE (1851 - 1914)	750-70000+	F
PEARCE, EDGAR LEWIS (1885 -)	200-1200	X (F)
PEARLSTEIN, PHILIP	*500-15000	
PEARLSTEIN, PHILIP (1924 -)	2500-40000	A,F
PEARSON, CORNELIUS (1805 - 1891)	*200-1500	L
PEARSON, HENRY (1914 -)	200-1000	X (A?)
PEARSON, JAMES (1900 -)	100-500	X

* Denotes Mixed Media, Watercolors, Gouaches, Pastels, and/or Drawings.

```
PEARSON, MARGUERITE STUBER (1898 - 1978)    300-9000      F,S
PEARSON, ROBERT (        - 1891)            500-3500      X (M)
PEASE, G.M. (19TH C)                        200-1500      X (L)
PEBBLES, FRANK M. (1839 -      )            200-1500      F,L
PECK, CHARLES E. (19TH C)                   300-1800      L
PECK, HENRY JARVIS (1880 - 1964)            200-1200      I
PECK, SHELDON (1797 - 1868)                 5000-100000   P
PECKHAM, DEACON ROBERT                      *300-1200
PECKHAM, DEACON ROBERT (1785 -      )       900-12000     F
PECKHAM, LEWIS (1788 - 1822)                500-6000      F
PEELE, JOHN THOMAS (1822 - 1897)            1000-10000    G,F
PEETERS, E. (19TH C)                        *100-700      X (L,S)
PEIRCE, H. WINTHROP (1850 - 1935)           300-2000      X (F,I)
PEIRCE, WALDO (1884 - 1970)                 300-4000      G,F
PEIXOTTO, ERNEST CLIFFORD (1869 - 1940)     200-1800      I,L
PEIXOTTO, FLORIAN (19TH C)                  300-1500      X (L)
PELL, ELLA FERRIS (1846 -      )            400-2000      X (F,I)
PELTON, AGNES (1881 - 1961)                 100-900       X (F)
PENE DU BOIS, GUY (1884 - 1958)             3000-60000    G,F
PENFIELD, EDWARD (1866 - 1925)              *200-2500     I
PENNELL, HARRY (early 20TH C)               250-3500      L
PENNELL, JOSEPH (1860 - 1926)               *250-2500     I
PENNINGTON, HARPER (1854 - 1920)            500-4500      F
PENNOYER, ALBERT SHELDON (1888 - 1957)      200-1500      L,F
PEPPER, BEVERLY (1924 -      )              *500-3500     A
PEPPER, CHARLES HOVEY (1864 - 1950)         *100-600      L
PERCIVAL, EDWIN (1793 -      )              400-1000      F
PERCONI, D.F. (20TH C)                      400-2000      X (G)
PEREIRA, IRENE RICE                         *100-5000
PEREIRA, IRENE RICE (1901 - 1971)           400-7500      A
PERELLI, ACHILLE (1822 - 1891)              400-3000      S,W
PERILLO, GREG (20TH C)                      500-3000      F,G
PERKINS, D.H. (20TH C)                      *100-700      X (L)
PERKINS, GRANVILLE                          *200-2000
PERKINS, GRANVILLE (1830 - 1895)            600-7500      L,M,I
PERKINS, RUTH HUNTER (1911 -      )         300-2500      P
PERKINS, SARAH (1771 - 1831)                *800-2500     F
PERLE, F. (early 20TH C)                    100-850       X (M)
PERRAULT, JOSEPH (20TH C)                   100-300       X (M)
PERRINE, VAN DEARING (1869 - 1955)          900-5000      A
PERRY, CLARA FAIRFIELD (        - 1941)     200-1000      L
PERRY, CLARA GREENLEAF (1871 -      )       300-1800      L,G
PERRY, ENOCH WOOD                           *500-6000
PERRY, ENOCH WOOD (1831 - 1915)             500-45000     F,G,L
PERRY, LILLA CABOT (1848 - 1933)            700-12000     F,L
PERRY, WILLIAM C. (20TH C)                  100-600       X
PERSSON, FRITIOF (20TH C)                   100-600       L
PERU, ALTO (18TH C)                         1500-8000+    F
PETERDI, GABOR (1915 -      )               *100-700      A
PETERIS, J.H. (20TH C)                      100-700       X (M)
PETERS, CARL WILLIAM (1897 -      )         100-700       X
PETERS, CHARLES ROLLO (1862 - 1928)         600-3000      L,M
PETERSEN, L. (19TH C)                       1000-4500     M
PETERSEN, THOMAS (20TH C)                   300-1200      X (M)
PETERSON, JANE                              *400-3000+
```

* Denotes Mixed Media,Watercolors,Gouaches,Pastels, and/or Drawings.

PETERSON, JANE (1876 - 1965)	500-25000	M,F,L,S
PETICOLAS, ARTHUR EDWARD (1793 - 1853)	3000-15000	L
PETO, JOHN FREDERICK (1854 - 1907)	2500-50000+	S
PETTET, WILLIAM (1942 -)	700-5000	A
PETTIBONE, RICHARD (1938 -)	150-950	X
PEW, GERTRUDE (20TH C)	*100-1200	X (F)
PEYRAUD, FRANK C. (1858 - 1948)	500-4500	L,F
PEYSTER, EVA DE (early 19TH C)	*400-1000	P
PFEIFFER, FRITZ (1875 - 1960)	500-4500	X
PHARES, FRANK (20TH C)	100-600	I
PHELAN, CHARLES T. (1840 -)	200-1500	W,L
PHELAN, HAROLD LEE (1881 -)	100-800	L
PHELPS, EDITH CATLIN (1879 - 1961)	200-1500	X
PHELPS, WILLIAM PRESTON (1848 - 1923)	300-6500	L,G
PHILIP, FREDERICK WILLIAM (1814 - 1841)	400-3500	F,S
PHILIPP, ROBERT (1895 - 1981)	300-9000	F,G,M,S
PHILIPPOTEAUX, PAUL D. (1846 -)	700-5500	G,F,L
PHILIPS, FRANK ALBERT (19TH C)	400-3500	X
PHILLIPS, AARON FRANCIS (1848 - 1899)	300-1500	L,F
PHILLIPS, AMMI (1788 - 1865)	1500-250000+	P
PHILLIPS, BERT GREER (1868 - 1956)	1000-70000	F,L,S,I
PHILLIPS, C. (mid 19TH C)	100-800	X (S)
PHILLIPS, GORDON (1927 -)	1000-12000	G,F
PHILLIPS, JOHN CAMPBELL (1873 - 1949)	100-1800	F,L
PHILLIPS, R. (20TH C)	200-1000	X (S)
PHILLIPS, S. GEORGE (- 1965)	100-700	L,F
PHILLIPS, WALTER JOSEPH (1884 - 1963)	*800-8500	L
PHIPPEN, GEORGE (1916 - 1966)	10000-60000	I,L,F
PIAZZONI, GOTTARDO (1872 - 1945)	600-3500	X (L)
PICKARD, C.G. (20TH C)	100-800	L
PICKETT, JOSEPH (1848 - 1918)	8000-35000	P
PICKNELL, GEORGE W. (1864 - 1943)	200-1500	L
PICKNELL, WILLIAM LAMB (1853 - 1897)	500-6500	L
PIENE, OTTO (1928 -)	300-1200	A
PIENKOWSKI, JONI (20TH C)	300-1200	X
PIERCE, CHARLES FRANKLIN (1844 - 1920)	100-1500	L,W
PIERCE, WALDO (20TH C)	200-1000	X (F)
PIERSON, ALDEN (1874 - 1921)	600-4500	X (L)
PIG, ROBERT (20TH C)	100-700	X (M)
PIKE, MARION HEWLETT (1914 -)	300-1200	X (S)
PILES, L.M. (late 19TH C)	300-2500	L
PILLSBURY, FRANKLIN C. (20TH C)	100-500	X (F)
PINE, THEODORE E. (1828 - 1905)	250-1200	F
PINNEY, EUNICE (1770 - 1849)	*500-12000	P
PIPPIN, HORACE (1888 - 1946)	12000-75000	P
PITTMAN, HOBSON L. (1900 - 1972)	600-5000	X (I)
PITZ, HENRY CLARENCE (1895 - 1976)	300-2500	I,L
PLATT, CHARLES ADAMS (1861 - 1933)	400-4000	M
PLEASONTON, RUTH (20TH C)	100-500	X (F)
PLEISSNER, OGDEN MINTON	*700-25000	
PLEISSNER, OGDEN MINTON (1905 - 1983)	2500-50000	G,L
PLETKA, (20TH C)	100-600	F,L
PLIMPTON, W.E. (early 20TH C)	100-400	X (L)
PLUMB, HENRY GRANT (1847 - 1936)	*400-3000	X (F)
PLUMMER, WILLIAM H. (19TH - 20TH C)	700-4000	M

* Denotes Mixed Media,Watercolors,Gouaches,Pastels, and/or Drawings.

```
PODCHERNIKOFF, ALEXIS M. (1912 -      )      350-3000      L,F
POEHLMANN, THEO (20TH C)                     100-500       X (F)
POGANY, "WILLY" (1882 - 1955)                *150-1200     F,I
POHL, EDWARD H. (19TH - 20TH C)              200-1200      L
POHL, HUGO DAVID (1878 - 1960)               100-900       I,F
POINCY, PAUL (1833 - 1909)                   700-7500      G,F
POINDEXTER, JAMES THOMAS (1832 - 1891)       800-3500      F
POLK, ANITA (19TH C)                         400-1000      X (F)
POLK, CHARLES PEALE (1767 - 1822)            2500-75000    F,G
POLLACK, MARK A. (20TH C)                    100-600       X (S)
POLLOCK, CHARLES CECIL (1902 -      )        700-5000      L
POLLOCK, JACKSON                             *4500-575000
POLLOCK, JACKSON (1912 - 1956)               7500-325000   A
POND, DANA (1880 - 1962)                     100-750       F,L
POND, MABEL E. DICKINSON (early 20TH C)      100-700       X (L)
PONSEN, TUNIS (20TH C)                       100-900       X (M)
POOLE, E. ABRAM (1883 - 1961)                200-1800      L,F
POOLE, EARL LINCOLN (1891 - 1934)            *100-600      W,I
POONS, LARRY (1937 -      )                  2000-50000    A
POOR, ANN (1887 - 1970)                      100-700       X (F)
POOR, HENRY VARNUM                           *100-700
POOR, HENRY VARNUM (1888 - 1970)             300-2500      L,S
POORE, HARRY (19TH C)                        200-1200      X
POORE, HENRY RANKIN (1859 - 1940)            300-7000      L,F,I
POPE, ALEXANDER (1849 - 1924)                500-15000+    S,W,F
POPE, ARTHUR (1880 -      )                  *100-600      X (L)
POPE, JOHN (1820 - 1886)                     100-2000      L,G,F
POPE, THOMAS BENJAMIN (      - 1891)         300-2500      L,G,S
PORIN, T. (19TH C)                           100-600       X (M)
PORTER, DAVID (1780 - 1843)                  2000-15000    M
PORTER, FAIRFIELD                            *500-20000
PORTER, FAIRFIELD (1907 - 1975)              5000-140000   L,M,F
PORTER, MARY KING (1865 - 1930)              *100-600      X (F,L)
PORTER, R.W. (19TH - 20TH C)                 *100-600      X (L)
PORTER, RUFUS (1792 - 1884)                  4000-60000    P
PORTER, S.R. (19TH C)                        300-1200      L
PORTER, V.F. (20TH C)                        200-800       X (M)
PORTINOFF, ALEXANDER (1887 - 1949)           *100-500      X (L)
POSEN, STEPHEN (1939 -      )                8000-25000    A
POST, EDWARD C. (active 1850-60)             600-6500      L
POST, CHARLES JOHNSON (1873 -      )         300-1500      X (L,I)
POST, GEORGE BOOTH (1906 -      )            *100-600      L
POST, WILLIAM MERRITT (1856 - 1935)          300-2800      L
POTTER, EDNA (20TH C)                        100-750       L
POTTER, HARRY SPAFFORD (1870 -      )        100-600       L,I
POTTER, MARY HELEN (1862 - 1950)             100-800       L,S
POTTER, LOUIS MCCLELLAN (1873 - 1912)        600-5000      G,F
POTTER, WILLIAM J. (1883 - 1964)             400-1800      F,L,M
POTTHAST, EDWARD HENRY                       *300-5000
POTTHAST, EDWARD HENRY (1857 - 1927)         1500-175000   G,F,L
POTTS, WILLIAM SHERMAN (1867 - 1927)         100-700       F
POULSON, M.B. (19TH C)                       300-2500      X (M)
POUSETTE-DART, NATHANIEL J. (1886 - 1965)    *100-600      X (F)
POUSETTE-DART, RICHARD (1916 -      )        7500-60000    A
POWELL, ACE                                  *200-3500
```

* Denotes Mixed Media,Watercolors,Gouaches,Pastels, and/or Drawings.

POWELL, ACE (1912 - 1978)	700-6500	F
POWELL, ARTHUR JAMES EMERY (1864 - 1956)	250-2500	L
POWELL, LICIEN WHITING	*200-700	
POWELL, LUCIEN WHITING (1846 - 1930)	200-4500	L
POWELL, M. (- 1711)	700-3500	F
POWER, JAMES P. (19TH C)	100-600	G,L
POWERS, A.G. (active 1845-65)	1500-6500	F
POWERS, ASAHEL LYNDE (1813 - 1843)	2500-20000	P
POWERS, MARION KIRKPATRICK (20TH C)	100-600	X (F)
POWIS, PAUL (19TH - 20TH C)	300-2500	X (S)
PRATHER, WILLIAM E. (19TH - 20TH C)	100-750	X (S)
PRATT, A.M. (19TH C)	300-1500	X (L)
PRATT, CATHERINE (19TH C)	300-1200	X (S)
PRATT, HENRY CHEEVES (1803 - 1880)	1000-4500	F,L,M
PRATT, MATTHEW (1734 - 1805)	5000-25000	F
PRATT, ROBERT M. (1811 - 1888)	700-20000	G,F,S
PRENDERGAST, MAURICE BRAZIL	*5000-450000	
PRENDERGAST, MAURICE BRAZIL (1861 - 1924)	10000-175000	A,L,F
PRENTICE, LEVI WELLS (1851 - 1935)	800-25000	S,L
PRENTISS, LILLIAN (20TH C)	100-700	X (G)
PRESCOTT, F.R. (early 19TH C)	100-700	X (L)
PRESSER, JOSEF (20TH C)	*100-600	X
PRESTON, MAY WILSON (1873 - 1949)	*250-1000	X (I)
PRESTON, WILLIAM (20TH C)	*150-1000	X
PRESTOPINO, GREGORIO (1907 -)	150-900	F
PREY, JUAN DE' (20TH C?)	*100-600	X (L)
PRICE, CLAYTON S. (1874 - 1950)	1500-12000	F,G
PRICE, GARRETT (20TH C)	*150-900	F,S
PRICE, L.A. (19TH - 20TH C)	200-800	X (W)
PRICE, M. ELIZABETH (20TH C)	100-700	X (L)
PRICE, NORMAN MILLS (1877 - 1951)	*200-1800	I
PRICE, WILLIAM HENRY (1864 - 1940)	100-1200	L,F
PRIEBE, KARL (1914 -)	*100-850	F
PRIESTMAN, BERTRAM WALTER (1868 -)	100-1000	M,L
PRINCE, L.E. (late 19TH C)	100-750	L
PRINGLE, JAMES FULTON (1788 - 1847)	2500-12000	M
PRIOR, WILLIAM MATTHEW (1806 - 1873)	1200-45000	P
PRITCHARD, GEORGE THOMPSON (1878 -)	200-1200	L
PRITCHARD, J. AMBROSE (1858 - 1905)	200-1200	L
PROBST, JOACHIM (1913 -)	100-500	X
PROBST, THORWALD A. (1886 - 1948)	100-500	X (I)
PROCTOR, ALEXANDER PHIMISTER (1862-1950)	*200-1000	W,F,L
PROHASKA, RAYMOND (1901 - 1981)	200-1500	I
PROOM, AL (1933 -)	100-800	X (S)
PUDOR, HEINRICH (19TH C)	400-2000	F
PURDY, DONALD ROY (1924 -)	100-750	F,L,S
PURWIN, SIGMUND (20TH C)	100-500	X
PUSHMAN, HOVSEP T. (1877 - 1966)	2500-25000	F,S
PUTHUFF, HANSON DUVALL (1875 - 1972)	300-5500	L
PUTMAN, DONALD (1927 -)	500-4500	F
PYLE, HOWARD	*500-10000	
PYLE, HOWARD (1853 - 1911)	2000-20000+	I

* Denotes Mixed Media,Watercolors,Gouaches,Pastels, and/or Drawings.

Q

QUARTLEY, ARTHUR (1839 - 1886)	800-5000	M
QUIDOR, JOHN (1801 - 1881)	20000-175000	F
QUIGLEY, EDWARD B. (1895 -)	500-6000	G,F
QUINLAN, WILL J. (1877 -)	250-1200	L
QUINN, EDMOND T. (1868 - 1926)	200-1000	F
QUIRT, WALTER W. (1902 -)	300-1800	A

R

RAAB, GEORGE (1866 - 1943)	*100-300	L
RABORG, BENJAMIN (1871 - 1918)	100-800	L
RACHMIEL, JEAN (1871 -)	150-1000	X
RAFFAEL, JOSEPH	*600-8500	
RAFFAEL, JOSEPH (1933 -)	2000-35000	A
RAIN, CHARLES WHEEDON (1911 -)	200-2500	X (S)
RALEIGH, CHARLES SIDNEY (1830 - 1925)	2500-35000	P
RALEIGH, HENRY PATRICK (1880 - 1945)	*200-1500	I,F
RAMME, H. (early 20TH C)	150-850	X (F)
RAMOS, MEL (1935 -)	3000-25000	A
RAMSDELL, FRED WINTHROP (1865 - 1915)	300-2500	L,F
RAMSEY, MILNE (1846 - 1915)	900-35000	S,L
RAND, ELLEN G. EMMET (1876 - 1941)	*100-700	X (F)
RAND, HENRY ASBURY (1886 -)	250-1200	L
RANDOLPH, JOHN (19TH - 20TH C)	200-1200	X (W)
RANDOLPH, LEE F. (1880 -)	300-1800	L,F
RANGER, HENRY WARD	*250-2000	
RANGER, HENRY WARD (1858 - 1916)	500-20000	L
RANN, VOLLIAN BURR (1897 - 1956)	150-1000	X (F)
RANNEY, WILLIAM TYLEE (1813 - 1857)	15000-300000+	G,F
RANSOM, ALEXANDER (19TH C)	300-1500	L,F
RANSOM, CAROLINE L. ORMES (1838 - 1910)	400-3500	L,S,F
RAPHAEL, JOSEPH (1872 - 1950)	700-20000	L,F
RAPP, J. (19TH - 20TH C)	200-1200	X (L)
RASCHEN, HENRY (1857 - 1937)	4500-60000	G,F
RASER, J. HEYL (19TH C)	250-1500	X (L)
RASKIN, JOSEPH (1897 -)	100-700	X (L,F)

* Denotes Mixed Media,Watercolors,Gouaches,Pastels, and/or Drawings.

RATNER, JOHN RYKOFF (1934 -)	500-6000	X (A)
RATTNER, ABRAHAM (1895 - 1978)	700-12000	A
RATTRAY, ALEXANDER WELLWOOD (1849 - 1902)	300-1800	L,F
RAUGHT, JOHN WILLARD (20TH C)	300-1000	X (L)
RAUSCHENBERG, ROBERT	*1500-425000	
RAUSCHENBERG, ROBERT (1925 -)	18000-175000	A
RAVLIN, GRACE (1885 - 1956)	600-5000	G,F
RAWSON, ALBERT LEIGHTON (1829 - 1902)	400-3000	L
RAWSON, CARL W. (1884 - 1970)	100-700	L,F
RAY, MAN (see MAN RAY)		
RAY, RUTH (20TH C)	100-500	A
RAYMOND, GRACE RUSSELL (1877 -)	100-900	X (M)
REA, LEWIS EDWARD (1868 -)	300-1200	L
READ, JAMES B. (1803 - 1870)	500-2500	F
READ, THOMAS BUCHANAN (1822 - 1872)	600-4000	F
REAM, CARDUCIUS PLANTAGENET (1837 - 1917)	800-6000	S
REAM, MORSTON CONSTANTINE (1840 - 1898)	600-8000	S
REASER, WILBUR AARON (1860 - 1942)	*150-700	L,F
RECKHARD, GARDNER ARNOLD (1858 - 1908)	300-1200	L,F
REDEIN, ALEX (1912 - 1965)	100-400	X (F)
REDELIUS, F.H. (20TH C)	100-900	X (S)
REDFIELD, EDWARD WILLIS (1869 - 1965)	2500-60000	L
REDMAN, B. (19TH - 20TH C)	700-3000	M
REDMOND, GRANVILLE (1871 - 1935)	400-2500	L,M
REDMOND, MARGARET (1867 - 1948)	300-4500	F,S
REDWOOD, ALLEN CARTER (1834 - 1922)	800-6500	F,G,I
REED, EARL H. (1863 -)	600-3000	L,W
REED, ETHEL (1876 -)	*200-1200	F
REED, MARJORIE (1915 -)	150-600	G,F
REED, PETER FISHE (1817 - 1887)	200-1000	L,F
REEDY, LEONARD HOWARD	100-1000	
REEDY, LEONARD HOWARD (1899 - 1956)	500-4000	I
REESE, BERNARD (JR) (19TH - 20TH C)	150-850	X (F)
REHN, FRANK KNOX MORTON	*150-950	
REHN, FRANK KNOX MORTON (1848 - 1914)	150-2500	M,L
REID, ROBERT LOUIS	*300-35000	
REID, ROBERT LOUIS (1862 - 1929)	1500-110000	F,L
REIFFEL, CHARLES (1862 - 1942)	600-3000	L
REINDEL, EDNA (1900 -)	800-3000	X (S)
REINEZ, S.A. (19TH C)	*100-400	G,F
REINHARDT, AD	*1500-15000	
REINHARDT, AD (1913 - 1967)	5000-175000	A
REINHARDT, SIEGFRIED GERHARD (1925 -)	600-6000	A
REINHART, BENJAMIN FRANKLIN (1829 - 1885)	3000-20000	G,F,L
REINHART, CHARLES STANLEY (1844 - 1896)	*200-1500	I
REISS, FRITZ WINOLD (1886 - 1953)	*300-18000	F
RELYEA. CHARLES M. (1863 -)	100-700	L,I
REMENICK, SEYMOUR (1923 -)	250-2000	A
REMINGTON, FREDERIC S.	*500-150000	
REMINGTON, FREDERIC S. (1861 - 1909)	12000-625000	G,F
REMINGTON, S.J. (19TH C)	400-2500	L
RENOUARD, GEORGE (19TH C)	100-500	L,F
RENSHAW, ALICE (19TH C)	*100-500	X (F)
RESNICK, MILTON (1917 -)	800-7500	A
RETTIG, JOHN (1860 -)	200-750	F,L

* Denotes Mixed Media,Watercolors,Gouaches,Pastels, and/or Drawings.

```
REUSSWIG, WILLIAM                                       *300-4000
REUSSWIG, WILLIAM (1902 - 1978)                          400-9000      I,G,F
REUTERDAHL, HENRY                                       *300-2000
REUTERDAHL, HENRY (1871 - 1925)                          400-5000      M,I
REYNARD, GRANT TYSON (1887 - 1968)                      *100-1500      I
REYNOLDS, JAMES (1926 -      )                          7000-60000     X (G)
REYNOLDS, W.S. (19TH - 20TH C)                           700-3500      X (S)
REYNOLDS, WELLINGTON JARED (1866 -      )               *500-6500      X (F)
RHEAD, LOUIS JOHN (1857 - 1926)                         *200-5000      X (I,F)
RIBAK, LOUIS (1903 - 1979)                              1000-7500      G,F
RIBCOWSKY, DEY DE (1880 - 1935)                          200-1800      M,L,F
RICCIARDI, CAESARE (1892 -      )                        100-500       L,S,F
RICE, G.S. (late 19TH C)                                 500-5000      F
RICE, HENRY W. (1853 - 1934)                            *100-500       X (M)
RICE, WILLIAM CLARKE (1875 - 1928)                       150-950       F,I
RICE, WILLIAM MORTON JACKSON (1854 - 1922)               500-2500      S,F
RICE-PEREIRA, IRENE                                     *100-5000
RICE-PEREIRA, IRENE (1901 - 1971)                        400-7500      A
RICH, JOHN HUBBARD (1876 - 1954)                         900-30000     X (F)
RICHARDS, FREDERICK DEBOURG (1822 - 1903)                700-7000      L,M
RICHARDS, JOHN (1935 -      )                            100-650       X (F)
RICHARDS, THOMAS ADDISON (1820 - 1900)                  1000-20000     L,F,S,I
RICHARDS, WILLIAM TROST                                 *200-40000
RICHARDS, WILLIAM TROST (1833 - 1905)                    500-45000+    M,L,S,F
RICHARDSON, ALLAN (early 20TH C)                         500-3500      X (F)
RICHARDSON, FRANCIS HENRY (1859 - 1934)                  250-4000      M,L,F
RICHARDSON, JOHN (20TH C)                                150-900       X (F)
RICHARDSON, MARGARET FOSTER (1881 -      )               700-6500      F
RICHARDSON, MARY CURTIS (1848 - 1931)                    300-4500      F
RICHARDSON, THEODORE J.                                 *250-1000
RICHARDSON, THEODORE J. (1855 - 1914)                    500-3500      L
RICHARDT, FERDINAND JOACHIM (1819 - 1895)                650-15000     L
RICHENBURG, ROBERT B. (1917 -      )                     500-6500      A
RICHERT, CHARLES HENRY                                  *100-350
RICHERT, CHARLES HENRY (1880 -      )                    100-600       L,M
RICHES, WILLIAM J. (late 19TH C)                         100-600       X (F)
RICHMOND, AGNES M. (1870 - 1964)                         300-15000     F
RICHTER, HANS (20TH C)                                  *500-1500      A
RICHTER, HENRY L. (1870 -      )                         100-600       L
RICKARDS, F. (early 19TH C)                              600-2500      F
RICKLE, T. (early 19TH C)                                400-2000      X (L)
RICKMAN, PHILIP (1891 -      )                          *400-2000      X (W)
RICKS, DOUGLAS (20TH C)                                 1000-6500      L,G
RIDDEL, JAMES (      - 1928)                            *100-700       X
RIDER, ARTHUR G. (20TH C)                                100-900       X (M)
RIDER, HENRY ORNE (1860 -      )                         100-600       L
RIECKE, GEORGE A.E. (1848 - 1930)                        200-900       L,W
RIECKE, JOHANN GEORGE LODEWYK (1817-1898)                300-2500      L,G,W
RIESENBERG, SIDNEY (1885 - 1962)                         350-3500      I
RIGGS, ROBERT (1896 - 1970)                             1000-7500      G,F,I
RILEY, KENNETH (1919 -      )                            700-50000     I
RILEY, MARY G. (1883 - 1939)                             100-600       X (L)
RILEY, NICHOLAS F. (1900 - 1944)                        *200-1500      I,F
RIMMER, WILLIAM (1816 - 1879)                           2500-60000     G,F,L
RINCK, ADOLPH D. (active 1835-60)                        200-800
```

* Denotes Mixed Media,Watercolors,Gouaches,Pastels, and/or Drawings.

Name	Price	Code
RIPLEY, AIDEN LASSELL (1896 - 1969)	*250-4000	W,L,F
RISING, C.P. (early 20TH C)	*100-600	L
RITSCHEL, WILLIAM P. (1864 - 1949)	400-6500	M,L,S
RITTENBERG, HENRY R. (1879 -)	500-2000	S,F
RITTER, ALONZO W. (1898 -)	100-400	X (F)
RITTER, HENRY (1816 - 1853)	1000-6000	G,F
RITTER, PAUL (19TH C)	400-2500	L
RIVERS, GEORGIE THURSTON (1878 -)	*100-400	X (F,L)
RIVERS, LARRY	*1000-75000	
RIVERS, LARRY (1923 -)	5000-100000	A
RIX, JULIAN WALGRIDGE (1850 - 1903)	300-5000	L
ROBBINS, ELLEN (1828 - 1905)	*400-3000	S
ROBBINS, HORACE WOLCOTT (1842 - 1904)	700-18000	L
ROBBINS, RAIS A. (20TH C)	300-2000	X
ROBERTS, MORTON (1927 - 1964)	800-15000	I
ROBERTS, NATHAN B. (19TH C)	600-3500	F
ROBERTSON, ANNA MARY (see "MOSES")		
ROBERTSON, ANNE L. (1844 - 1933)	600-45000	G,F
ROBERTSON, ARCHIBALD (1765 - 1835)	*450-3500	F
ROBERTSON, ROBERT (20TH C)	150-750	I
ROBINSON, ALEXANDER (1867 -)	*100-600	M,L
ROBINSON, BOARDMAN (1876 - 1952)	*100-700	I
ROBINSON, CHARLES DORMAN (1847 - 1933)	300-3000	L,M
ROBINSON, FLORENCE VINCENT (1874 - 1937)	*100-600	L,F
ROBINSON, GLADYS LLOYD (20TH C)	100-500	X (S)
ROBINSON, HAL (1875 - 1933)	150-3500	L
ROBINSON, MRS. A.K. (19TH C)	200-1000	X (W)
ROBINSON, THEODORE (1852 - 1896)	7500-250000	L,F
ROBINSON, THOMAS (1835 - 1888)	200-1800	L,G,W
ROBINSON, WILLIAM S. (1861 - 1945)	200-2000	L
ROBINSON, WILLIAM T. (1852 -)	200-1500	L,G
ROCKLINE, VERA (1896 - 1934)	600-3800	F
ROCKMORE, NOEL (20TH C)	400-1200	X (F)
ROCKWELL, AUGUSTUS (19TH C)	400-2500	L,F
ROCKWELL, CLEVELAND	*200-4500	
ROCKWELL, CLEVELAND (1837 - 1907)	700-6000	M,L
ROCKWELL, NORMAN	*1000-50000	
ROCKWELL, NORMAN (1894 - 1978)	2000-100000+	I
ROEDING, FRANCES (1910 -)	300-1200	X (F)
ROESEN, SEVERIN (1815 -)	8000-75000	S
ROGER, CHARLES A. (1866 - 1907)	100-700	L,F
ROGERS, FRANKLIN WHITING (1854 -)	200-1200	W,L
ROGERS, GRETCHEN W. (20TH C)	400-1200	F
ROGERS, WILLIAM ALLEN (1854 - 1931)	*300-2000	I
ROHDE, H. (20TH C)	100-600	L,W
ROHLAND, PAUL (20TH C)	100-400	X (S)
ROHOWSKY, MEYERS (1900 - 1974)	350-1500	X
ROLFE, EDMUND (19TH - 20TH C)	350-1800	S
ROLLE, AUGUST H.O. (1875 - 1941)	250-2000	L
ROLLINS, WARREN E. (1861 - 1962)	500-5500	F,L
ROLSHOVEN, JULIUS (1858 - 1930)	250-4500	F,L
ROMANO, UMBERTO (1905 -)	200-1200	F
ROMANSKI, HARRY (1861 -)	200-1200	X (L)
RONDEL, FREDERICK (1826 - 1892)	400-7500	L
ROOS, PETER (1850 -)	200-1500	L

* Denotes Mixed Media,Watercolors,Gouaches,Pastels, and/or Drawings.

```
ROOSEVELT, S. MONTGOMERY (1863 - 1929)        *100-600     X (F)
ROPES, JOSEPH (1812 - 1885)                    400-2000     L
ROSATI, JAMES (1912 -       )                  *100-900     A
ROSE, ANTHONY LEWIS DE (1803 - 1836)           350-1200     F
ROSE, GUY (1867 - 1925)                        1000-15000   L
ROSE, HERMAN (1909 -     )                      250-2000     L
ROSE, HORACE L. (19TH - 20TH C)                100-600      X
ROSE, W. (    - 1938)                          300-1800     X
ROSELAND, HARRY (1868 - 1950)                  700-25000    F,G
ROSEN, CHARLES (1878 - 1950)                   500-6000     L
ROSENBERG, HENRY MORTIKAR (1858 - 1947)        150-1000     X (F)
ROSENKRANZ, CLARENCE C. (19TH - 20TH C)        200-1000     L
ROSENQUIST, JAMES                              *1500-35000
ROSENQUIST, JAMES (1933 -     )                3000-70000   A
ROSENTHAL, ALBERT (1863 - 1939)                200-3500     F
ROSENTHAL, DORIS (1895 - 1971)                 150-600      G,F,L
ROSENTHAL, MAX (1833 - 1918)                   300-1500     F,M
ROSENTHAL, TOBY EDWARD (1848 - 1917)           700-20000    F,G
ROSNER, CHARLES (1894 - 1975)                  *150-500     M
ROSS, DENMAN WALDO (1853 - 1935)               400-1500     L
ROSS, LILLI (20TH C)                           100-300      X
ROSSEAU, PERCIVAL LEONARD (1859 - 1937)        1000-25000   W,L
ROSSITER, THOMAS PRITCHARD (1818 - 1871)       900-6000     G,F,L,M
ROTCH, BENJAMIN SMITH (1817 - 1882)            400-2000     L
ROTENBERG, HAROLD (20TH C)                     100-600      X
ROTH, ERNEST DAVID (1879 -     )               100-650      X (L)
ROTHBORT, SAMUEL (1882 - 1971)                 100-700      L
ROTHERMEL, PETER FREDERICK (1817 - 1895)       300-3000     F
ROTHKO, MARK                                   *1500-90000
ROTHKO, MARK (1903 - 1970)                     3000-750000+ A
ROTHSTEIN, E. (1907 -     )                    100-400      X (G)
ROUILLION, M.W. (19TH - 20TH C)                100-900      X (L)
ROUSSEFF, W. VLADMIR (1890 - 1934)             100-600      X (L)
ROUZEE, W. (19TH C)                            100-600      L,M
ROWE, J. STAPLES (1856 - 1905)                 *100-350     X (F)
RUBEN, RICHARD (1925 -     )                   150-800      A
RUCKER, ROBERT (20TH C)                        200-1000     X (L)
RUDELL, PETER EDWARD (1854 - 1899)             150-900      L
RUDOLPH, ERNEST (19TH - 20TH C)                400-2000     X (L)
RUFF, BEATRICE (20TH C)                        100-650      X (L)
RUGE, CARL (20TH C)                            *250-1000    X
RUIZ, B.Y. (20TH C)                            200-1200     L
RUMMELL, RICHARD (1848 - 1924)                 *350-3800    M
RUNGIUS, CARL (1869 - 1959)                    1000-80000   W,L
RUSALL, J.L. (19TH C)                          100-500      L
RUSCHA, EDWARD                                 *1000-6500
RUSCHA, EDWARD (1937 -     )                   4000-30000   A
RUSH, OLIVE (20TH C)                           *100-650     X (L)
RUSS, C.B. (active 1880-1920)                  350-2500     L
RUSSELL, ALFRED (20TH C)                       100-500      L,F
RUSSELL, BENJAMIN (1804 - 1885)                *2500-7500   M
RUSSELL, CHARLES MARION                        *1500-175000
RUSSELL, CHARLES MARION (1865 - 1926)          15000-275000 G,F,I
RUSSELL, EDWARD JOHN (1832 - 1906)             *1000-3000   M
RUSSELL, GRACE L. (20TH C)                     100-500      X (M)
```

* Denotes Mixed Media,Watercolors,Gouaches,Pastels, and/or Drawings.

```
RUSSELL, MORGAN (1886 - 1953)               450-4800     A
RUSSELL, MOSES B. (early 19TH C)            150-600      F
RUSSELL, WALTER (1871 - 1963)               400-10000    F,M,I
RUSSELL, WILLIAM GEORGE (1860 -     )       *100-850     X (M)
RUTLEDGE, JANE (20TH C)                      100-500      X (L)
RYAN, ANNE (1889 - 1954)                    *1800-6500   A
RYAN, TOM                                   *2500-40000
RYAN, TOM (1922 -     )                      3500-50000   I
RYDEN, HENNING (1869 - 1939)                 350-2500     F,M
RYDER, ALBERT PINKHAM (1847 - 1917)         ??????       F,L,M
RYDER, CHAUNCEY FOSTER (1868 - 1949)         600-10000+   L,F
RYDER, HENRY ORNE (19TH C)                   200-1200     L,M
RYDER, PLATT POWELL (1821 - 1896)            600-12000    G,F
RYLAND, ROBERT KNIGHT (1873 - 1951)          600-8500     F,I
RYMAN, ROBERT (1930 -     )                 *10000-45000  A
```

S

```
SACCO, LUCA (1858 - 1912)                    150-750      X (L)
SACKS, WALTER T. (1895 -     )              *100-800      L
SAGE, KAY (1898 - 1963)                      2000-25000   A
SAINT-PHALLE, NIKI DE (1930 -     )         *650-4000     A
SALEMME, ATTILIO (1911 - 1955)               1500-10000   A
SALINAS, PORFIRIO (1910 -     )              800-20000    L
SALLE, DAVID (20TH C)                        2000-35000   A
SALMON, ROBERT (1775 - 1848)                 3500-95000   M,L
SALT, JOHN (1937 -     )                      4000-25000   A
SALZMANN, E. (19TH C)                         500-1800     X (L)
SAMARAS, LUCAS (1936 -     )                 *1000-6000    A
SAMMONS, CARL (20TH C)                        300-1500     L,M
SAMMONS, FREDERICK HARRINGTON C.(1853-1917)  400-2000     X (S)
SAMPLE, PAUL STARRETT                        *300-1500
SAMPLE, PAUL STARRETT (1896 - 1974)          450-9000     G,L,M,I
SANBORN, PERCY (1849 - 1929)                 100-700      M
SAND, PERCY TSISETE (1918 -     )           *100-300      X (F)
SANDER, LUDWIG (1906 - 1975)                 750-5500     A
SANDERSON, CHARLES WESLEY (1838 - 1905)     *100-450      L
SANDZEN, SVEN BIRGER (1871 - 1954)           400-2000     X (L)
SANFORD, GEORGE T. (active 1840-1850)       *800-4500     M
SANGER, WILLIAM (1875 -     )               *100-600      X (F)
SANTRY, DANIEL (1867 - 1951)                 100-1500     L
SARG, TONY (1882 - 1942)                     *100-750     I
SARGENT, HENRY (1770 - 1845)                 3000-25000   G,F
SARGENT, PAUL TURNER (1880 -     )           1500-12000   X (L)
```

* Denotes Mixed Media,Watercolors,Gouaches,Pastels, and/or Drawings.

```
SARGENT, JOHN SINGER                              *600-135000
SARGENT, JOHN SINGER (1856 - 1925)                3000-550000   F,L
SARISKY, MICHAEL (20TH C)                         100-400       X (S)
SARKISIAN, SARKIS (1909 - 1977)                   400-1500      F
SARNOFF, ARTHUR (20TH C)                          *100-600      X
SARRAZIN, LOUISE (20TH C)                         *100-600      X
SARTAIN, WILLIAM (1843 - 1924)                    200-1800      L
SARTELLE, HERBERT (20TH C)                        100-600       L
SASLOW, HERBERT (1920 -      )                     200-1000      X (S)
SATTERLEE, WALTER (1844 - 1908)                   *400-1200     F
SAUERWEIN, FRANK PETER                            *650-2000
SAUERWEIN, FRANK PETER (1871 - 1910)              1000-6500     L
SAUL, PETER (1934 -      )                  ?      700-2500      A
SAVAGE, EUGENE FRANCIS (1883 -      )             200-1800      G,F
SAVAGE, R.A. (19TH C)                             200-1500      X (F)
SAVITSKY, JACK (1910 -      )                     350-1800      P
SAWTELLE, ELIZABETH A. (20TH C)                   200-1200      X (S)
SAWYER, HELEN ALTON (1900 -      )               100-600       L,S
SAWYER, W.B. (20TH C)                             250-1500      L
SAWYER, WELLS M. (1863 - 1961)                    100-600       X (M)
SAYER, RAYMOND (19TH - 20TH C)                    *100-450      X (M)
SAYRE, FRED GRAYSON (1879 - 1938)                 300-2500      L
SCALELLA, JULES (1895 -      )                    100-450       X (L)
SCHABELITZ, RUDOLPH FREDERICK (1884- 1959)        *100-850      G,I
SCHAEFFER, MEAD (1898 - 1980)                     500-7500      I
SCHAETTE, LOUIS (    - 1917)                      200-2000      F
SCHAFER, FREDERICK FERDINAND (1841 - 1917)        400-8500      L
SCHALDACH, WILLIAM J. (19TH - 20TH C)             *100-600      W
SCHANKER, LOUIS (1903 - 1981)                     1000-6500     A
SCHANS, S.V.D. (19TH C)                           3000-25000    F
SCHARY, SUSAN (20TH C)                            100-600       X (F)
SCHATER, F. (19TH C)                              500-4000      X (L,F)
SCHATTENSTEIN, NIKOL (1877 - 1954)                400-4000      F
SCHELL, FRANCIS H. (1834 - 1909)                  *100-600      I
SCHELL, FREDERICK H. (1838 - 1905)                *400-5000     M
SCHEUERLE, JOE (1873 - 1948)                      *350-2800     F
SCHINDLER, A. ZENO (1815 - 1880)                  *700-2500     L,F
SCHLAIKJER, JES WILLIAM (1897 -      )           400-4500      F,L
SCHLEETER, HOWARD BEHLING (1903 -      )         100-750       X (L)
SCHLEGEL, FRIDOLIN (19TH C)                       400-1200      F
SCHLENIER, T.M. (1820 - 1880)                     200-1200      L
SCHMEDTGEN, WILLIAM HERMAN (1862 - 1936)          *150-900      I
SCHMID, RICHARD ALLAN (1934 -      )             150-1000      L,F
SCHMIDT, CHRISTAIN FRIEDRICH (18TH-19TH C)        400-3500      G,F,L
SCHMIDT, HAROLD VON (1893 - 1982)                 900-50000     I,G
SCHMIDT, J.W. (20TH C)                            450-2500      M
SCHMIDT, KARL (1890 -      )                      100-350       X (M)
SCHMIDT, M.A. (20TH C)                            100-600       X (L)
SCHMITT, ALBERT F. (1873 -      )                400-1800      X (S)
SCHMITT, CARL (1889 -      )                      100-1200      X (L)
SCHNABEL, JULIAN (20TH C)                         *1500-100000  A
SCHNAKENBERG, HENRY (1892 - 1970)                 400-5500      W,L,S
SCHNEIDER, ARTHUR (20TH C)                        100-700       L,I
SCHNEIDER, FRANK (1935 -      )                   100-750       X (M)
SCHNEIDER, SUSAN HAYWARD (1876 -      )          100-700       X (L)
```

* Denotes Mixed Media,Watercolors,Gouaches,Pastels, and/or Drawings.

SCHNEIDER, THEOPHOLE (1872 -)	100-400	X
SCHOEN, CELESTE (20TH C)	100-500	F
SCHOEN, EUGENE (1880 - 1957)	200-1500	X (F)
SCHOFIELD, WALTER ELMER (1867 - 1944)	1000-25000	L
SCHOLDER, FRITZ (1937 -)	1000-12000	A
SCHONZEIT, BEN (1942 -)	3000-25000	A
SCHOONOVER, FRANK EARLE (1877 - 1972)	350-18000	I
SCHOTT, MAX (19TH - 20TH C)	700-3500	X (F)
SCHOTTLE, MARK (20TH C)	100-850	X
SCHRAG, KARL (1912 -)	*300-3500	A
SCHREIBER, GEORGES	*150-2500	
SCHREIBER, GEORGES (1904 -)	500-4500	G,I
SCHREYVOGEL, CHARLES (1861 - 1912)	3000-200000	G,F,L
SCHUESSLER, MARY (20TH C)	100-700	X (L)
SCHULTE, ANTOINETTE (1897 - 1981)	100-500	X (S)
SCHULTZ, CARL (19TH C)	*400-2000	F
SCHULTZ, GEORGE F. (1869 -)	150-3000	F,L,M
SCHUMACHER, WILLIAM E. (1870 - 1931)	150-1200	L
SCHUSSELE, CHRISTIAN	*400-2000	
SCHUSSELE, CHRISTIAN (1824 - 1879)	600-20000	G,F,L
SCHUSTER, DONNA N. (1883 - 1953)	350-5500	F,L
SCHUYLER, REMINGTON (1887 - 1955)	250-2500	F,G
SCHWABE, HENRY AUGUST (1843 - 1916)	200-1500	F
SCHWARTZ, A.W. (20TH C)	300-1000	X (L)
SCHWARTZ, ANDREW THOMAS (1867 - 1942)	100-900	L
SCHWARTZ, DANIEL (1929 -)	200-1500	I
SCHWARTZ, WILLIAM S. (1895 -)	600-6500	G,F
SCHWEIDER, ARTHUR (20TH C)	100-600	X (M)
SCIOCCHETTI, L. (20TH C)	100-600	X (L)
SCIVER, PEARL A. VAN (20TH C)	100-500	X (S)
SCOFIELD, K.M. (19TH C)	100-400	X (L)
SCOFIELD, WILLIAM BACON (1864 - 1930)	300-1800	L
SCOTT, CHARLES T. (1876 -)	400-2500	L,F
SCOTT, EMILY MARIA SPAFORD (1832 - 1915)	*200-1500	S
SCOTT, FRANK EDWIN (1863 - 1929)	200-1500	X (F)
SCOTT, G. (19TH C)	150-1200	L
SCOTT, HOWARD (1902 - 1983)	200-1500	I
SCOTT, JOHN WHITE ALLEN (1815 - 1907)	500-5500	L,M,F
SCOTT, JULIAN (1846 - 1901)	500-8500+	F,L
SCOTT, THOMAS J. (19TH C)	200-900	X (W)
SCOTT, WILLIAM EDOUARD (1884 -)	150-2500	X
SCOTT, WILLIAM J. (1879 - 1940)	*400-2500	F
SEAVEY, E. LEONE (19TH C)	250-1800	X
SEAVEY, GEORGE W. (1841 - 1916)	150-3000	X (S)
SECUNDA, ARTHUR (20TH C)	300-1500	L,F
SEERY, JOHN (1941 -)	800-7500	A
SEGAL, GEORGE (1924 -)	*500-3500	F
SEGALMAN, RICHARD (20TH C)	*150-600	X (F)
SEIBERT, J.O. (19TH - 20TH C)	100-500	X (F)
SEIFERT, PAUL (1840 - 1921)	*2500-10000	L
SELDEN, DIXIE (20TH C)	200-1000	L
SELDEN, HENRY BILL (1886 - 1934)	100-750	X (L,F)
SELF, COLIN (1941 -)	*400-2000	F
SELINGER, JEAN PAUL (1850 - 1909)	600-4500	F,S
SELLERS, ANNA (1824 - 1905)	700-3500	X (S)

* Denotes Mixed Media,Watercolors,Gouaches,Pastels, and/or Drawings.

SELTZER, OLAF CARL (1877 - 1957)	*2000-75000	G,F
SELZER, F. (19TH - 20TH C)	200-1200	X (F)
SENAT, PROSPER LOUIS (1852 - 1925)	*100-650	L
SENSEMAN, RAPHAEL (1870 - 1965)	*100-500	X (L)
SEPESHY, ZOLTAN L. (1898 - 1934)	150-3500	F,S,L
SERGER, FREDERICK B. (1889 - 1965)	100-850	X (F)
SERISAWA, SUEO (1910 -)	350-2500	X (L)
SERRA, RICHARD	*1200-4500	
SERRA, RICHARD (1938 -)	4000-20000	A
SERRA-BADUE, DANIEL (1914 -)	400-2000	X
SESSIONS, JAMES (20TH C)	*400-3200	L,F,M
SETHER, G. (early 20TH C)	*150-900	L
SEVERN, ARTHUR (?)	*100-350	X (M)
SEWELL, AMANDA BREWSTER	400-4500	F
SEWELL, AMOS (1901 - 1983)	250-1500	I
SEWELL, ROBERT VAN VORST (1860 - 1924)	200-5000	F,L
SEXTON, FREDERICK LESTER (1889 -)	300-1800	L,I
SEYFFERT, LEOPOLD (1887 - 1956)	100-750	F
SEYMOUR, RUTH (20TH C)	100-600	L,S
SHACKENBERG, HENRY E. (19TH C)	150-900	X (L)
SHACKLETON, CHARLES (- 1920)	250-1000	X (L)
SHADE, WILLIAM AUGUST (1848 - 1890)	800-4500	F,G
SHAHN, BEN	*600-65000	
SHAHN, BEN (1898 - 1969)	2000-100000	A,I
SHAPLEIGH, FRANK HENRY (1842 - 1906)	300-4000	L,M
SHARP, JAMES CLEMENT (1818 - 1897)	8000-35000	X (S)
SHARP, JOSEPH HENRY	*3500-20000	
SHARP, JOSEPH HENRY (1859 - 1953)	1500-125000	F,I
SHARP, LOUIS HOVEY (1875 - 1946)	250-2000	L,F
SHARP, W.A. (20TH C)	*100-300	X (L)
SHARP, WILLIAM (active 1840-90)	800-8000	G,I
SHARPLES, FELIX THOMAS (1786 -)	*500-5000	F
SHARPLES, JAMES (1751 - 1811)	*2500-8500	F
SHATTUCK, AARON DRAPER (1832 - 1928)	400-12000	L,F,W
SHAW, CHARLES GREEN (1892 - 1974)	500-6500	A
SHAW, G. (19TH C)	800-6500	L
SHAW, JOSHUA (1777 - 1860)	3500-75000	L,F,S,W
SHAW, SIDNEY DALE (1879 - 1946)	*100-750	L
SHAW, SUSAN M. (19TH C)	600-2500	X (S)
SHEARER, CHRISTOPHER H. (1840 - 1926)	100-4000	L
SHEBLE, H. (20TH C)	*300-2500	F
SHEELER, CHARLES	*500-20000+	
SHEELER, CHARLES (1883 - 1965)	3500-200000+	A,L
SHEETS, MILLARD (1907 -)	*500-5000	A,L
SHEFFER, GLEN C. (1881 - 1948)	100-1500	F
SHEFFERS, PETER W. (1894 - 1949)	200-1500	X
SHEFFIELD, ISAAC (1798 - 1845)	6000-30000	P
SHEPHARD, CLARENCE E. (1869 -)	100-900	L,F
SHEPHERD, J. CLINTON (1888 - 1975)	300-2500	F,G
SHEPPARD, JOSEPH SHERLY (1930 -)	250-1000	X
SHEPLEY, ANNIE B. (19TH C)	350-2000	X (F)
SHEPPARD, WARREN (1858 - 1937)	350-6000	M
SHEPPARD, WILLIAM LUDLOW (1833 - 1912)	*400-2800	F,G,I
SHERMUND, BARBARA (20TH C)	*100-800	X (F)
SHERWOOD, MARY CLARE (1868 - 1943)	1500-7500	L,F

* Denotes Mixed Media,Watercolors,Gouaches,Pastels, and/or Drawings.

SHIELDS, THOMAS W. (1850 - 1920)	*100-800	X
SHIKLER, AARON (1922 -)	*150-4500	X
SHINN, EVERETT	*250-70000	
SHINN, EVERETT (1876 - 1953)	1200-125000	G,F,I
SHIRLAW, WALTER	*100-650	
SHIRLAW, WALTER (1838 - 1909)	200-6000	F,G,I
SHITE, JULIA (20TH C)	*200-1000	X (F)
SHOKLER, HARRY (1896 -)	200-1500	X (L)
SHOOK, WILLIS (20TH C)	100-400	X (L)
SHOPE, SHORTY (1900 -)	2500-8500	X (F)
SHRADER, EDWIN ROSCOE (1879 - 1960)	350-1800	X (I)
SHRIVER, CRANE (late 19TH C)	300-1500	X
SHUCKER, JAMES W. (19TH - 20TH C)	100-500	X (F)
SHULL, DELLA (19TH - 20TH C)	300-1800	F
SHULTZ, ADOLPH ROBERT (1869 -)	100-750	L,S
SHURTLEFF, ROSWELL MORSE (1838 - 1915)	300-2500	L,M,I
SHUSTER, WILLIAM HOWARD (1893 - 1969)	400-2800	L,F
SHUTE, R.W. and S.A.	*3000-40000	
SHUTE, R.W. and S.A. (early 19TH C)	5000-35000	P
SIBBEL, SUSANNA (active 1800-15)	*2000-8500	P
SIEBEL, FRED (20TH C)	*150-750	X (G)
SIEBERT, EDWARD S. (1856 - 1938)	250-2000	L,F
SIEGRIEST, LUNDY (19TH - 20TH C)	*200-1200	X (F)
SIES, WALTER (19TH C)	400-2500	L,F
SIEVAN, MAURICE (1898 -)	100-700	X (L)
SIGLING, GEORGE ADAM (19TH - 20TH C)	300-1500	F
SILVA, FRANCIS AUGUSTUS	*1500-30000	
SILVA, FRANCIS AUGUSTUS (1835 - 1886)	3500-150000	M
SILVA, WILLIAM PASEY (1859 - 1948)	200-1200	L
SIMKHOVITCH, SIMKA (20TH C)	100-500	L
SIMMONS, EDWARD EMERSON (1852 - 1931)	750-18000	G,F
SIMON, HOWARD (1902 - 1979)	100-600	I
SIMPSON, CHARLES (19TH C)	100-600	X (G)
SIMPSON, JAMES ALEXANDER (1775 - 1848)	800-3500	F
SIMS, F. (19TH C)	300-1800	F,L
SINCLAIR, GERRIT VAN W. (1890 - 1955)	100-800	L
SINCLAIR, IRVING (20TH C)	100-750	X (M)
SINGER, CLYDE (20TH C)	300-2000	G
SINGER, WILLIAM HENRY (JR) (1868 - 1943)	450-3500	L
SIPORIN, MITCHELL (1910 -)	*100-700	F,I
SISSON, LAWRENCE P. (1928 -)	*250-1800	L,M
SITZMAN, EDWARD R. (1874 -)	100-800	L
SKEELE, HANNAH BROWN (1829 - 1901)	400-1200	F
SKIDMORE, THORNTON (1884 -)	600-4500	I,L
SKILLING, WILLIAM (20TH C)	500-2500	X (W)
SKIRVING, JOHN (active 1835-65)	300-1800	M
SKOU, SIGURD (- 1929)	*200-2000	A
SLADE, CALEB ARNOLD (1882 - 1961)	250-1500	L
SLADE, CONRAD (1871 - 1949)	150-900	X
SLOAN, JOHN	*600-6500	
SLOAN, JOHN (1871 - 1951)	700-150000	G,F,I
SLOAN, SAMUEL (1815 - 1884)	350-1800	F
SLOANE, ERIC (1910 -)	450-7000	L,W,I
SLOANE, MARION (19TH - 20TH C)	100-750	L
SLOMAN, JOSEPH (1883 -)	150-750	I

* Denotes Mixed Media,Watercolors,Gouaches,Pastels, and/or Drawings.

```
SLOUN, FRANK VAN (1879 - 1938)                  500-3500      F,G
SMEDLEY, WILL LARYMORE (1871 - 1958)            100-700       X (L,I)
SMEDLEY, WILLIAM THOMAS (1858 - 1920)           200-3000      F,I
SMIBERT, JOHN (1688 - 1751)                     2000-35000    F
SMILEY, HOWARD P. (20TH C)                      *100-450      L
SMILLIE, GEORGE HENRY                           *100-2500
SMILLIE, GEORGE HENRY (1840 - 1921)             300-12000     L
SMILLIE, JAMES (1807 - 1885)                    700-3000      F,L
SMILLIE, JAMES DAVID                            *400-8500
SMILLIE, JAMES DAVID (1833 - 1909)              600-6500      L,I
SMITH, ALFRED E. (1863 - 1955)                  100-700       X (S,I)
SMITH, ARCHIBALD CARY (1837 - 1911)             350-2500'     M
SMITH, CALVIN RAE (1850 - 1918)                 600-3500      X (F)
SMITH, CHARLES L.A.                             *100-450
SMITH, CHARLES L.A. (1871 - 1937)               150-900       L
SMITH, CHARLES WILLIAM (1893 -      )           300-1800      I
SMITH, DAN (1865 - 1934)                        *200-1200     I
SMITH, DAVID                                    *1000-12000
SMITH, DAVID (1906 - 1965)                      6000-20000    A
SMITH, DUNCAN (1877 - 1934)                     100-700       X (F)
SMITH, ELMER BOYD (1860 - 1943)                 100-500       F,I
SMITH, FRANCIS HOPKINSON (1838 - 1915)          *250-5000     L
SMITH, FRANK HILL (1841 - 1904)                 400-2000      F
SMITH, FRANK VINING                             *400-2000
SMITH, FRANK VINING (1879 - 1967)               500-5000      M
SMITH, FREDERICK CARL (1868 - 1955)             250-1200      X (F)
SMITH, GEAN (1851 - 1928)                       250-3000      W,F,G
SMITH, HARRY KNOX (1879 -      )                100-700       F
SMITH, HASSEL W. (1915 -      )                 500-5000      A
SMITH, HENRY PEMBER                             *200-3000
SMITH, HENRY PEMBER (1854 - 1907)               350-6500      L,M
SMITH, HOPE (1879 -      )                      300-1800      L
SMITH, HOUGHTON CRANFORD (19TH - 20TH C)        150-950       L
SMITH, HOWARD EVERETT (1885 - 1970)             350-3500      I,F,L
SMITH, JACK WILKINSON (1873 - 1949)             250-3000      L
SMITH, JEROME HOWARD (1861 - 1941)              100-850       X (L)
SMITH, JESSIE WILCOX (1863 - 1935)              600-3500      L,M
SMITH, JOHN FRANCIS (1868 - 1941)               250-3000      L,M
SMITH, JOSEPH B. (1798 - 1876)                  2500-12000    M
SMITH, JOSEPH LINDON (1863 - 1950)              150-4500      F
SMITH, LEON POLK                                *350-3000
SMITH, LEON POLK (1906 -      )                 1000-10000    A
SMITH, LETTA CRAPO (1862 - 1921)                400-2500      L,S
SMITH, LILLIAN GERTRUDE (19TH - 20TH C)         *300-1000     L
SMITH, LOWELL ELLSWORTH (1924 -      )          *3000-20000   L,F,G
SMITH, MARY (1842 - 1878)                       600-12000     W,L,S
SMITH, OLIVER (1896 -      )                     *450-2000     X (F)
SMITH, OLIVER PHELPS (1867 - 1953)              *300-2500     L
SMITH, PAUL WILLIAMSON (      - 1949)           150-700       L,S
SMITH, RUFUS WAY (1900 -      )                  300-1200      L
SMITH, RUSSELL (WILLIAM RUSSELL)(1812-1896)     300-5000      L,M,F
SMITH, THOMAS LOCHLAN (1835 - 1884)             500-4500      G,L
SMITH, WALTER GRANVILLE                         *150-2800
SMITH, WALTER GRANVILLE (1870 - 1938)           350-30000     L,F,I
SMITH, (WILLIAM) RUSSELL (1812 - 1896)   see "Russell Smith"
```

* Denotes Mixed Media,Watercolors,Gouaches,Pastels, and/or Drawings.

SMITH, WUANITA (1866 -)	*100-700	I
SMITH, XANTHUS (1839 - 1929)	400-28000	M,L,F
SMITHSON, ROBERT (1938 -1973)	500-2000	A
SMUKLER, BARBARA (20TH C)	*100-650	A
SMUTNY, JOSEPH (1855 - 1903)	300-1200	X (F)
SMYTHE, EUGENE LESLIE (1857 - 1932)	150-850	L
SNELL, HENRY BAYLEY (1858 - 1943)	100-1200	M,L
SNELL, IDA (19TH C)	400-2500	X (S)
SNIDOW, GORDON	*5000-45000	
SNIDOW, GORDON (1936 -)	10000-50000	G,F
SNOW, EDWARD TAYLOR (1844 - 1913)	800-9500	X (S)
SNYDER, CLARENCE (1873 -)	*100-450	X (L)
SNYDER, JOAN (20TH C)	*400-8000	X
SNYDER, WILLIAM HENRY (1829 - 1910)	700-8000	G,L
SOBLE, JOHN JACOB (20TH C)	600-4800	X (L,F)
SOELEN, THEODORE VAN (1890 - 1964)	450-6000	L,F
SOGLOW, OTTO (1900 -)	*100-850	X (I)
SOHIER, ALICE RUGGLES (1880 -)	400-3000	F
SOLDIER, ANDREW STANDING (20TH C)	100-600	X (F)
SOLING, PAUL (20TH C)	300-1200	L
SOLMAN, JOSEPH (1909 -)	700-5000	A
SOLOMON, HARRY (1873 -)	350-1200	X (F)
SOLOMON, HYDE (1911 -)	200-2500	A
SOMERBY, LORENZO (early 19TH C)	1200-5000	L
SOMMER, CHARLES A. (1829 - 1894)	450-3000	L
SOMMER, OTTO (19TH C)	450-3200	W,L
SOMMER, WILLIAM (1867 - 1949)	*150-1200	X (F)
SONN, ALBERT H. (1869 - 1936)	*150-1200	X (F)
SONNTAG, WILLIAM LOUIS (JR.)(1870 -)	*350-2000	L,F
SONNTAG, WILLIAM LOUIS (SR.)	*500-2500	
SONNTAG, WILLIAM LOUIS (SR.)(1822 - 1900)	1000-18000	L
SOREN, JOHN JOHNSTON (- 1889)	400-4500	M,L
SOULEN, HENRY JAMES (1888 - 1965)	350-3000	I
SOUTER, JOHN B. (19TH - 20TH C)	500-3000	F,L
SOUTHWARD, GEORGE (1803 - 1876)	300-4500	L,S,F
SOYER, ISAAC (20TH C)	300-1800	G,L
SOYER, MOSES	*100-2000	
SOYER, MOSES (1899 - 1974)	350-15000	F
SOYER, RAPHAEL	*200-3500	
SOYER, RAPHAEL (1899 -)	600-45000	F
SPACKMAN, CYRIL SAUNDERS (1887 -)	400-3500	X (F)
SPADER, WILLIAM EDGAR (1875 -)	200-1000	F,I
SPAHR, JOHN (20TH C)	150-800	X (L)
SPANG, FREDERICK (1834 - 1891)	100-500	X (F)
SPARHAWK-JONES, ELIZABETH (1885 -)	500-8500	F
SPARKS, ARTHUR WATSON (1870 - 1919)	350-3000	L,F
SPARKS, WILL (1862 - 1937)	350-3500	L,M,F
SPAULDING, HENRY PLYMPTON	100-500	L
SPEAR, ARTHUR PRINCE (1879 - 1959)	300-1800	X (L)
SPEAR, THOMAS TRUMAN (1803 - 1882)	300-1800	F
SPEER, WILLIAM W. (1877 -)	100-700	L
SPEICHER, EUGENE EDWARD (1883 - 1962)	500-15000	F,L,S
SPEIGHT, FRANCIS (1896 -)	250-1200	L
SPELMAN, JOHN A. (1880 -)	100-850	L
SPENCER, ASA (1805 -)	100-500	X (L)

* Denotes Mixed Media,Watercolors,Gouaches,Pastels, and/or Drawings.

```
SPENCER, FREDERICK R. (1806 - 1875)          300-2800      F,G
SPENCER, HOWARD BONNELL (20TH C)             300-2000      X (M)
SPENCER, JOHN C.(19TH - 20TH C)              500-3500      S
SPENCER, LILLY MARTIN (1822 - 1902)          700-15000+    G,F,S
SPENCER, MARGARET FULTON (1882 -    )        150-900       S
SPENCER, NILES (1893 - 1952)                 3500-45000    A
SPENCER, ROBERT S. (1879 - 1931)             400-20000     L,G,M
SPICUZZA, FRANCESCO J.                       *100-600
SPICUZZA, FRANCESCO J. (1883 - 1962)         100-900       F,M,L,S
SPIEGAL, A. (20TH C)                         200-900       X
SPIERS, HARRY                                *100-500
SPIERS, HARRY (1869 - 1934)                  250-950       L,F
SPIRO, EUGENE (1874 - 1972)                  200-1500      L
SPRINCHORN, CARL                             *150-1800
SPRINCHORN, CARL (1887 - 1971)               500-3200      A
SPRINGER, CHARLES HENRY (1857 - 1920)        100-700       X (M)
SPRUANCE, BENTON M. (1904 -    )             *400-2000     X (L)
SQUINT-EYE, (active 1880-90)                 *150-800      X
SQUIRE, E.P. (19TH C)                        500-3000      X (L)
SQUIRE, MAUD H. (early 20TH C)               150-800       F,L
SRULL, DONALD (20TH C)                       100-500       X
STABLER, ?    (19TH C)                       150-650       X (L)
STACEY, ANNA LEE (early 20TH C)              250-1500      L
STAGER, B. (19TH - 20TH C)                   100-600       X (L)
STAHL, BENJAMIN ALBERT (1910 -    )          100-1000      I
STAHLEY, JOSEPH (20TH C)                      100-600       X (F)
STAHR, PAUL C. (1883 - 1953)                 400-6000      I
STAIGER, PAUL (1941 -    )                    600-3500      A
STAIGG, RICHARD MORRELL (1817 - 1881)        400-3500      G,F,L
STAMOS, THEODOROS                            *1000-8000
STAMOS, THEODOROS (1922 -    )               5000-125000   A
STANCLIFF, J.W. (1814 - 1879)                500-4500      M,L
STANCZAK, JULIAN (1928 -    )                700-9000      A
STANLAWS, PENRHYN (1877 - 1957)              400-8000      I
STANLEY, CHARLES ST.GEORGE (active 1870-80)*200-800       F
STANLEY, JOHN MIX (1814 - 1872)              2500-40000    F,L
STANLEY, ROBERT (BOB) (1932 -    )           400-1000      A
STANTON, GEORGE CURTIN (1885 -    )          200-1200      L,F
STANWOOD, FRANKLIN (1856 - 1888)             350-2500      X (M)
STARK, OTTO (1859 - 1926)                    500-15000     F,L,I
STARKWEATHER, WILLIAM E. B. (1879 - 1969)    150-900       L,F
STARR, SIDNEY (1857 - 1925)                  *250-3000     X (F)
STEARNS, JUNIUS BRUTUS (1810 - 1885)         2000-30000    G,F,L
STEELE, THEODORE CLEMENT (1847 - 1926)       700-5000      L,F
STEENE, WILLIAM (1888 - 1965)                400-4000      F
STEENKS, L. (19TH - 20TH C)                  100-600       X (L)
STEFAN, ROSS (20TH C)                        600-4500      X (G,F)
STEICHEN, EDWARD J. (1879 - 1973)            2000-35000    L
STEIG, WILLIAM (1907 -    )                   *100-700      I
STEIN, LEO (19TH - 20TH C)                   200-950       L
STEINBERG, SAUL (1914 -    )                  *1000-30000+  A
STELLA, FRANK                                *2000-475000
STELLA, FRANK (1936 -    )                    4000-125000   A
STELLA, JOSEPH                               *450-25000
STELLA, JOSEPH (1877 - 1946)                 1200-40000    L,S,F
```

* Denotes Mixed Media,Watercolors,Gouaches,Pastels, and/or Drawings.

STENGEL, G.L. (1872 - 1937)	200-1200	X (L)
STEPHAN, GARY	*500-2500	
STEPHAN, GARY (1942 -)	1000-7000	A
STEPHENS, ALICE BARBER (1858 - 1932)	*300-4000	I
STEPHENS, ANSON R. (19TH C)	100-600	X
STERN, J. (19TH C)	300-1200	X (G)
STERNE, HEDDA (1916 -)	800-7500	A
STERNE, MAURICE	*300-1500	
STERNE, MAURICE (1878 - 1957)	400-3200	A,L
STERNER, ALBERT EDWARD	*200-5000	
STERNER, ALBERT EDWARD (1863 - 1946)	600-5000	F,L,I
STERRIS, JEROME L. (19TH - 20TH C)	100-700	X (L)
STETSON, CHARLES WALTER (1858 - 1911)	150-1500	F,L,S
STETTHEIMER, FLORINE (1871 - 1944)	*400-1500	X (S)
STEVENS, JOHN CALVIN (1855 -)	250-1200	X (L)
STEVENS, WILLIAM CHARLES (1854 - 1917)	150-1000	L
STEVENS, WILLIAM LESTER	*150-1200	
STEVENS, WILLIAM LESTER (1888 - 1969)	400-4500+	L,M,S
STEVER, JOSEPHINE (19TH C)	200-1000	X (L)
STEWARD, JOSEPH (1753 - 1822)	5000-40000	P
STEWARD, SETH W. (19TH - 20TH C)	400-4500	L,S
STEWART, JAMES LAWSON	*400-3000	
STEWART, JAMES LAWSON (1855 - 1919)	700-35000	F
STEWART, JEANETTE (1867 -)	250-1200	X (L,F)
STEWART, JULIUS L.	*400-3000	
STEWART, JULIUS L. (1855 - 1919)	700-35000+	F
STEWART, MALCOLM (1829 - 1916)	300-1200	X (F)
STICK, FRANK (1884 - 1966)	300-1500	X (L,G)
STILL, CLYFFORD (1904 - 1980)	15000-825000	A
STIMSON, JOHN WARD (1850 - 1930)	200-1200	F,I
STINSON, CHARLES (20TH C)	100-700	X (L)
STITT, HERBERT D. (1880 -)	400-3500	X (L)
STOCK, FRANK (20TH C)	300-1000	X
STOCK, JOSEPH WHITING (1815 - 1855)	3500-35000	P
STODDARD, ALICE KENT (1893 -)	800-10000	X (F)
STODDARD, FREDERICK LINCOLN (1861 - 1940)	350-2500	F,I
STOKES, FRANK WILBERT (1858 -)	300-2000	X (L)
STOLL, JOHN THEODORE E. (1889 -)	150-900	F,L,I
STOLTENBERG, HANS J. (1879 -)	100-900	L
STONER, HARRY A. (1880 -)	100-750	L
STOOPS, HERBERT MORTON (1888 - 1948)	500-25000	I
STORER, CHARLES (19TH C)	500-3000	X (S)
STORRS, JOHN BRADLEY	*600-4000	
STORRS, JOHN BRADLEY (1887 - 1966)	3500-8500	A
STORY, GEORGE HENRY (1835 - 1923)	1200-15000	F,G
STORY, JULIAN RUSSEL (1857 - 1919)	400-4000	F
STRAIN, DANIEL (active 1865-90)	300-2000	F
STRANG, RAY C. (1893 - 1957)	300-1500	I
STRAUS, F. (19TH C)	300-1500	L
STRAUS, MEYER (1831 - 1905)	300-1500	L
STRAUSS, CARL SUMNER (1873 -)	600-3500	X (L)
STREATOR, HAROLD A. (1861 - 1926)	400-2000	L
STREET, FRANK (1893 - 1944)	250-2000	I,L,F
STREET, ROBERT (1796 - 1865)	1200-28000	L,F
STRISIK, PAUL (1918 -)	400-10000	L,M

* Denotes Mixed Media,Watercolors,Gouaches,Pastels, and/or Drawings.

```
STROBEL, OSCAR (20TH C)                        100-500     X (L)
STRONG, ELIZABETH (1855 - 1941)                400-1800    L,S
STRONG, JOSEPH D. (1852 - 1900)                400-2500    L,F
STRUCK, HERMAN (1887 - 1954)                   300-1800    X (L,G)
STUART, ALEXANDER CHARLES (1831 - 1898)        400-1500    X (M)
STUART, GILBERT (1755 - 1828)                  1500-275000 F
STUART, JAMES EVERETT (1852 - 1941)            150-5000    L
STUART, JANE (1812 - 1888)                     1500-4000   F
STUBBS, WILLIAM PIERCE (1842 - 1909)           1000-8000   M,G
STUBER, DEDRICK BRANDES (1878 - 1954)          350-2800    L,M
STUECKMANN, FREDERICK C. (20TH C)              600-2500    X (F)
STUEMPFIG, WALTER (1914 - 1970)                300-5000    L,S,M,F
STULL, HENRY (1851 - 1913)                     500-8500    W
STURTEVANT, HELENA (1872 - 1946)               100-700     X (L)
SULLIVAN, DENIS (19TH C)                       *100-600    X (G)
SULLIVANT, THOMAS STARLING (1854 - 1926)       *100-500    I
SULLY, ALFRED (1820 - 1879)                    400-3800    F
SULLY, JANE COOPER (1807 - 1877)               350-1500    X (F)
SULLY, THOMAS                                  *800-18000
SULLY, THOMAS (1783 - 1872)                    700-40000   F
SUNDBLOM, HADDON HUBBARD (1899 - 1976)         300-2500+   I
SUPLIN, ANN (19TH C)                           150-850     P
SURENDORF, CHARLES FREDERICK (1906 -    ) *100-500    L,F,G
SUTER, E.V. (19TH - 20TH C)                    *100-700    X (F)
SUTTER, SAMUEL (20TH C)                        100-700     L
SUTZ, ROBERT                                   *300-2500
SUTZ, ROBERT (19TH - 20TH C)                   1000-8500   F
SUYDAM, HENRY (1817 - 1865)                    800-3500    L
SUYDAM, JAMES AUGUSTUS (1819 - 1865)           2000-8000   L,M
SUZUKI, JAMES HIROSHI (1933 -       )          500-3500    A
SVENDSEN, SVEND (1864 -       )                150-2500    L
SVOBODA, VINCENT A. (1877 - 1961)              *100-700    X (L,F)
SWAIN, C. (19TH - 20TH C)                      *100-700    L,G
SWANSON, GLORIA (1899 - 1983)                  200-1200    L,F,S
SWANSON, JACK (1927 -       )                  400-3500    G,F
SWANSON, RAY (1937 -       )                   6500-25000  F,G
SWEENEY, S.C. (1876 -       )                  100-800     X (M)
SWEET, CHARLES A. (20TH C)                     300-1500    X (L)
SWEET, F.H. (active 1880 - 1895)               100-600     X (L)
SWEET, GEORGE (1876 -       )                  300-1200    G,L
SWERINGEN, RON VAN (20TH C)                    300-1800    F,G
SWETT, WILLIAM OTIS (JR) (1859 - 1939)         100-900     L,W
SWIFT, CLEMENT N. (19TH C)                     150-750     L
SWIFT, IVAN (1873 - 1945)                      200-1200    L
SWINNERTON, JAMES GUILFORD (1875 - 1974)       400-9000    L
SWOPE, DAVID (18TH C)                          *500-3500   F
SWOPE, KATE F. (19TH - 20TH C)                 250-1500    X (L)
SWORD, JAMES BRADE (1839 - 1915)               250-8000    L,M,F
SWORDS, CRAMER (20TH C)                        100-800     X (S)
SYKES, ANNIE G. (20TH C)                       *100-600    X (S)
SYLVESTER, FREDERICK OAKES (1869 - 1915)       300-2500    L
SYLVESTER, H. M. (19TH - 20TH C)               100-600     L
SYMONS, GEORGE GARDNER (1863 - 1930)           250-35000   L
SZANTO, A. KAROLY L. (20TH C)                  *300-1500   X (G)
SZYK, ARTHUR (1894 - 1951)                     *500-3000   I
```

* Denotes Mixed Media, Watercolors, Gouaches, Pastels, and/or Drawings.

T

Name	Value	Code
TACK, AUGUSTUS VINCENT (1870 - 1949)	1000-4000+	A,F
TAGGART, JOHN G. (active 1845-65)	150-1000	X (F)
TAHY, JANOS DE (1865 - 1928)	100-800	X (F)
TAIT, ARTHUR FITZWILLIAM (1819 - 1905)	500-250000	F,G,W
TALBOT, JESSE (1806 - 1879)	2000-12000	F,L
TALLANT, RICHARD H. (1853 - 1934)	100-600	X (L)
TANGUY, YVES	*600-45000	
TANGUY, YVES (1900 - 1955)	5000-300000	A
TANNER, HENRY OSSAWA (1859 - 1937)	2000-15000+	G,L,F,W
TANNING, DOROTHEA	*250-2500	
TANNING, DOROTHEA (1912 -)	1000-18000	A
TANT, CHARLES DU (20TH C)	300-2000	X (F)
TARBELL, EDMUND CHARLES	*250-5500	
TARBELL, EDMUND CHARLES (1862 - 1938)	4000-200000	F,G,S
TAUBES, FREDERICK (1900 - 1981)	350-2500	F,L,S
TAUSZKY, DAVID ANTHONY (1878 -)	300-1500	F
TAVE, DO (19TH - 20TH C)	300-1500	X (F)
TAVERNIER, JULES (1844 - 1899)	800-20000	X (L)
TAYLOR, ANNA HEYWARD (1879 -)	*100-600	X (F)
TAYLOR, CHARLES JAY (1855 - 1929)	250-1800	I
TAYLOR, EDGAR J. (1862 -)	100-700	I
TAYLOR, FRANK H. (19TH - 20TH C)	*100-1500	L
TAYLOR, HENRY FITCH (1853 - 1925)	400-4000	X (L)
TAYLOR, JAY C. (19TH C)	100-750	L
TAYLOR, M.A. (early 19TH C)	500-3500	G,L
TAYLOR, WALTER (20TH C)	*100-700	F
TAYLOR, WILLIAM FRANCIS (1883 - 1934)	300-1500	X (L,I)
TAYLOR, WILLIAM LADD (1854 - 1926)	*150-1800	I,M,L
TCHACBASOC, NAHUM (20TH C)	200-1000	X (F)
TCHELITCHEW, PAVEL	*200-18000	
TCHELITCHEW, PAVEL (1898 - 1957)	400-15000	A
TEAGUE, DONALD (1897 -)	*500-35000	I,F,L
TEATER, ARCHIE B. (20TH C)	100-650	X (L)
TEED, DOUGLAS ARTHUR (1864 - 1929)	400-4500	F,G,L,S
TEICHMAN, SABINA (1905 -)	300-5000	X (F)
TERPNING, HOWARD A. (1927 -)	15000-150000	F,I
THAL, SAM	*100-600	
THAL, SAM (20TH C)	300-1000	X (F,M)
THALINGER, E. OSCAR (1885 -)	100-900	L,M,S
THATCHER, EARL (19TH - 20TH C)	*100-500	X (F)
THAYER, ABBOTT HANDERSON (1849 - 1921)	500-10000	F,L,W
THAYER, ALBERT R. (19TH - 20TH C)	300-1500	X
THEIL, E. DU (20TH C)	100-300	X (L)
THEOBALD, ELISABETH STUTEVANT (1876 -)	100-600	L
THEOBALD, SAMUEL (JR) (19HT - 20TH C)	300-1200	X (L)
THERIAT, CHARLES JAMES (1860 -)	400-3000	X (F)
THEUS, JEREMIAH (1719 - 1774)	2000-15000	P
THEVENAZ, PAUL (20TH C)	*100-600	X (S)

```
THIEBAUD, WAYNE                            *1500-40000
THIEBAUD, WAYNE (1920 -      )              5000-150000  A
THEIME, ANTHONY (1888 - 1954)              350-6500     M,L
THOM, JAMES CRAWFORD (1835 - 1898)         450-5000     G,F,L
THOMAS, A. (19TH - 20TH C)                 400-3500     X (L)
THOMAS, BYRON (1902 -     )                 400-2000     X (L)
THOMAS, GROSVENOR (20TH C)                 100-600      L,F
THOMAS, REYNOLDS (20TH C)                  *100-600     X
THOMAS, RICHARD D. (20TH C)                100-850      G,L
THOMAS, STEPHEN SEYMOUR (1868 - 1956)      300-3000     F,L
THOMPSON, (ALFRED) WORDSWORTH (1840-1896)  300-25000    M,G,F,L
THOMPSON, BOB                              *300-1000
THOMPSON, BOB (1937 - 1966)                600-6000     A
THOMPSON, CEPHAS GIOVANNI (1809 - 1888)    500-8500     G,F,L
THOMPSON, CHARLES A. (active 1850-60)      250-950      X (L,G)
THOMPSON, ELOISE REID (20TH C)            *100-650      X (S)
THOMPSON, FREDERICK LOUIS (1868 -     )    200-1800     M,L
THOMPSON, GEORGE ALBERT                    *100-500
THOMPSON, GEORGE ALBERT (1868 -     )      250-1200     L,M
THOMPSON, HARRY IVES (1840 -1906)          800-4500     F,L
THOMPSON, J. HARRY (19TH - 20TH C)         100-650      X (L)
THOMPSON, JEROME B. (1814 - 1886)          1500-70000   L,G,F
THOMPSON, WALTER W. (1881 - 1948)          100-800      X (L)
THOMPSON-PRITCHARD, E. (20TH C)            150-850      X (L)
THON, WILLIAM                             *100-750
THON, WILLIAM (1906 -     )                350-1800     L
THONY, GUSTAV (1888 - 1949)                1000-8500    L
THORN, JAMES CRAWFORD (1835 - 1898)        350-1500     F,L
THORNE, ANNA LOUISE (1878 -     )         *100-750      X (F)
THORNE, DIANA (1895 -     )                250-1000     X (W)
THORNE, S.A. (early 19TH C)               *600-2000     L
THOURON, HENRY J. (1851 - 1915)            600-6000     X (G)
THULSTRUP, THURE DE                       *250-1800
THULSTRUP, THURE DE (1849 - 1930)          700-6000     F.M.I
THURBER, JAMES (1894 - 1961)              *200-1000     X (I)
THURN, ERNEST (1889 -     )                100-650      X (S)
THURSTON, JOHN K. (1865 - 1955)           *100-800      M
TICE, CHARLES WINFIELD (1810 - 1870)       1000-6500    L,F,S
TIETJANS, M.H. (20TH C)                    150-900      X (F)
TIFFANY, LOUIS COMFORT                    *800-7000
TIFFANY, LOUIS COMFORT (1848 - 1933)       700-12000    F,L,M
TILTON, JOHN ROLLIN (1828 - 1888)          300-1800     L
TILYARD, PHILLIP (1785 - 1827)             500-2000     F
TIMMINS, HARRY LAVERNE (1887 - 1963)       200-1500     I
TIMMONS, EDWARD J. FINLEY (1882 -     )    200-1000     L
TING, WALASSE                             *300-2000
TING, WALASSE (1929 -     )                600-5000     A
TINGLEY, FRANK FOSTER (20TH C)            *200-850      X
TINSLEY, F. (19TH - 20TH C)                100-600      X (F)
TIRRELL, G. (19TH C)                       2000-8500    M
TITCOMB, MARY BRADISH (1856 - 1927)        1000-12000   F,I
TITCOMB, WILLIAM HENRY (1824 - 1888)       400-3000     L,F
TITLOW, HARRIET WOODFIN (20TH C)           300-1500     X (F)
TITTLE, WALTER ERNEST (1883 -     )       *150-700      L,I
TOBEY, ALTON (20TH C)                     *100-500      X
```

* Denotes Mixed Media,Watercolors,Gouaches,Pastels, and/or Drawings.

Name	Price	Code
TOBEY, MARK	*500-18000	
TOBEY, MARK (1890 - 1976)	900-50000	A,F
TODD, CHARLES S. (1885 -)	*400-1000	X (W)
TODD, HENRY STANLEY (1871 -)	150-750	F
TOFT, P. (19TH C)	*150-850	L
TOJETTI, D. (19TH - 20TH C)	100-500	X (F)
TOJETTI, EDWARD (19TH C)	100-650	X (F)
TOJETTI, M. (19TH C)	100-700	X (F)
TOJETTI, VIRGILIO (1851 - 1901)	300-8500	F
TOLEGIAN, MANUEL J. (20TH C)	200-1200	F,L
TOLMAN, STACY (1860 - 1935)	100-650	S,F
TOMANECK, J. (19TH - 20TH C)	100-1000	F
TOMLIN, BRADLEY WALKER	*500-15000	
TOMLIN, BRADLEY WALKER (1899 - 1953)	2500-65000	A,I
TOMPKINS, FRANK HECTOR (1847 - 1922)	400-6000	X (F)
TONEY, ANTHONY (1913 -)	100-750	X
TONK, ERNEST (1889 -)	850-6500	X (G)
TOOKER, GEORGE	*3000-8000	
TOOKER, GEORGE (1920 -)	10000-85000	G,F
TOPPAN, CHARLES (1796 - 1874)	200-900	X
TORLAKSON, JIM	*200-1200	
TORLAKSON, JIM (20TH C)	400-4500	X
TORREY, ELLIOT BOUTON (1867 - 1949)	300-2500	F,G,L
TORREY, GEORGE B. (1863 -)	100-600	M,F
TOSSEY, VERNE (20TH C)	200-1000	I
TOUSSAINT, RAYMOND (1875 - 1939)	*100-400	X (F)
TOWNSEND, ERNEST (1893 - 1945)	350-5000	F,L,I
TOWNSEND, HARRY EVERETT (1879 - 1941)	250-2500	I
TOWNSHEND, H.R. (early 20TH C)	100-500	X (L)
TOWNSLEY, CHANNEL PICKERING (1867 - 1921)	1000-7500	L,F
TRACY, CHARLES (1881 - 1955)	*100-700	X
TRACY, JOHN M. (1844 - 1893)	700-5000+	G
TRAVER, GEORGE A.	*100-750	
TRAVER, GEORGE A. (1864 - 1928)	150-1000	L,G
TRAVER, MARION GRAY (1896 - 1934)	100-700	L
TRAVIS, PAUL BOUGH (1891 - 1975)	*100-700	L,F
TREAT, ASA (19TH C)	700-3000	X (S)
TREBILCOCK, PAUL (1902 -)	200-2500	F
TREDUPP, CHARLES (19TH - 20TH C)	100-700	M
TREIDLER, ADOLPH (1886 - 1981)	*100-850	I
TRENT, VICTOR PEDRETTI (1891 -)	100-600	L
TREVILLE, DE (20TH C)	100-500	X (L)
TRIBE, GEORGE T. (19TH - 20TH C)	100-600	X (L)
TRIESTE, JOANSOVITCH (19TH C)	400-2500	M
TRISCOTT, SAMUEL PETER ROLT (1846 - 1925)	*150-1500	M,L
TROTTER, NEWBOLD HOUGH (1827 - 1898)	200-5000+	W,L
TROUBETZKOY, PIERRE (1864 -)	300-1200	F
TROUSSER, L. (19TH C)	*500-3000	X
TROVA, ERNEST	*600-2500	
TROVA, ERNEST (1927 -)	1200-12000	A
TROYE, EDWARD (1808 - 1874)	2500-50000	W
TRUESDELL, GAYLORD SANGSTON (1850 - 1899)	200-2500	W,F,L
TRUITT, ANNE (1921 -)	600-5000	A
TRUMBULL, EDWARD (early 20TH C)	*150-700	X (I)
TRUMBULL, JOHN (1756 - 1843)	1500-50000	F,L

* Denotes Mixed Media, Watercolors, Gouaches, Pastels, and/or Drawings.

```
TRYON, DWIGHT WILLIAM (1849 - 1925)          500-35000      L
TSCHACBASOV, NAHUM (1899 -      )             100-500        X (F)
TSCHUDI, RUDOLF (1855 - 1923)                300-1500       X (F,G)
TSCHUDY, HERBERT BOLIVAR (1874 -     )       100-1200       X (L,I)
TUBBY, J.T. (20TH C)                         *150-850       X
TUCKER, ALLEN (1866 - 1939)                  600-10000      L,F
TUCKER, MARY B. (19TH C)                     *700-4500      F
TUPPER, ALEXANDER GARFIELD (1885 -     )     100-500        L,M
TURNBULL, GRACE H. (1880 - 1976)             200-1000       L,F,S
TURNBULL, JAMES B. (1909 - 1976)             400-3000       X (F)
TURNER, A.L. (19TH C)                        100-700        X (L,M)
TURNER, CHARLES YARDLEY (1850 - 1919)        500-7500       G,F,L
TURNER, HARRIET FRENCH (1886 - 1967)         100-400        X
TURNER, HELEN MARY (1858 -     )             700-4500       F,L
TURNER, ROSS STERLING (1847 - 1915)          *200-1000      M,L
TURNEY, WINTHROP D. (1884 -     )            100-850        X
TUTTLE, RICHARD (1941 -     )                *400-2500      A
TWACHTMAN, JOHN HENRY                        *200-15000
TWACHTMAN, JOHN HENRY (1853 - 1902)          2500-150000    L
TWACHTMAN, JULIAN ALDEN (1935 -     )        200-900        X (L)
TWARDOWICZ, STANLEY (1917 -     )            300-1200       A
TWOHY, JULIUS (20TH C)                       100-500        X (F)
TWOMBLY, CY                                  *4500-185000
TWOMBLY, CY (1929 -     )                    2500-200000    A
TWORKOV, JACK                                *500-2500
TWORKOV, JACK (1900 -     )                  5000-50000     A
TYLER, BAYARD HENRY (1855 - 1931)            200-2500       L,F
TYLER, HATTIE (20TH C)                       150-950        X (W)
TYLER, JAMES GALE (1855 - 1931)              300-20000      M,I
TYNG, GRISWALD (1883 -     )                 100-800        X
TYSON, CARROLL SARGENT (JR) (1878 - 1956)    600-5000       L
```

U

```
UFER, WALTER (1876 - 1936)                   2500-375000    F,L
UHL, S. JEROME (1842 - 1911)                 250-2000       L,F
UHLE, BERNHARD (1847 - 1930)                 100-700        F
ULLMAN, EUGENE PAUL (1877 - 1953)            100-1000       F,L,M
ULRICH, CHARLES FREDERIC (1858 - 1908)       2500-32000     F,L
UPJOHN, ANNA MILO (20TH C)                   *100-500       F
URBAN, JOSEPH (1872 - 1933)                  *200-2500      I
URSULESCU, MIHAI (1913 -     )               100-500        X (F)
URWICK, WALTER C. (1864 -     )              400-2500       F,L
USHER, RUBY W. (20TH C)                      *100-450       X (F)
UTZ, THORNTON (1914 -     )                  300-3500       I
```

* Denotes Mixed Media,Watercolors,Gouaches,Pastels, and/or Drawings.

V

Name	Price	Code
VAIL, EUGENE LAURENT (1857 - 1934)	300-3500	M,F
VALENCIA, MANUEL (1856 - 1935)	200-2800	L
VALENCIA, RAMONA (20TH C)	200-1200	X (L)
VALENKAMPH, THEODORE VICTOR CARL(1868-1924)	200-2500	M,L
VALENTINE, ALBERT R. (1862 - 1925)	100-700	F,S
VALLEE, JEAN FRANCOIS DE (18TH - 19TH C)	2000-6500	F
VAN ELTEN, HENDRICK D.K. (1829 - 1904)	500-3500	L
VAN INGEN, HENRY A. (1833 - 1898)	500-4000	L,W
VAN LAER, ALEXANDER T. (1857 - 1920)	*150-700	L,M
VAN SCRIVEN PEARL A. (1896 -)	100-600	X (S)
VAN SOELEN, THEODORE (1890 - 1964)	450-6000	L,F
VAN VEEN, PIETER J. L. (1875 - 1961)	350-7000	F,L
VARADY, FREDERIC (1908 -)	*100-750	I
VARIAN, GEORGE EDMUND (1865 - 1923)	300-2000	I
VASILIEF, NICHOLAS IVANOVITCH (1892-1970)	200-2500	M,S
VAUGHAN, CHARLES A. (active 1845-60)	200-800	F
VAWTER, JOHN WILLIAM (1871 -)	100-700	L,I
VEDDER, ELIHU	*200-3500	
VEDDER, ELIHU (1836 - 1923)	600-35000	F,I
VER BECK, FRANK (1858 - 1933)	*200-1200	I
VERNER, ELIZABETH O'NEILL (1884 -)	*250-950	X (F)
VETTER, CORNELIA COWLES (1881 -)	100-300	X (L,S)
VEZIN, CHARLES (1858 - 1942)	500-6500	L
VEZIN, FREDERICK (1859 -)	300-2000	X
VIANDEN, HEINRICH (1814 - 1899)	300-2000	L
VIAVANT, GEORGE L. (1872 - 1925)	*400-3500	W
VICENTE, ESTEBAN	*1000-3500	
VICENTE, ESTEBAN (1904 -)	1500-15000	A
VICKREY, ROBERT REMSEN (1926 -)	1000-15000	F
VIGIL, VELOY (20TH C)	400-3000	X (F)
VIGNARI, JOHN T. (20TH C)	100-600	X (M)
VILLA, HERNANDO GONZALLO (1881 - 1952)	200-3000	F,L
VILLA, THEODORE B. (20TH C)	*500-4500	X
VILLACRES, CESAR A. (20TH C)	1000-5500	F,L
VINCENT, HARRY AIKEN	*250-850	
VINCENT, HARRY AIKEN (1864 - 1931)	400-3000	M,L,F
VINTON, FREDERIC PORTER (1846 - 1911)	500-5000	L,F
VOELCKER, RUDOLPH A. (1873 -)	200-1000	X (L)
VOGT, ADOLF (1843 - 1871)	200-2500	L,F
VOGT, FRITZ G. (1842 - 1900)	*600-9500	P
VOGT, LOUIS CHARLES (1864 -)	*100-500	L
VOLK, DOUGLAS (1856 - 1935)	400-3800	L,F
VOLKERT, EDWARD CHARLES (1871 - 1935)	500-4500	G,F,W
VOLKMAR, CHARLES (1809 - 1890/95)	250-2500	L,F
VOLL, F. USHER DE (20TH C)	*100-600	X
VONDROUS, JOHN C. (1884 -)	100-900	X (I)
VONNOH, ROBERT WILLIAM (1858 - 1933)	700-20000	L,F
VOORHEES, CLARK GREENWOOD (1871 - 1933)	400-3500	L

* Denotes Mixed Media,Watercolors,Gouaches,Pastels, and/or Drawings.

```
VOS, HUBERT                                *300-1800
VOS, HUBERT (1855 - 1935)                  400-3500    S,F
VREELAND, ANDERSON (19TH - 20TH C)         300-2000    X (M)
VREELAND, FRANCIS VAN (1879 -     )        *200-800    F,L
VUKOVIC, MARKO (20TH C)                    200-1000    X (S)
VYTLACIL, VACLAV                           *300-1500
VYTLACIL, VACLAV (1892 -     )             700-4500    A
```

W

```
WACHTEL, ELMER (1864 - 1929)               500-4500    L
WACHTEL, MARION K.                         *300-1800
WACHTEL, MARION K. (1875 - 1954)           500-4800    F,L
WADSWORTH, FRANK RUSSELL (1874 - 1905)     300-2500    L,F
WADSWORTH, WEDWORTH (1846 - 1927)          100-800     L,I
WAGNER, FRED                               *100-800
WAGNER, FRED (1864 - 1940)                 250-1500    L
WAGNER, JACOB (1852 - 1898)                400-2500    X (L)
WAGNER, JOSEF DE (20TH C)                  100-500     X (F)
WAGONER, HARRY B. (1889 - 1950)            200-1000    L
WAGUE, J.R. (19TH C)                       100-700     X (L)
WAITE, A.A. (19TH C)                       150-850     X (F)
WAITE, EMILY BURLING (1887 -     )         600-4500
WAITE, LUCRETIA ANN (1820 - 1868)[see CHANDLER, MRS.J.GOODHUE]
WAITT, MARION MARTHA PARKHURST (19TH C)    300-1500    L
WALDEN, LIONEL (1861 - 1933)               500-5000    X (M)
WALDMAN, PAUL (1936 -     )                600-5000    A
WALDO, J. FRANK (active 1870-80)           300-1200    L
WALDO, SAMUEL LOVETT (1783 - 1861)         400-5500+   F,M
WALES, NATHANIEL F. (active 1800-15)       2000-8500   F
WALES, SUSAN MAKEPIECE LARKIN (1839-1927)  *100-600    L,M
WALKER, CHARLES ALVAH (1848 - 1920)        300-2000    L
WALKER, FRANCIS S. (1872 - 1916)           400-2500    L
WALKER, HAROLD (1890 -     )               100-700     L
WALKER, HENRY OLIVER (1843 - 1929)         250-2500    F,L
WALKER, INEZ NATHANIEL (1911 -     )       *400-1500   P
WALKER, JAMES S. (early 20TH C)            *100-300    L
WALKER, SAMUEL (active 1850-70)            300-2000    M,F
WALKER, WILLIAM AIKEN                      *500-4500
WALKER, WILLIAM AIKEN (1838 - 1921)        700-60000   G,F,M,S
WALKLEY, DAVID BIRDSEY (1849 - 1934)       400-2800    F,L
WALKOWITZ, ABRAHAM                         *250-1500
```

* Denotes Mixed Media,Watercolors,Gouaches,Pastels, and/or Drawings.

Name	Price	Media
WALKOWITZ, ABRAHAM (1878 - 1965)	400-5000	A,F
WALL, A. BRYAN (1872 - 1937)	300-2000	X (F)
WALL, ALFRED S. (1809 - 1896)	350-3500	L
WALL, HERMAN C. (1875 -)	300-1500	X (F)
WALL, WILLIAM ALLEN	*200-1000	
WALL, WILLIAM ALLEN (1801 - 1885)	400-2500	F,L,M
WALL, WILLIAM ARCHIBALD (1828 - 1875)	300-1500	F,L
WALL, WILLIAM GUY (1792 - 1864)	400-4500	L
WALLER, FRANK (1842 - 1923)	200-1800	L,M
WALLINGER, CECIL A. (19TH C)	100-300	X (L)
WALLIS, FRANK (- 1934)	300-1000	X (L)
WALTENSPERGER, CHARLES E. (1871 - 1931)	150-850	X (F)
WALTER, CHRISTIAN J. (1872 - 1938)	300-4500	L
WALTER, L. (19TH C)	300-1500	X (M)
WALTER, MARTHA (1875 - 1976)	600-20000	F,L
WALTERS, EMILE (1893 -)	400-5000	L
WALTERS, H. (19TH C)	100-600	X (L)
WALTERS, JOSEPHINE (- 1883)	500-2500	L
WALTMAN, HARRY FRANKLIN (1871 - 1951)	200-850	X (L)
WALTON, HENRY (- 1865)	*500-5000	P
WALTON, WILLIAM (1843 - 1915)	200-1000	X (S)
WANDESFORDE, JAMES B. (1817 - 1872)	500-4000	G,L,F,
WARD, CHARLES (1900 -)	200-1200	X (L)
WARD, CHARLES CALEB	*1000-7500	
WARD, CHARLES CALEB (1831 - 1896)	1500-15000	G,F,L
WARD, EDGAR MELVILLE (1839 - 1915)	800-7500	G,L
WARD, EDMUND F. (1892 -)	800-5000	I
WARE, THOMAS (19TH C)	800-3000	P
WARHOL, ANDY	*350-100000	
WARHOL, ANDY (1928 -)	2000-175000	A
WARNER, EVERETT LONGLEY (1877 - 1963)	200-3000	L
WARREN, ANDREW W. (- 1873)	600-6500	M,L
WARREN, CONSTANCE WHITNEY (1888 - 1948)	*100-500	F
WARREN, HAROLD BROADFIELD (1859 - 1934)	*100-700	L,M,F
WARREN, J. C. (19TH C)	300-1200	X (W)
WARREN, MELVIN CHARLES	*4000-20000	
WARREN, MELVIN CHARLES (1920 -)	15000-150000	F,G
WARREN, WESLEY (20TH C)	100-500	X (M)
WARSHAWSKY, ABEL GEORGE (1883 - 1962)	200-2000	L,F
WARSHAWSKY, ALEXANDER (1887 - 1962)	200-1200	X (L)
WASHBURN, CADWALLADER (- 1965)	200-1000	X (F)
WASHBURN, JESSIE M. (20TH C)	100-600	X (L)
WASHES, J. (19TH - 20TH C)	*100-500	X (S)
WASSON, GEORGE SAVARY (1855 - 1926)	100-850	M,L
WATERMAN, MARCUS A. (1834 - 1914)	200-2800	F,L
WATERS, GEORGE W. (1832 - 1912)	300-2500	L,F
WATERS, SUSAN C. (1823 - 1900)	700-45000	P,F,L,W
WATKINS, CATHERINE W. (20TH C)	250-1500	L
WATKINS, FRANKLIN CHENAULT (1894 - 1972)	300-2800	G,F,L
WATROUS, HARRY WILSON (1857 - 1940)	500-40000	F,I,S
WATSON, A. FRANCIS (19TH C)	100-600	X (L)
WATSON, AMELIA MONTAGUE (1856 - 1934)	*200-950	L,I
WATSON, DAWSON (1864 - 1939)	200-1500	X (L)
WATSON, EDITH SARAH (1861 -)	*100-300	X (L)
WATSON, ELIZABETH VILA TAYLOR (-1934)	100-600	F

* Denotes Mixed Media, Watercolors, Gouaches, Pastels, and/or Drawings.

```
WATSON, HENRY SUMNER (1868 - 1933)           300-2000       I,W
WATSON, W. (19TH - 20TH C)                   200-1500       X (L)
WAUD, ALFRED R. (1828 - 1891)               *200-2500       I,M
WAUGH, COULTON                              *100-450
WAUGH, COULTON (1896 - 1973)                 200-900        I
WAUGH, FREDERICK JUDD (1861 - 1940)          400-40000      M,F,S
WAUGH, IDA (    - 1919)                       300-1800       G,F
WAUGH, SAMUEL BELL (1814 - 1885)             350-4000       L,F
WAY, ANDREW JOHN HENRY (1826 - 1888)         400-5000       S,L,F
WEBB, A.C. (1888 -    )                       300-2000       F,I
WEBBER, CHARLES T. (1825 - 1911)             600-4500       F,L
WEBBER, WESLEY (1841 - 1914)                 250-4500       M,L
WEBER, C. PHILIP (1849 -    )                 300-1200       L
WEBER, CARL                                 *150-1500
WEBER, CARL (1850 - 1921)                    300-5000       L
WEBER, CARL T. (19TH - 20TH C)               100-500        X
WEBER, FREDERICK T. (1883 - 1956)            100-650        M
WEBER, MAX                                  *300-15000
WEBER, MAX (1881 - 1961)                     500-65000      A,F
WEBER, OTIS S.                              *100-600
WEBER, OTIS S. (late 19TH C)                 200-2500       M
WEBER,PAUL(GOTTLIEB DANIEL PAUL)(1823-1916) 400-12000       L,F,W
WEBER, PHILIPP (1849 -    )                   500-9500       L
WEEKS, EDWIN LORD (1849 - 1903)              500-30000+     F,L
WEEKS, JAMES (1922 -    )                     3500-12000     X
WEGER, MARIE (1882 -    )                     100-600        X (S)
WEIGAND, GUSTAVE A.(1870 - 1957) [see WIEGAND, GUSTAVE ADOLPH]
WEINBERG, EMILIE SIEVERT (20TH C)            150-850        X (L)
WEINREICH, AGNES (early 20TH C)              200-900        X (L)
WEIR, JOHN FERGUSON (1841 - 1926)            600-25000      L,S,F
WEIR, JULIAN ALDEN                          *500-15000
WEIR, JULIAN ALDEN (1852 - 1919)             1500-70000     F,L,S
WEIR, ROBERT WALTER (1803 - 1889)            600-60000      G,F,L,I
WEISER, MARY E. (19TH - 20TH C)              100-600        X (S)
WEISS, BERNARD J. (20TH C)                   100-600        X (L)
WEISS, MARY L. (early 20TH C)                100-450        X (S)
WEISS, S.A. (early 20TH C)                   100-750        X
WELBECK, G.A. (19TH - 20TH C)                150-950        X (L,F)
WELCH, LUDMILLA P. (19TH - 20TH C)           300-2000       X (L)
WELCH, MABEL R. (    - 1959)                  150-1000       X (F)
WELCH, THADDEUS                             *300-2000
WELCH, THADDEUS (1844 - 1919)                400-7500       L,F
WELDON, CHARLES DATER (1844 - 1935)          1000-8500      I
WELDON, H.A. (19TH - 20TH C)                 150-850        L
WELLER, CARL F. (1853 - 1920)               *100-500        X (L)
WELLIVER, NEIL (1929 -    )                   3000-35000     A
WELLS, BENJAMIN B. (20TH C)                 *100-800        X
WELLS, BETTY (20TH C)                       *100-800        X
WELLS, LYNTON (1940 -    )                    2000-20000     A
WELLS, NEWTON ALONZO (1852 -    )            300-1500       L,S
WENBAN, SION LONGLEY (1848 - 1897)           300-2000       L
WENDEL, THEODORE (1857 -    )                 800-40000      L,M
WENDEROTH, AUGUSTUS (1825 -    )             400-4500       F,W,L
WENDEROTH, FREDERICK A. (19TH - 20TH C)      300-1800       X (S)
WENDT, WILLIAM (1865 - 1946)                 600-12000      L,F
```

* Denotes Mixed Media,Watercolors,Gouaches,Pastels, and/or Drawings.

WENGENROTH, STOW (1906 -)	300-1500	L,M
WENGER, JOHN	*100-600	
WENGER, JOHN (1887 -)	300-1500	X (F)
WENTWORTH, DANIEL F. (1850 - 1934)	400-2500	L
WENZELL, ALBERT BECK (1864 - 1917)	*100-3000	I
WERNER-BEHN, HANS (early 20TH C)	100-600	X
WERTINFIELD, JOSEPH (20TH C)	100-350	X (F)
WESCOTT, PAUL (1904 - 1970)	300-1500	X (L,M
WESLEY, JOHN (1928 -)	300-2500	A
WESSELMANN, TOM	*700-30000	
WESSELMANN, TOM (1931 -)	2000-50000	A
WESSON, ROBERT (19TH C)	100-500	L
WEST, BENJAMIN	*400-20000+	
WEST, BENJAMIN (1738 - 1820)	600-??????	F,G,L
WEST, LEVON (1900 -)	*200-1200	F
WEST, PETER B. (1833 - 1913)	300-2000	G,W,L
WEST, RAPHAEL LAMARR (1769 - 1850)	*350-2500	F,I,L
WEST, WILLIAM EDWARD (1788 - 1857)	400-2500	F,M
WESTERMANN, HORACE CLIFFORD (1922 -)	*500-6000	A
WESTON, MORRIS (19TH - 20TH C)	100-500	X (L)
WETHERBEE, GEORGE FAULKNER (1851 - 1920)	500-7500	F,L
WETHERBY, ISAAC AUGUSTUS (1819 - 1904)	800-6000	P
WETHERILL, ELISHA KENT KANE (1874 - 1925)	150-2500+	M,L,F
WEYDEN, HARRY VAN DER (1868 -)	100-700	X (L)
WEYL, MAX (1837 - 1914)	400-3500	L
WHEELER, CHARLES ARTHUR (1881 -)	150-750	X (F)
WHEELER, WILLLIAM R. (1832 - 1894)	250-950	F
WHEELOCK, MERRILL GREENE (1822 - 1866)	*200-1200	M,L
WHEELOCK, WALTER W. (early 19TH C)	250-950	F
WHEELOCK, WARREN (1880 - 1960)	150-1500	F,L
WHELAN, THOMAS (20TH C)	150-950	X (L)
WHISTLER, JAMES ABBOTT MCNEIL	*500-85000	
WHISTLER, JAMES ABBOTT MCNEIL (1834-1903)	1000-??????	L,F
WHITAKER, CHARLES W. (20TH C)	150-800	X (L)
WHITAKER, GEORGE WILLIAM	*300-1500	
WHITAKER, GEORGE WILLIAM (1841 - 1916)	100-1500	M,S,L,I
WHITCOMB, JON	*200-800	
WHITCOMB, JON (1906 -)	200-4500	I
WHITE, CHARLES (1918 - 1980)	*800-6000	F
WHITE, CHARLES HENRY (1878 -)	600-3500	X (L,F)
WHITE, CLARENCE SCOTT (1872 -)	300-2500	L
WHITE, EDWIN (1817 - 1877)	500-10000	F,G
WHITE, HENRY COOKE (1861 - 1952)	200-1000	L
WHITE, ORRIN AUGUSTINE (1883 - 1969)	400-3500	L
WHITE, THOMAS GILBERT (1877 - 1939)	100-700	F,L
WHITEHORNE, JAMES A. (1803 - 1888)	300-900	F
WHITEMAN, SAMUEL EDWIN (1860 - 1922)	200-1200	L
WHITESIDE, FRANK REED (1866 - 1929)	100-750	L,M
WHITING, HENRY W. (19TH C)	150-2000	L
WHITMAN, A.M. (19TH - 20TH C)	*100-800	X (L)
WHITMAN, EDWIN (20TH C)	100-700	X (G)
WHITMORE, M. COBURN (1913 -)	300-5000	I
WHITTAKER, JOHN BARNARD (1836 - 1926)	300-3500	F,L
WHITTEMORE, WILLIAM JOHN (1860 - 1955)	100-1000	F,M
WHITTREDGE, THOMAS WORTHINGTON (1820-1910)	1000-90000+	L,M

* Denotes Mixed Media,Watercolors,Gouaches,Pastels, and/or Drawings.

```
WHORF, JOHN                                           *250-4000
WHORF, JOHN (1903 - 1959)                              500-4000    L,M,F
WICKEY, HARRY (1892 -      )                           *100-600     X (F)
WIDFORSS, GUNNAR MAURITZ (1879 - 1934)                *300-3000    L,F
WIDNER, G.O. (19TH C)                                  800-6000    L
WIEGAND, CHARMION VON (1899 -      )                  *300-1200    A
WIEGAND, GUSTAVE ADOLPH (1870 - 1957)                 200-3000    L
WIEGHORST, OLAF CARL                                  *500-9000
WIEGHORST, OLAF CARL (1899 -      )                  4000-80000    F,G,W
WIES, W. (19TH - 20TH C)                               100-600     X (L)
WIESSLER, WILLIAM (1887 -      )                       100-500     X (S)
WIGGINS, GUY CARLETON (1883 - 1962)                   500-30000   L
WIGGINS, (JOHN) CARLETON (1848 - 1932)                200-5000    L
WIGGINS, SIDNEY MILLER (1883 - 1940)                  150-950     X (L)
WIGHT, MOSES (1827 - 1895)                             300-4500    G,F
WILATCH, MICHA (1910 -      )                          300-2000    X (L)
WILBUR, THEODORE E. (19TH C)                           150-750     X (L)
WILCOX, FRANK NELSON (1887 -      )                   *150-850     X (L)
WILCOX (WILLCOX), WILLIAM (1831 -      )               200-800     L
WILDE (WILD), HAMILTON GIBBS (1827 - 1884)            200-1500    F,G,L
WILDER, ARTHUR B.                                     *150-600
WILDER, ARTHUR B. (1857 -      )                       300-2500    L
WILDER, F. H. (active 1845-50)                         400-1500    F
WILDER, FRANKLIN (19TH C)                             *2000-8500   P
WILES, IRVING RAMSAY                                  *250-3500
WILES, IRVING RAMSAY (1862 - 1948)                    400-10000   G,M,I
WILES, LEMUEL MAYNARD (1826 - 1905)                   500-15000   L
WILES, M. (20TH C)                                     100-600     X (S)
WILEY, WILLIAM T.                                     *800-15000
WILEY, WILLIAM T. (1937 -      )                     1000-20000   A
WILFORD, LORAN FREDERICK                              *100-650
WILFORD, LORAN FREDERICK (1893 - 1972)                250-2500    F,I
WILKIE,ROBERT D. (1828 - 1903)                        500-10000   G,L,S,W
WILKINSON, J. WALTER (1892 -      )                    100-850     X (F)
WILL, JOHN M. AUGUST (1834 - 1910)                    *100-650     F,L
WILLARD, ARCHIBALD M. (1836 - 1918)                   800-??????   F,L
WILLEY, PHILO "CHIEF" (1886 - 1980)                   500-5000    P
WILLIAMS, CHARLES DAVID (1875 - 1954)                *200-1500    I
WILLIAMS, FREDERICK BALLARD (1871 - 1956)             250-2500    F,G,L
WILLIAMS, FREDERICK DICKINSON (1829-1915)             250-1800    F,L
WILLIAMS, GEORGE ALFRED (1875 - 1932)                *100-800     F
WILLIAMS, HENRY (1787 - 1830)                          300-2800    F
WILLIAMS, ISAAC L. (1817 - 1895)                       300-3000    F,L
WILLIAMS, JOHN SCOTT (1877 -      )                   *100-1000    L,I
WILLIAMS, M.C. (19TH C)                                100-1000    G
WILLIAMS, MARY BELLE (19TH - 20TH C)                  200-1500    L
WILLIAMS, MICAH                                       *700-3000
WILLIAMS, MICAH (active 1815-30)                      1000-6500   F
WILLIAMS, VIRGIL (1830 - 1886)                         300-3500    G,F,L
WILLIAMS, WILLIAM (c.1710 - 1790)                      400-3000    F,L
WILLIAMS, WILLIAM JOSEPH (1759 - 1823)                500-4500    F
WILLIAMSON, CHARTERS (1856 -      )                    250-1200    L
WILLIAMSON, JOHN (1826 - 1885)                         400-8500    L,F,S
WILLIS, EDMUND AYLBURTON (VAN) (1808-1899)            300-2000    G,L,W
WILLIS, THOMAS (1850 - 1912)                          *1500-5000   M
```

* Denotes Mixed Media,Watercolors,Gouaches,Pastels, and/or Drawings.

WILLSON, B. (19TH C)	200-1200	L
WILLSON, JAMES MALLERY (1890 -)	100-700	X (L,M)
WILLSON, MARY ANN (active 1810-30)	*1000-7500	P
WILMARTH, LEMUEL EVERETT (1835 - 1918)	700-15000	G,S
WILSON, DONALD ROLLER (20TH C)	300-1500	X (F)
WILSON, GAHAN (20TH C)	*100-1000	X (F)
WILSON, H.M. (20TH C)	100-600	X (L)
WILSON, HARRIET (20TH C)	*100-600	X (S)
WILSON, JAMES (19TH C)	1000-6500	L
WILSON, JANE (1924 -)	2000-20000	A
WILSON, ROBERT BURNS (1851 - 1916)	*250-850	L
WILSON, SOL (20TH C)	100-750	X (L)
WILSON, T. (19TH C)	100-650	L
WILTZ, ARNOLD (1889 - 1937)	200-1000	L
WIMAR.CHARLES(or KARL FERDINAND)(1828-1863)	5000-75000	F,M,W,L
WINGERT, EDWARD OSWALD (1864 - 1934)	100-650	X (L)
WINNER, WILLIAM E. (1815 - 1883)	500-8000	G,F
WINSLOW, HENRY (1874 -)	400-3500	X (L,M)
WINSOR, HELEN A. (19TH C)	300-1800	X
WINTER, ALICE BEACH (1877 -)	400-3500	F,I
WINTER, ANDREW (1893 - 1958)	150-850	L
WINTER, CHARLES ALLAN (1869 -1942)	300-5000	F,I
WISBY, JACK (20TH C)	300-2000	L,M
WITHERSTINE, DONALD FREDERICK (1896-)	200-700	L
WITKOWSKI, KARL	*300-1500	
WITKOWSKI, KARL (1860 - 1910)	1000-12000	G
WITT, JOHN H. (1840 - 1901)	600-4500	F,L
WOELFLE, ARTHUR WILLIAM (1873 - 1936)	250-2000+	M,L,F,S
WOLCOTT, HAROLD (20TH C)	300-1200	X (F,L)
WOLCOTT, JOHN GILMORE (1891 -)	100-700	X (F)
WOLCOTT, ROGER A. (20TH C)	150-850	F
WOLCOTT, ROGER H. (20TH C)	150-800	X (L)
WOLF, BEN (20TH C)	100-450	X (F)
WOLF, CHAS. H. (early 19TH C)	10000-40000	P
WOLF, F.H. (20TH C)	200-800	X (S)
WOLF, GEORG (1882 - 1962)	500-7500	G,W,F,L
WOLF, HENRY (1852 - 1916)	150-650	L,F,S
WOLF, LONE	*600-3500	
WOLF, LONE (1882 - 1965)	1000-18000	X (F)
WOLF, WALLACE L. DE (1854 - 1930)	250-1200	L
WOLFE, BYRON (1904 - 1973)	*1000-8500	X (F)
WOLFE, JACK (20TH C)	200-900	A
WOLFE, WAYNE (20TH C)	5000-30000	X (L)
WOLFF, B. (20TH C)	100-400	X (L)
WOLFF, GUSTAV (1863 - 1934)	300-3000	L,M
WOLLASTON, JOHN (active 1735-70)	2000-10000	F
WONNER, PAUL JOHN (1920 -)	*1000-4000	X
WOOD, A.M. (19TH C)	100-500	X (L)
WOOD, ALEXANDER (19TH - 20TH C)	300-6500	F,L
WOOD, GEORGE ALBERT (1840 -)	300-1200	L
WOOD, GEORGE BACON JR (1832 - 1910)	300-3500	G,L
WOOD, GRANT	*2000-325000	
WOOD, GRANT (1891 - 1942)	2500-1375000	F,L,G,W
WOOD, HOWARD (1922 -)	150-850	A
WOOD, HUNTER (1908 -)	400-2500	X (M)

* Denotes Mixed Media,Watercolors,Gouaches,Pastels, and/or Drawings.

```
WOOD, OGDEN (1851 - 1912)                         150-1500     L,W
WOOD, ROBERT (1889 - 1979)                        1000-8500    L,F
WOOD, ROBERT E. (1926 - 1979)                     1000-15000   L
WOOD, STANLEY L. (1860 - 1940)                    500-5000     X (I,F)
WOOD, THOMAS WATERMAN                             *2000-40000
WOOD, THOMAS WATERMAN (1823 - 1903)              700-75000     G,F
WOOD, VIRGINIA HARGRAVES                          *100-750      X (F)
WOOD, WORDEN                                      *250-1000
WOOD, WORDEN (active 1910-1940)                   500-3000      M,I
WOODBURN, STEPHEN (20TH C)                        300-2000      X
WOODBURY, CHARLES HERBERT (1864 - 1940)           400-9500      F,M,L
WOODBURY, MARCIA OAKES (1865 - 1913)              250-2000      F
WOODCOCK, HARTWELL L. (1853 - 1929)              *100-600       M,L
WOODRACH, KARL L. (20TH C)                        *100-350      X (M)
WOODRUFF, G.L. (19TH C)                           300-1000      X (S)
WOODSIDE, JOHN ARCHIBALD (1781 - 1852)            1000-7500+    P
WOODVILLE, RICHARD CATON (1825 - 1855)            2000-75000    G
WOODWARD, ELLSWORTH (1861 - 1939)                 *500-3000     G,M,I
WOODWARD, LAURA (19TH C)                           100-850      X (S)
WOODWARD, MABEL MAY (1877 - 1945)                 600-20000     F,M,L,S
WOODWARD, ROBERT STRONG (1885 - 1960)             400-3000      L
WOODWARD, STANLEY WINGATE (1890 -     )           300-1800      M,I
WOOLF, SAMUEL JOHNSON (1880 - 1948)               100-1800      L,F
WOOLRYCH, F. HUMPHRY W. (1868 -      )            100-800       F,L,S,I
WOOSTER, A.C. (19TH C)                            150-950       L
WORDEN, J. (20TH C)                               100-300       X (F)
WORES, THEODORE (1860 - 1939)                     500-3800      F,M,I
WORTH, THOMAS                                     *200-1200
WORTH, THOMAS (1834 - 1917)                       500-4500      G,L
WRENN, CHARLES LEWIS (1880 - 1952)                100-900       F,I
WRIGHT, CHARLES H. MONCRIEF (1870 - 1939)         500-6000      L,F,I
WRIGHT, CHARLES LENOX (1876 -      )              400-3800      X (L,I)
WRIGHT, GEORGE HAND                               *300-3000
WRIGHT, GEORGE HAND (1873 - 1951)                 900-32000     I,G,F
WRIGHT, GEORGE W. (1834 - 1934)                   1800-45000    G,F
WRIGHT, JAMES HENRY (1813 - 1883)                 500-6500      L,M,F,S
WRIGHT, RUFUS (1832 - 1895)                       500-4500      F,L,S
WRIGHT, STANTON MACDONALD [see MACDONALD-WRIGHT, STANTON]
WUERMER, CARL (1900 - 1982)                       1500-18000    L
WUERPEL, EDMUND HENRY (1866 - 1958)               200-1000      X (L)
WUIRT, WALTER (20TH C)                            400-2000      A
WUST, ALEXANDER (1837 - 1876)                     400-3500      L,M
WUST, CHRISTOFFEL (1801 -      )                  600-4500      F
WYAND, D.E. (19TH - 20TH C)                       *100-600      G,F
WYANT, ALEXANDER HELWIG                           *400-50000
WYANT, ALEXANDER HELWIG (1836 - 1892)             800-50000     L
WYCKOFF, H. (19TH C)                              100-600       X
WYDEVELD, A. (19TH C)                             200-1000      X (W,S)
WYETH, ANDREW                                     *2000-100000
WYETH, ANDREW (1917 -      )                       20000-75000+
WYETH, JAMES                                      *1500-7000
WYETH, NEWELL CONVERS (1882 - 1945)               2000-30000+   I,L
```

* Denotes Mixed Media,Watercolors,Gouaches,Pastels, and/or Drawings.

X

XCERON, JEAN (1890 - 1967) 1000-5000 A

Y

YARD, SYDNEY JANIS (1855 - 1909)	*200-950	X (L)
YARROW, WILLIAM HENRY KEMBLE (1891 -)	*200-950	L,M
YATES, CULLEN (1866 - 1945)	500-4500	M,L,S
YATES, WILLIAM HENRY (1845 - 1934)	300-5500	F,L
YECKLEY, NORMAN (19TH C - 20TH C)	100-700	X (L)
YELLAND, RAYMOND DABB (1848 - 1900)	400-6500	M,L
YENNAD, ADUASHA (20TH C)	100-600	X (M)
YENS, KARL (JULIUS HEINRICH) (1868 - 1945)	200-1000	F,I
YEWELL, GEORGE HENRY (1830 - 1923)	300-5000	G,F
YOHN, FREDERICK COFFAY (1875 - 1933)	300-4500	I
YONG, JOE DE	*100-2500	
YONG, JOE DE (1894 - 1975)	500-5000	G,F
YORKE, WILLIAM G. (19TH - 20TH C)	2000-15000	X (F)
YOUENS, CLEMEMT T. (19TH - 20TH C)	200-800	X (L)
YOUNG, AUGUST (1839 - 1913)	700-5000	G,F
YOUNG, B.S. (late 19TH C)	800-5000	X (M)
YOUNG, CHARLES MORRIS	*300-2500	
YOUNG, CHARLES MORRIS (1869 - 1964)	1000-7500	L
YOUNG, FRED GRANT (19TH - 20TH C)	100-700	X (S)
YOUNG, HARVEY B.	*300-1800	
YOUNG, HARVEY B. (1840 - 1901)	400-5000	L,F,W
YOUNG, JAMES HARVEY (1830 - 1918)	400-2000	F
YOUNG, MAHONRI MACKINTOSH	*100-700	
YOUNG, MAHONRI MACKINTOSH (1877 - 1957)	600-3000	F,L
YOUNG, OSCAR VAN (1906 -)	300-1500	X
YOUNG, PETER (20TH C)	800-15000	A
YOUNGERMAN, JACK	*400-1200	
YOUNGERMAN, JACK (1926 -)	800-8500	A

* Denotes Mixed Media,Watercolors,Gouaches,Pastels, and/or Drawings.

Z

```
ZAJAC, JACK (1929 -    )                       400-2500     A
ZAKANITCH, ROBERT S. (1935 -    )              4000-20000   A
ZANDT, THOMAS KIRBY VAN (active 1830-65)       400-4000     W
ZANDT, WILLIAM C. VAN (20TH C)                 300-2000     X (F)
ZANG, JOHN J. (19TH C)                         600-4000     F,L
ZELDIS, MELCAH (1931 -    )                    500-7500     P
ZELLINSKY, C.L. (19TH C)                       400-2000     X (F,W)
ZELTNER, WILLIAM (19TH C)                      *250-1200    X (F)
ZIEGLER, EUSTACE PAUL (1881 - 1941)            1000-18000   F,L,I
ZIMMELE, MARGARET SCULLY (1872 -    )          150-950      L,I
ZIMMERMAN, FREDERICK ALMOND (1886 - 1976)      150-750      X (L)
ZIMMERMAN, WILLIAM (20TH C)                    *150-650     X (W)
ZION, BEN (20TH C)                             100-600      X (S)
ZIROLI, NICOLA VICTOR (1908 -    )             300-3000     X (F)
ZOGBAUM, RUFUS FAIRCHILD                       *400-2500
ZOGBAUM, RUFUS FAIRCHILD (1849 - 1925)         800-6500     I,F,M
ZOGBAUM, WILFRID (1915 - 1965)                 900-6000     A
ZORACH, MARGUERITE THOMPSON (1888 - 1968)      400-3500     L,F,S
ZORACH, WILLIAM (1887 - 1966)                  *300-3000    A,L
ZOX, LARRY (1936 -    )                         800-8500     A
ZUCCARELLI, FRANK EDWARD (20TH C)              100-700      X (F)
ZUCKER, JOSEPH (1941 -    )                    *500-7000    A
ZUILL, ALICE I. (19TH C)                       250-1000     L,S
```

* Denotes Mixed Media,Watercolors,Gouaches,Pastels, and/or Drawings.

RECORD PRICES

The following prices are record AUCTION prices (as of 7/1/85) for each of the respective artists, and are isolated here because they are **well above** the "normal" price range for the artist. Within the alphabetical listings, the price range for each of these artists will be followed by a "+" to indicate your referral to the list below. [NOTE: Most prices include a 10% buyers premium.]

ARTIST	PRICE	SUBJECT	DATE
BIERSTADT, ALBERT	792,000	L (W)	6/83
BLUM, ROBERT FREDERICK	*104,000	F	12/82
BLUM, ROBERT FREDERICK	473,000	F	6/82
CHASE, WILLIAM MERRITT	*820,000	F	5/81
CHURCH, FREDERIC EDWIN	2,750,000	M	10/79
COATES, EDMUND C.	47,500	F	7/84
COOPER, COLIN CAMPBELL	33,000	L	6/82
DUNNING, ROBERT SPEAR	187,000	S	10/84
ENNEKING, JOHN JOSEPH	121,000	L	6/83
FECHIN, NICOLAI	154,000	F	4/80
HENRY, EDWARD LAMSON	275,000	G	7/80
JACOBSEN, ANTONIO	60,984	M	6/85
KENSETT, JOHN FREDERICK	594,000	M	12/83
KOONING, WILLIAM DE	*1,210,000	A	5/83
MAN-RAY	825,000	A	11/79
MELROSE, ANDREW W.	37,500	M	10/73
NEWELL, HUGH	27,500	G	5/81
NEWMAN, BARNETT	1,754,500	A	5/85
PEARCE, CHARLES SPRAGUE	247,500	F	6/81
PERU, ALTO	28,600	F	5/81
PETERSON, JANE	*30,800	F	5/85
PETO, JOHN FREDERICK	460,000	S	6/84
PHILLIPS, AMMI	682,000	P (F)	1/85
POPE, ALEXANDER	187,000	S	11/81
PYLE, HOWARD	49,500	I	1/80
RANNEY, WILLIAM TYLEE	748,000	G	10/80
RICHARDS, WILLIAM TROST	187,000	L	5/84
ROCKWELL, NORMAN	253,000	I	4/81
ROTHKO, MARK	1,815,000	A	11/83
RYDER, CHAUNCEY FOSTER	35,200	L	6/83
SCOTT, JULIAN	33,000	F	6/83
SHEELER, CHARLES	*209,000	A	6/83

* Denotes Mixed Media, Watercolors, Pastels, or Drawings

SHEELER, CHARLES	1,870,000	A (L)	6/83
SPENCER, LILLY MARTIN	99,000	F	12/83
STEINBERG, SAUL	*154,000	A	11/83
STEVENS, WILLIAM LESTER	10,450	L	12/80
STEWART, JULIUS L.	170,500	F	12/84
SUNDBLOM, HADDON HUBBARD	13,200	I	12/80
TACK, AUGUSTUS VINCENT	165,000	A	10/84
TANNER, HENRY OSSAWA	275,000	G	12/81
TRACY, JOHN M.	50,600	G	9/83
TROTTER, NEWBOLD H.	17,050	W	1/82
WALDO, SAMUEL LOVETT	33,000	F	10/78
WEEKS, EDWIN LORD	70,000	F	11/81
WEST, BENJAMIN	*165,000	F	5/84
WETHERILL, ELISHA KENT KANE	7,150	W	10/79
WHITTREDGE, THOMAS W.	280,000	L	9/81
WOELFLE, ARTHUR WILLIAM	9,350	L	12/80
WOODSIDE, JOHN ARCHIBALD	286,000	P (L)	6/82
WYETH, ANDREW	462,000	W	12/81
WYETH, NEWELL CONVERS	135,000	I	?/83

* Denotes Mixed Media, Watercolors, Pastels, or Drawings

APPENDIX

RESOURCES FOR PRICING

REFERENCE BOOKS

Prices for auction price guides can be very high - from $40 to $175. Unless you plan to buy and sell art regularly, you should check with a large public library, or art museum library for the titles you will need (next page).
For acomplete look at the references available, write or call the following book dealers and request their catalog. You should become familiar with all the art price guides and art reference books available to you, before you start buying. One note, I do not believe these "guides" are available in any familiar "chain" bookstores.
Here is a list, first, of art book dealers I am familiar with and would recommend, and second, of those price guides which are important listings of auction results of American art. You can look ahead, under **Biographical Resources** for a list of the important art dictionaries.

WILLEM G. FLIPPO
P.O. Box 8
Larchmont, N.Y. 10538

(914) 834-6351

DEALER'S CHOICE
6402 N. Nebraska
Tampa, Fl 33604

(800) 238-8288 (toll free)
In Fla.:AREA CODE (813)

HACKER ART BOOKS
54 West 57th St.
New York, N.Y. 10019

MUSEUM GALLERY BOOK SHOP
Box 121
SouthPort, CT 06490

(203) 259-7114

NEW ENGLAND GALLERY
R.F.D.2
Wolfeboro, N.H. 03894

(603) 569-3501

JOSLIN HALL CO.
663 Salem St.
Malden, MA 02148

(617) 321-9310

****

Important Art Price Sources:
(check each dealer - prices vary)

1. **AUCTION PRICES OF AMERICAN ARTISTS**
by Richard Hislop, Art Sales Index Ltd.,England.

   4 volumes available covering art sales from 1970
thru 1984. Prices from $40-$65.

2. **JACOBSEN'S SEVENTH PAINTING AND BRONZE PRICE GUIDE**
by Anita Jacobsen.

   Lists art sold at auction over a two year period -
American and European. Back volumes still available.
Present volume is $40 with most book dealers.

3. **LEONARD'S ANNUAL PRICE INDEX OF ART AUCTIONS**
by Auction Index, Inc., 30 Valentine Park,
West Newton, MA 02165

   Complete listing of sales results, American and European,
during 1983-84. Past volumes available. Price $175.

   They still issue quarterly volumes (softcover)
during the year. The price is $125 per year.

4. **E. MAYER 1985 INTERNATIONAL AUCTION RECORDS**
by Editions Publisol

   A very thick, well illustrated, international price guide
to paintings, prints, drawings, and sculptures.

   Covers auction results for preceding year. Back copies
available. Present price is $158 (hardcover).

   NOTE: My only complaint with "Mayer's" is they never
indicate in the entries, the nationality of the artist
or his date of birth and death.

5. **AMERICAN ART ANALOG** : Watch for it. It will be published
in January of 1986. Three volumes (hardcover),1200 pages total
with biographical and sales info on 850 leading American
artists. Priced retail at $350, pre-publication price of
$295.

"ON-LINE" DATABASES

For the "serious" art dealer,collector, appraiser, auctioneer, one of the two "on-line" databases listed below, is a must. You go to your terminal, touch a few keys ,and quickly, you have access to the world's most complete coverage of international auction sales. Let's look at each one.

ARTSCAN

Subscribers to ArtScan have a terminal provided free of charge. ARTSCAN's advertising literature claims that they provide the following services:

"INTERNATIONAL AUCTION RECORDS: EMAYER - just type an artist's name and receive a complete listing of his or her recent and past international auction sales".

"FASTFINDER - search the complete contents of upcoming auction catalogs...instantaneous access or add to an international inventory of artwork available for purchase, sale, exhibition or research".

"MAILBOX - communicate with other members of the ArtScan Network instantly! Send and receive general broadcasts and personalized messages".

"STOLEN WORKS - no longer should the buyer beware. Access this database and receive immediate world-wide listings of stolen works of art".

"CALENDAR - at the push of a button scan a directory listing the date, time, and location of upcoming auctions and consignment deadlines, gallery openings, sales, exhibitions, publications..."

"ARTCONTROL - select this service for all your inventory control and accounting needs. Unique security features ensure you total confidentiality".

If you would like to know more about ARTSCAN, or verify the claims above, please call or write to:

ARTSCAN INC.
125 Wolf Road
Albany, NY 12205

800-742-5500
(NY) 800-351-1300
(Outside USA, Collect) 518-438-1223

ARTQUEST

ARTQUEST, a subcription computer service, was compiled by Richard Hislop, editor of Art Sales Index (ASI). This database contains the international sale results of the past 15 years. Presently on the database are results from the sale of over 40,000 American paintings, and over 600,000 works of art world-wide.

Unlike Artscan, users must have their own terminals, and these terminals must have modems for telecommunications.

You can retrieve information in innumerable ways: by artist, title, size, medium, nationality, price (descending or ascending order), most recent sales, and much more. ARTQUEST will also give you an analysis of each artist's auction record during the past 15 years, year by year. Information can be accessed in seconds, important when you are paying between $1.00 - $1.75 per minute for "connect" time. It is worth the expense, though, because you can glean information in seconds from ARTQUEST which you could not gather from the "guide" books after weeks of investigation.

I subscribe to ARTQUEST, and whole heartedly recommend it to any "active" art dealer, collector, appraiser, or auctioneer. Any novice to computers can learn to use ARTQUEST successfully in a very short time. For more information call or write:

ARTQUEST
Art Sales Index, Ltd.
Pond House
Weybridge, Surrey KT13 8SP
ENGLAND

TELEPHONE: Weybridge 56426
TELEX: 946240 CMEASY G

NOTE: Although the ARTQUEST database is located in London, you can access it easily by using a "local" packet switching network. The literature you recieve from ARTQUEST will explain it more thoroughly.

MAJOR AMERICAN ART AUCTION HOUSES

Here is an alphabetical list, by state, of those auction houses which sell a large volume of art work each year. Most have in-house art specialists who do the research on each consignment,and prepare them for cataloging. If you are considering consigning your art to auction, send a clear color photograph (the larger the better) with a description of the piece to several of the auction houses herein. Make sure you tell them that: I am interested in possibly consigning to you the inclosed work of art. Could you please send me an estimate of the price you feel my (painting, drawing, watercolor, or whatever) might realize at your auction, and please advise my if it would be suitable for one of your upcoming sales.

Please keep in mind, most "major" auction houses will not take a "single" consignment unless it is valued at over $300. Check the policies of each when you initially contact them.

Here is our list:

CALIFORNIA

Butterfield & Butterfield
1244 Sutter Street
San Francisco, CA 94109
(415) 673-1362

Sotheby's
308 North Rodeo Drive
Beverly Hills, CA 90210
(213) 274-0340

D.C.

Adam A. Weschler and Sons
905 E. Street NW
Washington, DC 20004
(202) 628-1281

MAINE

Barridoff Galleries
242 Middle Street
Portland, Maine 04101
(207) 772-5011

MASSACHUSETTS

Richard A. Bourne Co., Inc.
Box 141
Hyannis Port, MA 02601
(617) 775-0797

Robert C. Eldred Co., Inc.
Box 796 1483 Route 6A
East Dennis, MA 02641
(617) 385-3116

Robert W. Skinner Inc.
Route 117
Bolton, MA 02116
(617) 779-5528

MICHIGAN

DuMouchelle's
409 East Jefferson Avenue
Detroit, MI 48226
(313) 963-6255

NEW HAMPSHIRE

Young Fine Arts Gallery, Inc.
56 Market Street
Portsmouth, NH 03801
(603) 436-8773

NEW YORK CITY

Christie, Manson & Woods,
International
502 Park Avenue
New York, NY 10022
(212) 546-1000

Christie's East
219 East 67th Street
New York, NY 10021
(212) 570-4141

William Doyle Galleries
175 East 87th Street
New York, NY 10028
(212) 427-2730

Phillips Son & Neale, Inc.
406 East 79th Street
New York, NY 10021
(212) 570-4830

Sotheby's Parke Bernet Inc.
1334 York Avenue
New York, NY 10021
(212) 606-7000

OHIO

Wolf's Auction Gallery
13015 Larchmere Boulevard
Shaker Heights, OH 44120
(216) 231- 3888

IMPORTANT AMERICAN GALLERIES

The following is a short list of reputable art dealers with whom I am familiar. If you decide to sell your art work through a reputable dealer, at a fair price, consider contacting one, or more, of the following.

AMERICAN 18TH, 19TH AND EARLY 20TH CENTURY ART

WEST COAST

Petersen Galleries
332 N. Rodeo Dr.
Beverley Hills, CA 90210
(213) 274-6705

Goldfield Galleries
8400 Melrose Avenue
Los Angeles, CA 90069
(213) 651-1122

De Ville Galleries
8751 Melrose Avenue
Los Angeles, CA 90069
(213) 652-0525

MID-WEST

R.H. Love Gallery
100-108 East Ohio Street
Chicago, IL 60611
(312) 664-9620

Keny and Johnson Gallery
300 East Beck Street
Columbus, OH 43320
(614) 464-1228

EAST COAST

Alexander Gallery
996 Madison Avenue
New York, NY 10021
(212) 472-1636

Coe Kerr Gallery
49 East 82nd Street
New York, NY 10028
(212) 628-1340

Graham Gallery
1014 Madison Avenue
New York, NY 10021
(212) 535-5767

Hirschl & Adler Galleries,Inc.
21 East 70th Street
New York, NY 10021
(212) 535-8810

Kennedy Galleries
40 West 57th Street,5th Floor
New York, NY 10019
(212) 541-9600

Wunderlich & Co. Inc.
41 East 57th Street
New York, NY 10022
(212) 838-2555

Vose Galleries of Boston, Inc.
238 Newbury Street
Boston, MA 02116
(617) 536-6176

Currier's Fine Art
Appraisals and Publishing
P.O. Box 2098
Brockton, MA 02403
(617) 588-4509

AMERICAN ILLUSTRATORS

Judy Goffman
American Paintings
18 East 77th Street
New York, NY 10021
(212) 744-5190 (NY)
(215) 643-4661 (PA)

AMERICAN FOLK ART

Peter Tillou Fine Arts
Prospect Street
Litchfield, CT 06759
(203) 567-6706

America Hurrah Antiques
766 Madison Avenue
New York, NY 10021
(212) 535-1930

Jay Johnson Gallery
1044 Madison Avenue
New York, NY 10021
(212) 628-7280

Steve Miller
17 East 96th Street
New York, NY 10028
(212) 348-5219

Steven Score, Inc.
159 Main Street
Essex, MA 01929
(617) 768-6252

Leo Castelli Gallery
420 West Broadway
New York, NY 10012
(212) 431-5160

Andre Emmerich Gallery
41 East 57th Street
New York, NY 10022
(212) 752-0124

Allan Frumkin Gallery
50 West 57th Street
New York, NY 10019
(212) 757-6655

Marlborough Gallery
40 West 57th Street
New York, NY 10019
(212) 541-4900

M. Knoedler & Co., Inc.
19 East 70th Street
New York, NY 10021
(212) 794-0050

Fischbach Gallery
24 West 57th street
New York, NY 10019
(212) 759-2345

The Pace Gallery
32 East 57th Street
New York, NY 10022
(212) 421-3292

CONTEMPORARY ART

The Harcus Gallery
7 Newbury Street
Boston, MA 02116
(617) 262-4445

BIOGRAPHICAL RESOURCES

DICTIONARIES OF ARTISTS

I will only list those dictionaries that apply specifically to American artists. The prices for these "dictionaries" may vary between $40-$120.

* **Dictionary of American Artists, Sculptors and Engravers,** Mantle Fielding, edited by Glenn B. Opitz

* **Who's Who in American Art,** Jaques Cattell Press

* **Dictionary of Contemporary American Artists,** Paul Cummings

* **Index of Artists,** Daniel Trowbridge Mallett (2 vol)

* **Dictionary of American Artists, Sculptors, and Engravers,** William Young

* **The New York Historical Society's Dictionary of Artists in America,** Groce and Wallace

* **Dictionary of American Artists of the 19th & 20th Century,** Alice Coe McGlauflin

* **Illustrated Biographical Encyclopedia of Artists of the American West,** Peggy and Harold Samuel

* **Who Was Who in American Art,** Hastings

* **Concise Dictionary of Artists Signatures,** Jackson

* **Dictionary of Marine Artists,** E.R. Brewington

* **Women Artists in America,** Glenn B.Opitz

* **Dictionary of American Artists,** F. Levy

AGENCIES

The leading resource nationally for biographical information is the National Museum of American Art, Washington, D.C. (a division of the Smithsonian Institution). It offers comprehensive details on American Paintings executed before the year 1914. Researchers can visit in person or make inquires through the mail. For your inspection, I have reproduced below the information available from the Smithsonian with regards to the Museum.

The Inventory of American Paintings Executed before 1914 is a computerized index listing over 230,000 records of paintings in public as well as private collections throughout the nation. Information is indexed by artist, owner/ location and subject matter. Complementing the descriptive indexes is an Image File of approximately 45,000 photographs and reproductions which are available for study in the Inventory office.

The Peter A. Juley and Son Collection of approximately 127,000 photographic negatives documents works of art and artists. Located in New York City and specializing in photography of fine arts, the Juley firm which was active from 1896 to 1975 produced many negatives of art historical significance which record works of art now lost, destroyed, or altered in appearance. Preliminary computer indexing of the collection has been completed. Generous support from the Samuel H. Kress Foundation, James Smithson Society, J. Paul Getty Trust, and others has enabled the museum to make prints from the negatives which will be made available for study in the NMAA Slide and Photograph Archives.

The Smithsonian Art Index was initiated in 1976 by the National Museum of American Art to identify and to record works of art -- drawings, prints, paintings and sculpture -- in Smithsonian divisions which were not part of the art museum collections. The Index was designed as a research tool or directory to a vast amount of material that had generally been overlooked by or was largely unknown to scholars and the public. A total of 9,565 records representing 207,208 objects in the Smithsonian Institution is indexed by artist, division, donor/source, and subject.

The Slide and Photograph Archives, a facility for the visual documentation of American art, consists of approximately 60,000 35mm color slides and 200,000 photographs and negatives (including the Peter A. Juley and Son Collection). Slides and photographs are available for research on the premises and a smaller collection of approximately 12,000 slides is available for borrowing by the public. A computerized information storage and retrieval system is employed in the cataloguing and classification of the collection permitting frequent updating of subject, artist/title and media indexes.

The Pre-1877 Art Exhibition Catalogue Index is a computerized project to index information from over 700 rare catalogues of exhibitions which were held between 1790 and 1876 at art unions, museums, state fairs, auctions, commercial galleries, and lotteries in the United States and Canada. When completed, the Index will provide valuable information on individual artists, patrons, art organizations, media, and subject matter as well as on the histories of specific works of art that my no longer be extant.

The Wang System: The Office of Research Support provides training and operational services for NMAA's present in-house office automation system, a Wang OIS 115 Model 3 minicomputer. The system is utilized by the museum staff for numerous office applications, including form letters, exhibition lists, in-house directories, manuscripts, exhibition checklists, label copy and museum publications.

The Permanent Collection Data Base, a computerized listing, provides information on the over 30,000 objects in the museum's permanent collection. The object records in the data base, which have been entered on computer by staff of the Office of Research Support, are indexed by artist, title, medium, department and other classifications.

Office of Research Support
National Museum of American Art
Smithsonian Institution
Washington, D.C. 20560

****

The Archives of American Art have seven offices nationwide.
They are another very important source of biographical material
on American artists. Here are their locations and telephone
numbers.

Boston, Massachusetts	617-223-0951
Detroit, Michigan	313-226-5744
Houston, Texas	713-526-1361
New York City	212-826-5722
San Francisco, California	415-556-2530
San Marino, California	818-405-7849
Washington, D.C.	202-357-2781 (Headquarters)

****

If you live in New York City, a wealth of art resources can be
found in **The Frick Art Reference Library**, located at:

10 East 71st Street
New York, NY 10021

212-288-8700

Last, but not least, are the Fine Arts Departments around the
country in our major public libraries and museums.

APPRAISAL ORGANIZATIONS

If have need of an art appraiser be sure he or she is a member in good standing with one of the respected appraisal organizations nationally. Here are your leading sources for qualified - ask for references - appraisers.

THE APPRAISERS ASSOCIATION
OF AMERICA
60 East 42nd Street
New York, NY   10165

THE NEW ENGLAND
APPRAISERS ASSOCIATION
104 Charles Street
Boston, MA   02114

(617) 523-6272

THE AMERICAN SOCIETY
OF APPRAISERS
11800 Sunrise Valley Drive
Suite 400
Reston, VA 22070

(703) 620-3838

THE INTERNATIONAL SOCIETY
OF APPRAISERS
BOX 726
Hoffman Estates, IL   60195

(312) 882-0706

THE ART DEALERS ASSOCIATION
575 Madison Avenue
New York, NY   10022

(212) 940-8590

In addition to the list above, the **MAJOR** auction houses also have appraisal services.

****

AUTHENTICATION SERVICES:

The **Art Dealers Association** will be helpful when you need an expert to authenticate a valuable work of art.

The **International Foundation for Art Research** (IFAR) provides an authentication service for valuable works of art. For more information on all their services write or call:

IFAR
Dr. Constance Lowenthal
Executive Director
46 East 70th Street
New York, NY 10021

(212) 879-1780

****

CONSULTANTS

After carefully searching for a directory which would list art consultants I realized that none exist. For me to suggest or recommend a list of art consultants at this time would be impossible. I am only acquainted with one local art consultant: MS Kathryn Corbin. MS Corbin recently left her post as painting specialist at Robert W. Skinner Inc.(auction house), Bolton, Massachusetts, to work privately as a consultant for clients with an interest in American and European art of the 19th and 20th Centuries. She is extremely knowledegable and possesses an eye for quality, and I would recommend her if you are in need of her services: market liaison, agent, consultant, appraisals, dealer. She can be reached at:

Kathryn Corbin
Box 343
Boston, MA 02117
(617) 266-6249

PAINTING CONSERVATORS

The following list of painting conservators was compiled with one important criterion in mind : that they be members of **The American Institute for Conservation of Historic and Artistic Works** (AIC). Although AIC members agree to abide by AIC's Code of Ethics and Standards of Practice, the author and AIC cannot guarantee compliance with this code and do not professionally endorse any member on the enclosed list.

Because of limitations of space, only a representative sample of conservators has been compiled from the United States and nine foreign countries. Only telephone numbers are given, and in some instances, you may find that you have contacted a conservator at a museum. If so, they may only be able to work on conservation projects for that particular museum. In all likelihood, they will certainly be able to recommend someone else.

Remember, the simplest and safest route to take in finding a competent conservator is to get a referral from a reputable art gallery or museum.

If you would like a complete list of AIC members, send for the **AIC Directory** (217 pages)($20 plus $1.75 postage). They also list conservators of paper, textiles, photographs, furniture, and more - over 2000 members in all.

AIC
3545 WILLIAMSBURG LANE, N.W.
WASHINGTON, D.C. 20008

Telephone: 202-364-1036

****

ALABAMA

Griggs, Brigitta	205-772-0569

ARIZONA

Giffords, Gloria	602-749-4070
O'Brien, Patrick	602-946-5471
Peters, Claude	602-778-4281

ARKANSAS

Pinkston, Dow G.	501-756-6994

CALIFORNIA

Alden, Gary	619-236-9702
Antognini,Alfredo	619-236-9702
Calabi, Dennis	707-829-2971
Court, Elizabeth	619-236-9702
Engel, Betty	619-236-9702
Greaves, James L.	213-857-6161
Haskins, Scott	805-963-4476
Johnson, Benjamin	213-451-9625
Knipe, John	213-384-8559
Leonard, Mark	213-459-7611
Littau, Karen	916-441-4656
Miller, Bruce	415-558-2887
Pinney, Edward B.	213-478-1422
Rieniets, Judith	415-931-5346

Smith, Nora 619-224-9019
Thompson, Tatyana 415-453-9126
Van Gelder, Mark 415-453-9126
White, Sherman H. 805-963-2442

COLORADO

Bria, Carmen F. 303-573-1973
Cornelius, F. Dupont 303-576-4360
Shank, J. William 303-573-1973
Swope, James 303-753-3218
Wanke, Connie R. 303-756-2575

CONNECTICUT

Connell, Susan 203-269-7722
Douglass, George A. 203-637-0797
Garland, Patricia 203-278-2670
Kiehart, Paul P. 203-379-7779
Mayer, Lance 203-443-2618
Myers, Gay 203-443-2618
Zagni, Tosca 203-379-9245

DELAWARE

Katz, Melissa 302-656-8591
Richard, Mervin J. 302-656-8591
Tallent, Carolyn 302-392-6837

DISTRICT OF COLUMBIA

Brock, David 312-922-3879
Conway, Susan W. 202-333-6343
Page, Arthur H. IV 202-333-6269
Scafetta, Stefano 202-357-2685
Silberfeld, Kay 202-842-6432

FLORIDA

Elliott, Dorothy 813-924-5563
Holmes, Kathleen 904-376-6077
Jordan, William 813-258-2932

Radcliffe, John 904-477-3943
Westcott, Doris 813-461-1925

GEORGIA

Crissey, Devant 404-432-0220

ILLINOIS

Bauman, Barry R. 312-944-5401
Grosz, Georgette 312-248-6935
Lukowsky, Francis J. 312-232-2479
Pomerantz, Louis 312-587-6578
Wrubel, Faye 312-443-3639
Zebala, Aneta 312-823-4577

INDIANA

Metzger, Catherine 812-335-5102
Miller, David 317-923-1331
Witkowski, Linda A. 317-923-1331

KENTUCKY

Kohlhepp, Norman

LOUISIANA

Hudson, Phyllis 504-523-4846

MAINE

Brooke, Stephen W. 207-289-2301
Snow, Nancy L. 207-751-2309

MARYLAND

Archer-Shee, Audrey 301-822-0703
Ash, Margaret R. 301-396-6334
Covey, Victor 301-235-0247
Cunningham, Roland 202-278-2670

Klatzo, Cornelia	301-530-0880
Milton, Kenneth M.	301-778-5252
Webster, Judith	301-654-8996
Wimsatt, Justine	301-564-1036

Ackerman, Alfred	603-436-2436
Beardsley, Barbara	603-895-2639
White, Mary Lou	603-895-2639

MASSACHUSETTS

Brink, Elise	617-566-5252
Coren, Simon	617-398-8415
Fieux, Robert	617-362-3301
Findley, David	617-799-4406
Heslip, Michael	413-458-5741
Hoepfner, Gerald	413-458-5173
Konefal, Irene	617-267-9300
Lockwood, Josephine	413-698-3318
O'Day, Susan	617-247-2757
Schnorr, Emil G.	413-733-4214
Tucker, Linda	617-868-9347
Wales, Carroll	617-536-2323
Webber, Sandra	413-458-5741

NEW JERSEY

Boncza, Richard	201-791-3030
Deflorio, Dante	201-744-1921
Duff, Suzanne	201-228-4701
Focer, Phillip	609-881-8569
Grace, Victor	201-567-6169
Koszewnik, Fred	609-397-8672
Nevistich, Tania	201-994-3374
Papadopulos, George	201-966-5559

NEW MEXICO

Munzenrider, Claire	505-827-2545

MICHIGAN

Field, Susan	313-398-4749
Hartmann, E. John	313-833-7920
Molnar, CindyLou	212-638-5000

MINNESOTA

Kamm, Patricia C.	202-364-8542

MISSISSIPPI

Brown, Frances DeBra	601-746-3034

MISSOURI

Bailey, Forrest	816-561-4000
Heffley, Scott	816-561-4000
Robertson, Clements	314-721-0067

NEW HAMPSHIRE

NEW YORK

Allston, George	914-949-9035
Aviram, Anny	212-708-9573
Blakney, Susan	315-685-8534
Brown, Edward	212-249-1713
Cranmer, Dana	212-246-4307
Eidelberg, Michael	212-410-5687
Iosifescu, Maria	212-879-2154
Kahl, Robert O.	914-454-1250
Mahon, Dorothy	212-879-5500
Sack, Susanne P.	718-858-2624
Steele, Elizabeth	212-842-6432
Sutton, Margaret	315-685-8534
Thomas, Gregory A.	607-547-8768
Yost, James	212-749-8457

NORTH CAROLINA

Bauer, David C.	919-833-1935
Baxter, Ellen	704-364-3113
Goist, David C.	919-833-1935
Kropp, Karen K.	704-373-0761

OHIO

Batchelor, Elisabeth	513-721-5204
Eisele, Douglas	513-321-1911
Katz, Kenneth	216-775-7331
Lodge, Robert	216-775-7331
Thompson, Paul	513-221-0400

OKLAHOMA

Garrison, Jane	918-245-0407
Wiesendanger, Martin	918-245-2439

PENNSYLVANIA

Amarotico, Joseph	215-972-7617
Bechtel, E. Eugene	215-489-3900
Butler, Marigene	215-763-8100
Crenshaw, Shaw	412-622-3267
Daulton, Christine	412-422-0277
Erisoty, Steven	215-765-2607
Penn, Suzanne	215-787-5418
Tucker, Mark	215-787-5418

PUERTO RICO

Bronold, Edeltraud	809-840-1510
Poli, Dominique	809-727-6202
Winnicke, Frank	809-840-1510

RHODE ISLAND

Bosworth, David	401-789-1309

SOUTH CAROLINA

Dibble, Virginia	803-254-1640
Rogers, Catherine	803-479-2225

TENNESSEE

Stow, Cynthia	615-269-3868

TEXAS

Billfaldt, Jeanne	713-621-5623
Flanagan, Jack	713-621-5623
Houp, Helen	817-332-8451
Huston, Perry	817-595-4131
Parkin, Helen	817-332-8451
White, Richard	504-945-6015

VIRGINIA

Casper, Foy C.	804-622-1211
Clover, Cecile	804-973-8126
Houlgrave, Carolyn	804-355-5516
Kniss, Stephen J.	703-356-4315
Olin, Charles	703-759-3581

WASHINGTON

DeLaney, Stuart	206-352-3390
Harrison, Alexander	604-732-5217
Jolles, Arnold	206-447-4710
Lucas, Jack	206-693-3415

WEST VIRGINIA

Carter, Thomas G.	304-535-6371

WISCONSIN

Munch, Charles	608-583-2431
Paynter, Janice	608-238-6607
Spangler, David	608-637-2326

FOREIGN LISTINGS

ARGENTINA		JAPAN	
Iturbe, Sara	801-3786	Koyano, Masako	03-383-1821

BRAZIL		NEW ZEALAND	
Duvivier, Edna May	021-245-4748	Hutchinson, Mervyn	792-020

CANADA

		SWITZERLAND	
Bantock, Keith	902-424-7542	Bosshard, Emil	012-512-486
Barclay, Marion	613-996-8274		
Barmall, June	416-844-9865		
Carlyle, Leslie	613-236-9363		
Daly, Debra	613-998-3721		
Douglas, Jane	204-786-6641		
Keyser, Barbara	416-977-0414		
Klemplan, Barbara	613-521-2882		
Legris, Patrick	613-836-1089		
Michaud, William	416-725-6754		
Ramsay, Barbara	613-996-8274		
Ruggles, Mary A.	613-996-8274		
Ruggles, Mervyn	613-234-2823		
Walsh, Betty	604-387-3686		
Zdzitowiecka, Maria	514-482-2009		
Zukowski, Eduard	416-977-0414		

ENGLAND

Finn, Veronica	235-1650
Sitwell, Christine	09-855-277
Woodgate-Jones, Kate	082-343-2643

HONG KONG

Castaneda, Anthony	524-7157

ITALY

Wicks, Elizabeth	05-557-1137

BASIC BIBLIOGRAPHY

IN PAINTING CONSERVATION

The Care of Pictures, Stout, George L.

The Cleaning of Pictures, Ruhemann, Helmut

Conservation and Scientific Analysis of Paintings, Hours, Madelaine

The Restorer's Handbook of Easel Painting, Emile-Male, Gilberte

A Handbook on the Care of Paintings, Keck, Caroline K.

AIDS IN DATING AND IDENTIFICATION

Antique Picture Frame Guide Book, Maranski

Book of Picture Frames, Grimm

Frames in America, 1700-1900: Survey of Fabrication, technique and style.

American Costume 1840-1920, Worrell

Costume and Fashion: A Concise History, Laver

****

IMPORTANT NOTES

IMPORTANT NOTES

IMPORTANT NOTES

IMPORTANT NOTES

IMPORTANT NOTES

IMPORTANT NOTES

IMPORTANT NOTES

IMPORTANT NOTES

IMPORTANT NOTES

IMPORTANT NOTES

☐ Please include me on your mailing list so that I will be notified when each new, updated and expanded edition is available.

NAME _____
ADDRESS _____
CITY _____ STATE _____
ZIP _____

Additional copies of this guide may be ordered directly from the publisher.

Enclose $14.95 plus $1.00 shipping, (MA residents add 5% sales tax,.75) make check payable CFAAP

☐ Please include me on your mailing list so that I will be notified when each new, updated and expanded edition is available.

NAME _____
ADDRESS _____
CITY _____ STATE _____
ZIP _____

Additional copies of this guide may be ordered directly from the publisher.

Enclose $14.95 plus $1.00 shipping, (MA residents add 5% sales tax,.75) make check payable CFAAP